SUGGESTIONS ON ACADEMICAL ORGANISATION

This is a volume in the Arno Press collection

THE ACADEMIC PROFESSION

Advisory Editor
Walter P. Metzger

Editorial Board
Dietrich Goldschmidt
A. H. Halsey
Martin Trow

See last pages of this volume
for a complete list of titles.

SUGGESTIONS

ON

ACADEMICAL ORGANISATION

WITH ESPECIAL REFERENCE TO OXFORD

MARK PATTISON

ARNO PRESS

A New York Times Company

New York / 1977

Editorial Supervision: MARIE STARECK

———◆———

Reprint Edition 1977 by Arno Press Inc.

Reprinted from a copy in
  The Princeton University Library

THE ACADEMIC PROFESSION
ISBN for complete set: 0-405-10000-0
See last pages of this volume for titles.

Manufactured in the United States of America

———◆———

Library of Congress Cataloging in Publication Data

Pattison, Mark, 1813-1884.
    Suggestions on academical organisation with especial
reference to Oxford.

    (The Academic profession)
    Reprint of the 1868 ed. published by Edmonston and
Douglas, Edinburgh.
    1. Oxford. University—Administration. I. Title.
II. Series.
LF504.P37 1977   378.425'74   76-55200
ISBN 0-405-10027-2

SUGGESTIONS

ACADEMICAL ORGANISATION.

Printed by R. Clark

FOR

EDMONSTON AND DOUGLAS, EDINBURGH.

LONDON . . . HAMILTON, ADAMS, AND CO.
CAMBRIDGE . . MACMILLAN AND CO.
DUBLIN . . . M'GLASHAN AND GILL.
GLASGOW . . JAMES MACLEHOSE.

SUGGESTIONS

ACADEMICAL ORGANISATION

WITH ESPECIAL REFERENCE TO OXFORD

BY

MARK PATTISON, B.D.
RECTOR OF LINCOLN COLLEGE, OXFORD

EDINBURGH
EDMONSTON AND DOUGLAS
1868

CONTENTS.

Contents. ix

b

Section 7.—Conclusion.

APPENDIX.

SUGGESTIONS

ON

ACADEMICAL ORGANISATION.

———◆———

Εστιν οὐκ ἔλαττον ἔργον τὸ ἐπανορθῶσαι πολιτείαν ἢ κατασκευάζειν ἐξ ἀρχῆς,
ὥσπερ καὶ τὸ μεταμανθάνειν τοῦ μανθάνειν ἐξ ἀρχῆς.—ARIST. *Pol.* 4. 1.

IN May 1866 a few Members of Convocation met in the
chambers of Mr. O. Morgan, Lincoln's Inn, to consider
some university matters. A wish was expressed by the
meeting for fuller information and suggestions. As no one
else could be readily found to undertake the task, I have
ventured to offer the following notes and hints. They are
but a very imperfect contribution towards a scheme for
making Oxford a university fully adequate to the wants of
the nation. Such a scheme can only be made complete by
the joint efforts of many advisers representing different
branches of knowledge. In the hope that these pages may
provoke others to come forward with more matured and
better directed proposals, they are given to the public.

SEC. 1.—OF LEGISLATIVE INTERVENTION.

Those who make it their business to watch the current
of opinion in this country, tell us that there are signs that

it is preparing to take up the universities, and that "the university question" may be soon expected to become matter of general discussion. In the reform of our whole system of education we began with elementary schools, and have slowly ascended through the middle and the grammar schools. The final stage of superior education has naturally been left to the last. Partly, it interests a much smaller class than any of the preliminary stages do; but chiefly, it is incomparably the most difficult of all the educational problems. The difficulties in which elementary education is implicated, great as they are, are difficulties of action—How to carry through what we know ought to be done. 1. How is the cost to be defrayed? 2. How is attendance to be secured? 3. How are the nonconformist children to be provided for? These questions exhaust the school problem for the elementary stage. How to do what we want is not easy, but we understand what we do want.

When we come to the university question it is quite otherwise. As we have here to deal, not with the masses, but with a small class amenable to reason, there would be little difficulty in getting anything done if we could see our way clearly to what we do want. But the subject has not been sufficiently ventilated, and opinion is not ripe for action. Even university men themselves betray rather an impression that something should be done, than a reasoned conviction as to what that something is. The ideas of the wider public, so far as it concerns itself with our affairs at all, are still more crude and inappropriate. The danger is, that the something that is done should be discovered under pressure of the necessity of doing it; that *any* reform should be adopted because *some* reform is required. Twice before, in the history of English endowments, has this error been committed. For two centuries the public conviction of the inutility of monastic endowments had been slowly ripening. In 1536 the monasteries fell before the advance of rational views of society, but the national property was carried off from the nation and appropriated to their private use by a powerful aristocracy. Had these endowments in the sixteenth century been devoted to national education, it is possible that our present social difficulty—a difficulty the chief element of which is the fact that our industrial and commercial development has been more rapid than our intellectual and moral development—might never have occurred. Again, for centuries our middle-class public were slowly travelling to the conviction of the inutility of cathedral chapters. In the crisis of the revolution of 1830 the chapters went to the ground. The advance of social science since 1530 was shown by the fact that this time there was no plunder. Wrecking was no longer permitted by public morality. The nation this time retained its property, but it appropriated it to parochial, not to educational purposes. Thus a second opportunity was lost; but the need of the parochial clergy was so great, that it overbore other considerations. Now, the turn of the college endowments is come. The same power which destroyed the monasteries, which destroyed the cathedrals, is beginning to ask—Of what use are college endowments ? The British public will not long ask this question without helping itself to the answer that they are of no use. Thereupon a new appropriation of the endowment will be made. Such appropriation will necessarily be unwise, because it has been made under pressure. The public will give away its property as trustees of a rich charity do, who relieve any applicant, deserving or undeserving, because the funds of the charity must be distributed to some one.

Before this crisis comes it may be well to consider what the college endowments can do for the nation, whose property they are.

The remarks which follow are not an answer to the question—" Of what use are college endowments as now administered?" Did I propose to myself a defence of the universities against their censors, I might endeavour to show that they were of use. This is not my purpose. The advocates of the chapters in 1832 took a confined view of their position, when they endeavoured to vindicate the cathedrals as they actually were. It would have been better to have admitted that the cathedrals had not done the work they might have done, and to have shown what that work was, and how chapters might be so remoulded as to do it in future. The friends of the universities might profit by this experience. They should not attempt to make a conservative fight for the colleges as they are, even though there is confessedly much to be said on their behalf.

The following sheets assume that the English nation, in the existing phase of its history, wants a certain provision for the higher culture, and on that assumption offer suggestions as to how Oxford may be adapted to meet that want. If to any competent persons any of the suggestions seem to demand too great an alteration, let them show how the same end can be effected by an easier change. But it is no recommendation of a change that it is a little one, if it does not answer the end proposed. As one who owes to college endowments all that he has and is in life, the present writer could never turn upon his university in a spirit of hostile attack. But Oxford needs no indulgence or consideration of filial piety. Her defects are, I think, defects not hers, but those of our ecclesiastical and social condition and policy. Her merits, on the other hand, are her own. All her recent reforms have been the work of a minority, it is true, but still a minority of her own family. The movement commenced from within. Is it too bold to say that more enlightened views as to her proper destiny and worth are entertained by those whom she has trained, than are to be found elsewhere in that public opinion by which she is most seriously arraigned? Our temper at this moment should not be one of animadversion and cavil, but of honourable ambition. There is a work sorely needing to be done for the social and intellectual welfare of a country which is rich, prosperous, powerful, but greatly wanting in mental and spiritual disposition and capacity. The universities are better able to do that work than any other extant machinery—the universities, not as they are, but as they may be made. Will Oxford have the ambition to seize the opportunity to fill the vacant place, to break the bonds that bind her, and offer to supply that intellectual and moral nourishment for want of which we are in danger of starving in the midst of all our gold?

The public outside is desirous to take away or to undo, but not instructed enough to point out what should be added or substituted. In this university it is a minority only who are conscious of dissatisfaction with what we are. The great majority seem to think that we are going on pretty well, and that a few trifling alterations in the examination-schools are the only changes to be desired. Over and above what is apathy or shortsightedness, there is a strong feeling against interference by Parliament. It is said we have only just been reformed, we cannot need to be over-hauled again; we must wait to see how the new system works.

We begin, then, by considering what it was that was done in 1854, and if effects of the Act of Vict. 17 and 18, cap. 81, are to be expected, which ought to be waited for before any further change is made in the constitution of the university.

The intervention of the Legislature in 1854 was made by it, and submitted to by us, in an unhappy spirit, which, in a great degree, falsified the relation between the parties. After two centuries of neglect, the House of Commons had been brought to the point of considering the state of the universities. The movement was by no means a spontaneous one on the part of the House or the Government. They were brought to it, reluctantly enough, by the patient persevering efforts of a minority of university men. Their reluctance to touch the case was intelligible, for it had all the characteristics which make a business distasteful to members of Parliament. It was wrapt up in new, intricate, esoteric details, requiring much study to master; it related to the transcendental parts of education ; it involved religious party and the Established Church. Ill understood, the question was ill cared for. So much of it as could be brought upon the platform was made into a party topic, and debated with excited temper and party exaggeration. The usual result followed. The House passed the Government bill, maiming it in vital points in its passage through committee.

Our mode of receiving the measure was still less worthy of our character. The University of Oxford, remembering that its last appearance on the stage of history had been in resistance to the encroachment of the Crown, took legal advice as to whether it could not resist even the preliminary inquiry. Besides withholding all information from the commission, a great deal of foolish bluster was talked about interference with private property and the illegality of the commission. So great is the territorial influence of our great educational endowments that this unconstitutional language made an impression. The House of Commons only touched the ark of our property with half a heart. The Act nowhere asserts the rights of the nation over the national domain. The preamble can scarcely be acquitted of dishonesty when, in professing to recite what it was expedient to do, it omits to mention that the Act took powers to deal with college property. In the same temper the executive commission, when it came to divert college-funds to new uses, only diverted an insignificant fraction.

It must be desirable that when the Legislature deals with our statutes or our property, it should do so with a clear conscience. Violence and confiscation, no less on a small than a large scale, must prejudice the moral interests of the country. The rapacious appropriation of the abbey lands probably overbalanced in moral effect on that generation the gain from the abolition of the system. Mr. William Stebbing, M.A., of the Chancery Bar, has drawn up a statement of the legal grounds on which Parliament may divert college-estates to new but cognate uses. This argument is, by his permission, here printed:—

" A college, *ex vi termini*, imports a corporation ; and in fact the colleges of Oxford are civil eleemosynary corporations. The University of Oxford, which is also a corporation, and a civil, but not an eleemosynary, corporation, is independent of the corporations of the colleges ; but the colleges are hardly independent of it. A corporator of the university is not necessarily a corporator of a college ; but the corporators of a college, who are those, and only those, on the foundation, are corporators of the university also, and are entitled to enjoy all its advantages.

" The colleges being eleemosynary institutions, and the charity which they are particularly designed to afford being educational aid, the estates given for their corporate enjoyment are presumed by law to have been dedicated by the donors to charity—and educational charity. But the corporate estates are, though eleemosynary, not trust, property. They are not trust-property, because no trust can be implied unless where the two interests—the beneficiary, or right to the enjoyment, and the legal, or right to the custody and management of the sub-stance—exist, or are capable of being contemplated as existing, separate from each other ; and here both interests are united in the corporation itself. Side by side, indeed, with its rights and powers, stand those of the visitor and of the individual corporators ; but the visitor is no trustee for the corporation, but a judge interposed, not between the public and the corpora-tion, but between the several individual corporators themselves, present and future ; and, on the other hand, the distribution by the corporation, whether or not under a special arrange-ment ordained by the founder, of its revenues among its in-dividual corporators, does not turn it into a trustee for them, but is simply a particular form of enjoyment by itself, from whose beneficiary interest that of its members is derived, and to whose interest theirs continues always subject.

" The conscience of the corporation thus being burdened with no trust for other than itself, complete ownership of its estates being enjoyed by it, and the visitatorial powers supplying, in accordance with the founder's intention, and with the compact between him and the State ratified by the charter of incorporation, a *forum domesticum* in cases of conflict of the interests of one individual corporator with those of another or of the corporation, no room is left for the superintending jurisdiction which the Court of Chancery ordinarily exercises on behalf of actual or possible objects of the trusts in the matter of charity estates, and which, indeed, it puts in motion against colleges themselves in regard to any property which they can be shown to hold actually on trust. The public has, it is true, an interest in the corporate estates of colleges, as in those of other charitable institutions, under the principle that such corporate estates must be supposed to have been intended by the donors for the benefit, not merely of the special educational charity, but of charity (in the present instance, educational charity) generally; and that, therefore, if the corporation be dissolved for breaches of its charter, or, as happened to Hertford College, through failure of members, the estates, or at any rate the beneficial interest in them, does not, as in the case of a like failure of a grant to a non-eleemosynary corporation, revert to the grantor's heirs, but the general charitable purpose affects the property into whatever hands it may have come.* But it seems that the public cannot claim the aid of

---

* It is laid down by the authorities that no right of escheat lies when a body politic or incorporate is dissolved, but that the donor has his land again, subject to the exception that, when the corporation is eleemosynary, estates given to it are presumed to have been dedicated to charity generally, and no reversion therefore, or at least no beneficial reversion, remains in the grantor. In the case, however, of the dissolution of Hertford College, a commission of escheat does seem to have issued, and to have found that the lands had escheated to the Crown. The 56 Geo. III. c. 136, which provides for a grant of the site of the late college to Magdalen Hall, does not state any circumstances which explain away the inconsistency of this proceeding with the accepted principle that a writ of escheat

the courts to protect this its contingent interest until failure of the original limitation. The public is entitled as against the donor's heirs, but it has no enforceable interest as against the corporation, any more than the Crown or lord, under the right of escheat, has against an actual tenant in fee-simple.

" The exemption of the corporate property of colleges from the ordinary charitable jurisdiction, however dissimilar the actual circumstances to those when the existing appropriation of the corporate resources was made, and however unanimous the members of the corporation itself in requiring a modification of the original arrangement, would seem to justify legislative interposition. But the primary ground of the interposition of the Legislature is not, as would have been that of the Court of Chancery, because there is a fund for charity in need of new regulation, but because there are chartered corporations, not perhaps wholly public, but still more certainly not wholly private, by whose mode of using such a fund, as originally prescribed, the national purposes for which they have received special privileges and prerogatives—for instance, immunity from the enactments respecting mortmain and perpetuities, and, in some cases, even endowments out of public property—are being mutilated and rendered abortive. At the same time, any legislative changes in the constitution of a body maintained out of a certain fund, which do not, by operating, as did the Reformation, directly upon the State, and only through the State upon eleemosynary and educational institutions, leave the old relations of the institutions both to the State and to their own special objects in the main intact, work a silent change in the direction of the fund itself, and invite direct legislative interference with it, in order—regard being had to the vested rights of

does not lie in such a case. Perhaps the commission found that the founder left no heirs to exercise the rights of re-entry ; and the legal interest thus escheating to the Crown, with a general trust for charity attaching to it, the Crown, instead of settling a new scheme under the sign-manual, carried it by the form of a statute.

existing corporators—to cement new relations for it in the place of those which the legislative changes in the objects of the corporations have dissolved. To have abolished, for instance, a founder's kin fellowship, without proceeding to appropriate to new objects the part of the corporate revenues formerly thus employed, would have been indefensible from any point of view. If it be conceded that the Legislature is morally entitled to refuse to let institutions with public duties and privileges be any longer hampered and blocked up by rules which formerly may have given them greater public utility, but now simply encumber them, it would have implied a dangerous and unreal distinction to have remodelled the corporation, but have shrunk from touching property given for corporate enjoyment and meant to follow the corporate fortunes. And if this be not conceded, but, on the contrary, it be maintained that the State is morally bound to abstain from making changes in the collegiate constitutions because they must tend to throw out of gear endowments bestowed on the faith of no such changes being made, yet, the changes once having been made, Parliament would, far from curing, have greatly aggravated its original alleged breach of public faith, and still further infringed the donor's presumable intentions, by abandoning a fund, the very existence of which as a surplus, through the failure of his expressed intentions as to it, was certainly not contemplated by him, but which he designed at all events for some distinct educational and charitable object, to the private enjoyment of the remnant of corporators, already as well endowed as before the changes were made, but who, unless hindered by legislative authority, would, as constituting the same corporation, however diminished the number of members, be entitled to divide such unappropriated surplus among themselves.

" There are various ways in which it is conceivable that the changes in the constitutions of the several colleges sanctioned by Parliament may have resulted in a surplus revenue, over and above the demands of the residuum of the original constitutions imposed by the founder. It may arise from the suppression of a family fellowship; or it may arise from the release of a college from the obligation to provide for the academical education of a county, to whose natives, now free of the foundations of other once-closed colleges, such an asylum is no longer necessary; and a foundation in which a score of fellowships, confined, perhaps, each to one particular county, were but just enough out of which to pick the indispensable staff for carrying on the college duties, may now find a dozen open ones amply sufficient. But in whatever way it may arise, having been created by Parliament, or assumed by Parliament to have been created by it, it is natural that Parliament should attempt forthwith to deal with it. With a surplus due to the gradual rise in the value of property beyond the wants of the corporation, measured by the standard of the donor's intentions, and of its office in the State, it is a question rather of expediency whether or when the Legislature should interfere, so as to utilise the fund for charity, without deadening all personal interest of those who are to remain guardians of it still in providing for its beneficial employment; and it appears a very proper occasion for the Legislature to interfere and appropriate such gradually-accumulated surplus to new objects when it is giving new objects to the institutions themselves. But, whatever the source of the surplus, or the right time for the State to compute and re-distribute it, the principles which we might expect Parliament, in conformity with its ordinary rules of action, to apply in appropriating it, when it does appropriate it, would be those by which equity supplements or interprets the intentions of benefactors of unchartered charities; and while Parliament merely puts aside obstacles to the application of equitable principles to a fund for charity employed in maintaining an eleemosynary corporation, no greater violence is done, at any rate to the expressed intentions of donors in regard to their estates, than when the Court of Chancery dictates a scheme for the employment of charity funds to trustees, in whose discretion there is no reason to presume the donor did not confide as much as benefactors to colleges in those of their corporators. It would be confiscation, possibly capable of full justification, but needing special justification, for Parliament to appropriate corporate property, whether a surplus or not, to uses bearing no analogy to the old, as though it had come into its hands unearmarked, as it were, by the donor. It may equally be confiscation (as, in one sense, any dealing by the Legislature, where the municipal law cannot deal, with property against the will of its owners, however ample the pecuniary compensation provided—a railway act, for instance, with compulsory powers—always must be) for Parliament, even when its enactments do in fact enlarge the corporators' liberty of choice and action, to prescribe at all what a corporation is to do, or is not to do, with its corporate property. But the two kinds of confiscation are separated by several degrees in moral rank as confiscation ; and so long as Parliament does with the property of incorporated charities only what the Court of Chancery, in its inherent jurisdiction as representing the sovereign, the *parens patriæ,* and proceeding on the express ground that it is thus compassing both the true intentions of the donor and the real benefit of the charity itself, does with the property of any private charity, the charge of confiscation is like an action for damages in which the defendant is proved to have overstepped his rights, but no loss can be shown by the plaintiff.

" Although regard to the wishes of a donor to charity is matter rather of courtesy than of absolute right (since a gift to a charitable purpose, which may from its nature last for ever, is a total abandonment of at least all beneficial interest in the property), the Court of Chancery, very properly, always acts as if it were his representative, and entrusted by him with the carrying out of his intentions. But, when not constrained by his expressed will, it interprets his presumed intentions somewhat liberally, seeking, under its *cy près* principles, what objects a person now wishing to benefit society would choose. It compels trustees for charity to perform the trusts; and, if no trustees have been appointed or have accepted, it nominates some itself. If the objects proposed by the donor be illegal or indefinite, or have become, through lapse of time or change of circumstances, unfitted for carrying out the presumable intention, it, or in certain cases, the sovereign's self by sign-manual, settles a new scheme. When there is a general dedication to charity, but the donor has not duly assigned some particular interest in the property to any special charitable purpose, or the fund has since outgrown the requirements of the original scheme, the Court disposes of the lapsed revenues. It may in its discretion grant a proportionate addition to the remuneration which any of the objects of the trust receive for duties imposed upon them; but it suffers neither trustees nor beneficiaries to enjoy the surplus as their right. It claims undoubted 'authority to alter the trust in the distribution of the increased revenues, if it thinks it expedient so to do,'* and 'not only to increase the objects of the charity, but to make an alteration in them.'†

"We might expect, then, that Parliament, in settling a scheme for the application of the corporate property of a college, would, if it accepts the principles which govern the exercise of the ordinary charitable jurisdiction in equity, direct the expenditure of the fund—first, for the purposes specified by the donor; but if these were originally, or have since become, impracticable, unlawful, or too meagre for the resources of the charity, then—secondly, on objects expressly next within the donor's contemplation; or, if there be none such legal, practicable, and advantageous to the society—thirdly, on those which it may be collected from the character of the originally designated

---

* Lord Chancellor Eldon, in *Att.-Gen.* v. *Mayor of Bristol*, 2 Jac. and Walk. 319.   † Lord Chancellor Hardwicke, *ibid.*

purposes, and from the presumption, without which no such appropriations of property would have been privileged by the State, of a general intention to benefit the country, that the donor, if he were living now, would be likely to select as, among charitable objects, the most generally beneficial at the present time.

"The donor's primary intention, and that which governs or tempers all guesses after his subordinate and presumable intentions, was, as expressed in, or necessarily to be inferred from, the nature of the gift itself, to devote his estates to the maintenance of the particular corporation, doubtless to its maintenance as an instrument for the perpetual carrying out of the special objects stated in the charter or his grant, but at all events to the perpetual maintenance of the corporation itself. The property once given became absorbed in the corporation, and was bound to follow its destinies so long as, however revolutionised, that retained its identity. The failure of the special objects would not render the intention to maintain and benefit the corporation nugatory or ineffectual; and any change—the abolition, for example, of the restriction, in the election to a fellowship, to the natives of one particular county —is, provided that it leaves the enjoyment of the corporate property to the same corporation, altered as may be its constitution and objects, less violent in principle than would be a measure for taking away the fund itself from the formerly close but now open college, and applying it to the endowment of schools in the once favoured district. And Parliament did, in fact, pay absolute deference to the donor's primary intention, so far as it implied the enjoyment of his property by the corporation. Its directions for the employment of college funds in aid of the university professoriate nowise litigated against this primary intention. A professorship in the university might be endowed with the proportion of the corporate revenues which perhaps previously maintained a couple of Fellows of founder's kin. But the professor, while adding the prestige of university rank and authority to the corporation, was to be, as fully as had been the founder's kin Fellows, a corporator of the college; and the fund which paid him was to remain as completely corporate property as the fund which had paid them.* Again, in declaring the uses to which the corporators should put the revenues which the corporation enjoyed, Parliament still respected the donor's expressed intention, so far as the objects specified by him were compatible with, and survived, the changes it had introduced into the constitution of the college; and, so far as these surviving specified objects did not suffice to exhaust the corporate resources, it complied with the implied intention of the donor, that the college should enjoy the whole benefit of his bounty, by directing search to be made for wants and possible improvements of the college and its own members, upon which to expend its remaining means, before diverting any part of the benefit to the enlargement of the basis of the University professoriate.   Whether all in-college wants and possible improvements were or were not adequately provided for by the commissioners' ordinances in every case, is a question of fact; but at least Parliament assumed that, in sanctioning an expenditure of college revenues on the professoriate, it was dealing with a surplus, with a fund which could not be employed, with a reasonable prospect of advantage, on recognised in-college objects.

" When there is a failure of direct objects of a charity, the Court of Chancery applies the fund to the benefit of a charity with similar ends and purposes; and even on this simple principle, without more, might be justified the diversion to

---

* On this subject, I allude to cases where the commissioners, under their parliamentary powers, appropriated to the professoriate college revenues not made chargeable at all by the founders with such duties. The apology for such an appropriation, where the founders themselves directed the delivery of lectures to the university at large, is much simpler.

the university professoriate, which, although the university itself is not an eleemosynary corporation, is of an analogous eleemosynary and educational character to the foundations of colleges, of college revenues, which the Legislature assumed to be incapable of profitable employment for direct in-college objects. But further, in fact, such an application of the corporate revenues did tend both to the general and indirect, and to the special and direct, advantage of the corporation which furnished them. It tended to the general advantage; for the university, which profited by having its educational staff strengthened through college revenues, is, though a distinct corporation independent of the colleges, a body so closely related to any college whose revenues may have so been appropriated, that it might be presumed to have been within the donor's own contemplation in the grant he made to the college—that is, to a society connecting, if not a place in, yet a certain very positive relation to, the university. It is of the college's very essence that, if not itself as a corporation, yet all those whom, through it and as members of it, he had an intention to benefit, whether express as to the foundationers, or presumable as to the unattached members, however long afterwards adopted by the corporation, belong to the university and partake in the advantages it has to bestow.

" The university is no rival of a college, as one college is of another. As it benefits by a benefit to a college, so, but much more immediately, a college benefits by a benefit to it, and is compromised by its bad discipline or ill repute. Parliament, then, might as reasonably have taxed the surplus corporate revenues of a college towards the support of the educational institutions of the university, if only on the ground of this relationship and perhaps somewhat one-sided interdependency of the two corporations, as Courts of Equity grant to a ward, and with a view to his especial welfare, a more liberal allowance for maintenance out of his estate, on the ground that his family, a parent, a brother, a sister, or, it

C

may be, a guardian, is poor and necessitous. But this appli-cation of college revenues to the extension of professorial teaching also, besides the general tendency, had, or, what is the same thing when the inquiry is as to the principles on which Parliament acts, was supposed by Parliament to have, a special and direct tendency to promote actual college interests. If, as seems, whether rightly or wrongly, to have been thought by the Legislature, the professoriate provides an instrument, for which no expenditure on simple in-college objects can be a substitute, and which is indispensable for completing and crowning the kind of education for furthering which colleges may be said to exist and be privileged by the State, it was as proper to use spare revenues for supplying the want, which the resources of the university were inadequate to supply, and which else would not have been supplied at all, as for meeting any other need of the college not especially provided for by the founder ; and surely not the less proper because members of neighbouring societies might share in the advantages of the new educational machinery, to which indeed many of them in other but analogous ways were made to contribute in their turn."

The suggestions, however, which are to follow do not rest on this basis. They do not require or imply the diver-sions of funds from the use of one corporation to that of another—from collegiate tuition to the university profes-soriate. My endeavour will be to show that the colleges are not now performing the functions designed by their founder, and to urge that they should be enabled by legis-lative interposition to resume that function. All that is required for this purpose is that changes which have taken place in the conditions of English social life should be recognised as facts, and the play of the college corpora-tions be allowed to adapt itself to those changes.

Indeed the cry that the colleges are not national property, and the universities not national institutions, loud enough in 1852, has been sensibly enfeebled since. It will hardly again be found in the mouths of any public men who have any claim to statesmanlike capacity, or who aim to argue the question on broad grounds of public welfare. It will no doubt reappear from time to time, and be made to do duty as a party weapon. But the Legislature of this country is now fairly in presence of the much more serious question, *What* it shall do with its seminaries of the higher education? That the Legislature should have clearly realised the extent of its rights is the best guarantee we can have that it will recognise their limitation. That there is a limit to the power of the State in its treatment of its one great scientific corporation will not be questioned. It is only by perfect freedom in its internal administration that such a corporation can discharge its trust. Even in German States, in which the Government undertakes far more extensive functions than with us, this freedom is recognised. One of the articles of the Prussian charter which the reactionary party have never sought to touch is, " Die Wissenschaft und ihre Lehre ist frei." And even as early as 1808 Schleiermacher had laid down limits of State interference in terms which must be always applicable. " Whatever belongs to the domestic life and internal management of the institution must be arranged by itself. Privileges or property, which the State has conferred, of these the corporation is only trustee " (*Gedanken über Universitäten, Werke,* i. p. 600).

As to the right of the Legislature to interfere at all times, no constitutional lawyer will probably question it. But I would submit to those who are more competent to judge on points of public policy, if such a right does not carry with it a corresponding obligation. Can the right of interference be properly exercised as a sort of appellate jurisdiction only where a party interested is able to carry a case as far as this High Court? The colleges are corporations enjoying property to certain uses. If this were all they are, Parliament, though it would still retain the right of interference, need not exercise the right till a case of abuse was alleged. But though colleges are this, they are more than this. They are endowed corporations, through the medium of which the social body performs one of its vital functions. The State has accorded to the colleges, as it has to the Bank of England, exceptional privileges to enable them to discharge those functions. They not only share the protection of the Government in common with all other sanctioned institutions, but they are an essential part of that public machinery by which the national life is carried on. Protection is not enough. It must be among the duties of Government, under its responsibility to the nation, to watch unintermittingly over the university, and to see that it does in practice efficiently discharge the functions assigned it. If the Legislature only steps in when crying abuses have accumulated, it is hardly possible that justice will be done by a popular assembly, heated with previous struggle between those who exaggerate in denouncing, and those who exaggerate in defending, the abuse. The university submits with discontent as to a tyrannical intruder, and the Legislature, unacquainted from disuse with the matter on which it has to legislate, gladly escapes from an unwelcome task by an Act, which passed, it dismisses the subject for an indefinite period.

This is the point at which the university question is found to be involved in that more general question which constitutes the governmental problem of the time, both in this country and in Europe at large, how to hold the balance, namely, between centralisation and self-government. Mr. Arnold (*A French Eton*, p. 74) has pointed out that neither State action nor local administration, as such, can be a principle in education. The limit of State interference with the universities must be the minimum of interference which will maintain the full efficiency of the institution which the State has established, or which it entrusts with public functions. "The citizens of a State are a partnership, a partnership in all science, in all art, in every virtue, in all perfection" (*Burke, quoted by Mr. Arnold*). Neither the university nor its colleges are a private enterprise, existing for their own purposes. Our independence and our self-respect must not be impaired, for they are elements of our success in the task assigned us. We must not, like a French *maître d'école*, be set to task-work. But a closer connection with the central power would quicken our zeal and concentrate our energies. The mediæval system provided a special organ of such connection in the Episcopal Chancellor; and the Court of Rome, the then central authority in spirituals, maintained a direct surveillance over universities. It may be true that there are no hands now in which the supervision formerly exercised by Rome can be lodged. Not in those of Parliament, as having too much else on its hands. Not in those of the Church of England, as having no proper organisation, and being, besides, too much of a party within the State. But why should the Crown not exercise such a function? Our relations with the State might be re-established, in a mode as little revolutionary as may be, by giving the Crown the nomination of the Chancellor. He should be a lay person nominated for life, be unpaid, but have a paid secretary and an office through which all communications should pass. An annual report should be laid before him by each university officer. It should be his duty to examine these reports, and to bring before the university Council any matters arising upon such reports. He should be *ex officio* a member of the Hebdomadal Council, and his motions, to be made *aut per se aut per alium*, should take precedence of those of any other member.

I do not venture to make any suggestion as to what the relations should be between the Chancellor and the Government, as this could not be done without opening the question of an education-office. In compensation for surrendering its right of electing its own Chancellor, the university should acquire an official recognition in place of the unofficial and somewhat *ex parte* championship expected of her Chancellor in his place as a Peer in Parliament.

Official recognition in the Government would supersede for the future spasmodic and occasional efforts of parliamentary legislation. Such intermittent government is to be deprecated. But for the moment an appeal to Parliament seems to be unavoidable. The arrears of two centuries require to be cleared off. But the colleges once started on a new career, powers of internal legislation should be entrusted to the university, which would enable it, under proper safeguards, to avoid for the future a repetition of the dead-lock which now necessitates an appeal to Parliament.

If this be a true view of the duty of Government towards the university, the Act of 1854 was by no means its discharge in full. It had at that time become urgent to relieve the universities from certain superincumbent disabilities which were crushing them. This the Act of 1854 did, but it could not and did not pretend to be a reform of the universities. The public and patent grievances which had been long urged by the minority above spoken of were—

1. The incompetence of the governing body—the old Hebdomadal Board of Heads of Houses and Proctors.
2. The close Fellowships and Scholarships.
3. Inadequate teaching—the tutors being incompetent and the professors silent.
4. The enforcement of religious tests.

These were the four points which had been always propounded by the reforming minority of enlightened academics. The Act of 1854 dealt with all four points. It treated 1 and 2 fully and confidently. 1. It abolished the Board of Heads of Houses and Proctors. 2. It abolished local claims for Fellowships, and partially for Scholarships. 3. It did little for No. 3—partly from the timidity in dealing with college property to which I have referred, partly also because it was hoped that the abolition of close Fellowships would of itself raise the teaching capacities of the tutors. 4. What it did under this head was the result of a compromise between parties in the House. The subscription was retained for the M.A. degree. How little of principle there was in the retention was shown by the Cambridge Act of the following year, which abolished all subscription for degrees.

It would be ungrateful to its framers and promoters not to recognise heartily the great benefits which have been derived from the Act of 7th August 1854. Its indirect effects in stimulating the spirit of improvement among us have been no less important than the specific reforms enacted by it. The last twenty years have seen more improvement in the temper and the teaching of Oxford than the three centuries since the Reformation. This improvement has undoubtedly been vastly promoted by the Reform Bill of 1854, or at least by one of its enactments. The abolition of close Fellowships has not only done more for us than all the other enactments of the measure together, but it is the only one which has completely answered the expectations then formed from it. But the Act of 1854 never could claim to be a settlement of the university. It was merely an enabling Act, removing two evils of long standing, and giving very inadequate relief from two others. It cannot be premature to apply again to the Legislature to complete the work begun, and only begun, in 1854.

Beginning with No. 4, it may be briefly disposed of. I am happily dispensed from the discussion of what is a question rather of imperial policy than of academical arrangement, by the fact that it is now under the consideration of the Legislature itself.

SEC. 2.—OF THE CONSTITUTION OF THE UNIVERSITY.

On the working of the new government of the university as constituted by the Act of 1854, twelve years have given us some, if not a conclusive, experience. As this memoir may be consulted by others than Oxford men, an account of the constitution of 1854 may not be superfluous. The University Senate called the Hebdomadal Council is an elective body. It numbers twenty-two persons. Of these four are *ex officio* members—viz. the Chancellor, the Vice-Chancellor, and the two Proctors. The Chancellorship is a life office, the Vice-Chancellor holds office for four years, the Proctors for one. The other eighteen members are elected by a defined constituency out of three qualified categories—six from the Heads of Houses, six from the Professors, and six from M.A.'s of not less than five years' standing. Of these eighteen half retire (but are re-eligible) at the end of three years. The vote is taken under a minority protective clause—*i.e.* for three vacancies each voter gives only two votes.

The constituency themselves compose a second and lower branch of our legislature. This is Congregation, a body of about 270 persons, and which may be said roughly to comprise all resident M.A.'s. All measures must originate in the Council, and, when passed by it, must be laid before Congregation. Congregation can discuss the measure as it stands, but cannot move or vote upon amendments. Nor may this body vote on the day on which it debates.

There is yet a third legislative chamber, Convocation, which every measure must go through before it can become law. Convocation consists of every M.A. who has his name on the books of any college or hall, whether he is resident or not.

Council.—With respect to the Hebdomadal Council, those who recollect the hopeless stagnation of legislation under the old Board of Heads will, I think, admit that the new Council has been a substantial gain. I cannot suggest any alteration in its composition or the mode of election. The question, however, has been raised, Do we want an Elective Council at all? Cannot the business of the university be transacted directly by Congregation—*i.e.* by the constituency itself, instead of the constituents meeting to appoint delegates? Mr. Goldwin Smith has urged this on the ground that the triennial elections themselves, with the caucuses, wire-pulling, and party spirit, which attend them, are an unmixed evil (*The Elections to the Hebdomadal Council*, Parker 1866). He would have Congregation fitted for the purpose of academical administration, by extruding from it the non-academical element which forms the main strength of the present party domination.

But if we may judge from our twelve years' experience of Congregation, it appears very doubtful if that body would be competent to the task of general administration of our affairs. The attendance of members is too fitful and irregular for the conduct of business. Nor would it be possible to enforce attendance by penalty, the most valuable members of Congregation being just those on whose time elsewhere exist the most, and the most imperative, demands. The business would inevitably fall into the hands of permanent delegacies or standing committees. These would necessarily be composed of the same class of men who now make up the Council, who would act without the sense of publicity and responsibility under which the Council now acts. Men like Mr. Goldwin Smith himself, whose time is engrossed by the literary or scientific studies proper to the place, cannot go into Council as it is, and would not in the other case be able to give the close and *suivi* attendance in Congregation which would then be necessary. The working tutor or professor *now* is glad to be able to delegate his share of the drudgery of business to his representative in Council. At the same time, whenever a question of importance is passing through our legislature, he has the opportunity of offering his advice upon it in person in Congregation. As to the displays of party-spirit, which take place on occasion of every election to Council, they are confessedly one of the abuses of the place. But it must be observed that elections to Council are only the occasions on which a spirit, the existence of which is due to much more deeply-seated causes, shows itself on the surface. Elections to Council at Cambridge do not stir up theological passions. If elections to Council ceased to be at Oxford, the same passions would only break out with still more disastrous effect in nominations to offices. And if Congregation has not public virtue enough to be trusted with a vote for representatives, how can it be trusted with the direct administration of its own affairs?

I should wish, then, to see an Elective Council continue to exist. In adapting it to the other parts of the scheme, as proposed in these " Suggestions," the threefold division into Heads, Professors, and Masters, would have to be replaced by a division according to the Faculties. But all councils have an inherent tendency to grasp at administration beyond their competency—to attempt to do too much. There is at least one department which requires a more special supervision than can be given by the Hebdomadal Council—viz. the Studies and the Examinations. A body elected for general purposes is obviously not fitted for the conduct of such an intricate machine as our examination system. Our treatment of this department has hitherto been too minute for legislation, too lax for administration. We have attempted to regulate by statute, details too minute to be capable of being fixed—*e.g.* even to enacting what books shall be used in the schools; while, on the other hand, there is no concerted action between the several boards of examiners. The whole of this department, "Studies and Examinations," should be placed under a special delegacy. An organic statute passed, defining the competency of this delegacy, and as few other points as possible, the Hebdomadal Council would be relieved from all further responsibility in respect of "the schools," and the university would be released from the anxiety of having the system of its studies always at the mercy of a party majority.

Congregation.—This body consists of all resident members of Convocation, with a few official persons—*e.g.* the Chancellor, High Steward, etc.—who are non-resident. Residence is defined as residing twenty weeks within a mile and a half of Carfax. The number of persons thus qualified is at present about 270. This body forms at once a member of the legislature, or House through which all statutes must pass before they can become law, and is also the constituency by which Council is elected. This body was called into being by the Act of 1854, and was calculated to have been one of the most useful of its enactments. That it has not been so is owing to an alteration, seemingly trifling, which was made in the bill in committee. Congregation was designed by Mr. Gladstone to be an assembly of the persons engaged in teaching —a Senatus Academicus. In committee this was enlarged

so as to include all residents. This alteration added to
the assembly about 100 members, not connected with the
studies of the place, and waterlogged Congregation at one
stroke. Had Mr. Gladstone's first draft been adopted,
Congregation would have been a revival of the old distinction between regent and non-regent masters. It would have
been a notable example of what I believe will be found to
be true, that, as the university revives, we shall find ourselves reviving old arrangements, not because they are old,
but because they were the results of much experience.
" All doctors and masters had originally a right to be
present in the general assembly of the university. But
after the middle of the thirteenth century, when these
degrees no longer necessarily implied that the person
holding them was actually engaged in teaching, the
lecturers or acting masters only (*magistri regentes*) ordinarily took a part in the general assembly " (Malden, *Origin
of Universities*, p. 25).

Mr. Goldwin Smith has proposed a double reform of
Congregation—the exclusion of all residents engaged in
any other profession than that of learning or education,
and the inclusion of non-residents having only those
interests. Both these amendments are desirable. The
congregational franchise is a strictly educational franchise,
and local residence can confer no right to it, any more
than non-residence can disqualify. But in this case, as in
that of all educational or fancy franchises, there will be a
difficulty in finding a definition. How can we ascertain
of any class of non-residents that in its mind the interests
of learning and science will be paramount to theological
party ? How can we say of any class of resident M.A.'s

that it is not engaged in study ?   Certainly this cannot be
affirmed of the city clergy, the class which is supposed to
be most directly under discipline to the wire-pullers of the
party.   For every Anglican clergyman, when ordained
priest, enters into an engagement that he will " be diligent
in prayers, and in reading of the Holy Scriptures, *and in
such studies* as help to the knowledge of the same" (*Ordination Service*).   An attempt of Mr. Gladstone's to confine
Congregation to "students" was upset in committee in
1854 by this very difficulty of defining students.   It was
then found impossible to procure a definition which did
not create as many anomalies as it removed—a definition
which shall exclude those who have no interest in knowledge without also excluding the class, *e.g.,* to which Mr.
Goldwin Smith himself belongs—of unattached M.A.'s resident for purposes of study.   This, however, may be a
matter of detail.   The important thing is to get the principle recognised in Parliament and elsewhere, that the
franchise, as entrusted to Congregation, is an educational,
not a local or a property franchise.   The substitution of
the words " all residents" in committee (in May 1854) was
made on Sir W. Heathcote's motion, who argued that
" Congregation ought to be an epitome of Convocation if it
were to be useful at all."   The policy of creating an inter-
mediate legislative corps between Council and Convocation
was, on the contrary, not to *repeat* Convocation, but to
correct Convocation.   This object of obtaining a more
enlightened vote was defeated by Sir W. Heathcote's
amendment.   Congregation has been, what he desired to
see it, "an epitome of Convocation."   All that is now
asked is that effect should be given to the original scheme

of Congregation—a scheme of which nothing but the name has ever been in operation. As if its usefulness was not sufficiently crushed by making it " an epitome of Convocation," jealousy of its power went the length of—(1), dividing the vote from the debate; and (2), denying it the power of amending. Both these disabilities should be abrogated. Congregation, purged of alien interests, ought to feel itself an integral and equal moiety of the legislature. When reconstituted as proposed, it would be a body not equal to the Council for the detailed conduct of business and shaping of measures, but likely to take broader views of principle and policy.

Convocation.—If Congregation were reinstated in its destined rights, it seems to follow that it would be necessary to put an end to the legislative functions of Convocation. This also Mr. Goldwin Smith contends for. He describes Convocation as " theoretically a body so large that scarcely a tenth part of it could get into the Convocation House, and scattered over the three kingdoms, which, if it could be brought together in a building large enough to hold it, and addressed by its most eminent members, might possibly come to a reasonable decision. Practically, saving in the case of some theological Armageddon, it is some thirty or forty staunch partisans, who, having leisure enough to come up whenever they are called, have put themselves into the pockets of two or three wire-pullers, and thus enabled the wire-pullers to coerce Congregation whenever it presumes to come to a decision of which they do not approve " (*Elections to the Hebdomadal Council*, p. 12). Before we ask for this change, we ought fully to place before our minds how great the change would be. It appears to me that this single measure, could it possibly be carried, would be a greater revolution in the university than all the reforms of 1854, or than any other reforms that are thought of now. Without professing to be able to foresee all the results of a change so momentous, is it not clear on the face of it that it would be to transfer at one stroke the foundation of the university from property to intelligence? As long as Convocation subsists as it is at present, though it may be seldom appealed to, it always can be, and it retains in its hands the ultimate decision on the whole conduct of the university, its internal government as well as its external relations. How is this body composed, in which is ultimately lodged the sovereign authority of the university? In discussions on the electoral franchise we always see the university constituency quoted as an example (and the only extant example) of the " educational franchise." It is so by contrast with the franchise which is founded on a combination of property and territorial circumscription. All the members of Convocation have this in common, that they have been educated at the university. But they have also other things in common, which influence their opinions more than the common attribute which constitutes their qualification. The majority of the Oxford Convocation are clergymen—beneficed clergymen, or having a fair prospect of becoming so. Their vote is not a purely clerical or professional vote, but one, partly professional, partly governed by that relation to the property of the country in which the beneficed clergyman stands. Such a constituency is capable of being, among the constituencies in this country, a very valuable electoral body, and Mr. Goldwin Smith does not propose to deprive it of the parliamentary franchise, though he passes an indignant condemnation on its occasional employment of that privilege. The sovereign authority in university affairs is, then, a body in which the educational element on which the qualification rests is very considerably tempered, or held in check, by professional or territorial interests. Now, Congregation, as we propose to reform it, would be a purely educational body, entirely divested of such interests. Are we prepared to sever the ties which at present bind our national universities to the country and its interests, and hand them over to intelligence? Is our country ripe for such a measure? I wish I could think so. I confess it seems to me there are possible risks in the attempt, which ought to be well weighed before the attempt is made. It is not, of course, meant that the conduct of the institution by an intelligent Congregation would not be greatly superior to legislation by a body composed as Convocation is composed. But would a great institution like Oxford, possessed of vast wealth, if its roots in the prejudices and interests of the country were cut at one stroke, and it was handed over to the conduct of a handful of intelligent men to manage upon rational principles, would it be safe for even a single session of Parliament? Intelligence is in a minority in this country in our general administration. It is aware that it is watched with fear and suspicion. It is prudent enough not to provoke a direct struggle between itself and the forces that resist it. Observers tell us that the culture of our highest class is not what it used to be. Mr. Arnold says—" The culture and intellectual life of our highest class seem to me to have somewhat flagged since the last century.

Their value for high culture, and their belief in its importance, is not what it used to be." He thinks " that this sleep
of the mind—this torpor of intellectual life—this dearth of
ideas—an indifference to fine culture, or disbelief· in its
necessity—is spreading through the bulk of our higher
class, and influencing the rising generation " (*French Eton*,
p. 102). The dearth of literature in the country houses of
England is a frequent source of complaint. I have heard
it said that there is not now a single nobleman's mansion
in which the company and the tone of society is literary.
If the country is thus going backwards in civilisation, the
towns are not going forward. Our middle class does not
seem to have made any advances towards taking up the
place which the aristocracy has abdicated. Dr. Donaldson's picture is of the man of business properly so called :—

" The man of business is prone to acquiesce in the consciousness of his own respectability. This, in some of its
outward manifestations, is the idol of his heart. If he is
ambitious to be fashionable or aristocratic, it is for the sake of
appearances, and he is generally found to imitate rather the
expensiveness, than the refinements, of the class above him. If
he lays down the law in politics or in religion he is the uncon-
scious mouthpiece of some short-sighted utilitarian or canting
bigot whom it is respectable to follow. When he sends his
boys to school, he cares less for their improvement than for
the credit which redounds to himself. When most satisfied
with his own position he seems to care for little beyond the
uncontradicted maintenance of the opinions he has adopted
from his newspaper or his preacher, his personal and domestic
comfort, and the decencies of his outward appearance. Abundant meals and good clothes, and a well-furnished parlour, are
the extent of his wishes." (*Classical Scholarship*, etc., p. 88.)

And a foreign observer describes us more generally :—

" L'esprit anglais est un des moins ouverts à la critique. Aucune nation dans le monde ne cherche davantage la verité qui a une utilité prochaine ; aucune n'a plus de secrets pour voir les choses comme elle les veut ; aucune n'est plus singulière et même admirable pour faire la verité à son image et à son usage. Cherchez un peuple qui sente moins le besoin de connaitre ce dont il ne voit pas l'utilité actuelle : cherchez-en un seul qui subordonne plus volontiers ses libres et vigoureuses facultés à cette utilité, un seul pour lequel ce qui a été pensé ailleurs ait moins de valeur et de poids. Prenez les écrivains anglais depuis 70 ans ; assurement il y en a beaucoup qui ont cherché et exprimé le vrai ; mais combien y en a-t-il qui n'avaient pas de raisons de parti pour le chercher et l'exprimer ? Ont ils souvent revendiqué un droit de la pensée sans courir aussitôt à la pratique ? Quand on travaille autant que le peuple anglais, on n'a pas le temps de penser, ou plutot un tel peuple pense en agissant, et sa pensée c'est de l'action." (*Revue des deux Mondes*, 1 *Avril* 1866.)

The clergy are often treated as obstacles to the diffusion of knowledge. As a *profession*, perhaps, they are at a disadvantage from their want of proper professional acquirement —acquirement which makes the practitioner of any other profession respectable, however slender his general attainment. But as a *class*, the clergy surely compare favourably with any other class in the country. Abstract the clergy from the rural parishes, and how much cultivation would you have left ? Literary men who lead a metropolitan life are apt to think depreciatingly of the clergy as a class. They would do well to consider the immense advantage which England enjoys, in comparison with a Catholic country, from the possession of a territorially endowed clergy, and the circumstance that the clergy receive a general, not a professional, education. Our immediate prospects for the moral improvement of the country must rest in great measure on this order. It is an error, I venture to think, on the part of educated and intelligent politicians, when they aim at social improvement without the clergy. Within the Church of England itself there is just now a strongly-pronounced tendency to turn the English clergyman into the Catholic priest. It would be playing into the hands of this party to do anything which should break the connection at present subsisting between the clergy and the universities. Our hope must be in acting more powerfully on the clergy, and not in alienating them. It may be at this moment the interest of Oxford to be relieved from the dead weight of Convocation. But in order to get an immediate benefit to the university, we must not risk the remoter hopes of the nation. The small minority of educated men exercise a great power in this country. But they exercise it on condition of remaining unobtrusive and invisible. They are not strong enough to contend single-handed as a party in a political struggle with the laity of the middle class and the clergy united, while the working class, ignorant of the merits, look on with indifference. If the Oxford Convocation chooses to resist suppression, it is very doubtful if its suppression would be carried through both Houses of Parliament. But it cannot be unwilling to hear reason, and to part with some of its powers. It must be obvious that a body of 4000 persons, from its mere number, cannot be competent to adjust and re-adjust the shifting details of a complex system like that which we have to work. Especially is this incompetence felt in the teaching and examining part of the system. If the suggestions made above were adopted, and an organic statute passed for professors and examiners, Convocation might be called upon to vote the heads of such a statute, the arrangement of details being left to an administrative board. Convocation would also do wisely to surrender of itself its right of electing to certain professorial chairs. I have already suggested that the Chancellor should be nominated by the Crown.

Vice-Chancellor.—After the legislation comes the administration. The most important officer of the university is the Vice-Chancellor. I am unable to define the powers now lodged in the hands of the Vice-Chancellor. Probably no definition is possible. The statute (tit. xiii. iii. 2) begins by conferring upon him all the powers vested in the Chancellor. But the powers which had just before (tit. xiii. i. 2) been conferred on the Chancellor, including an etc. of consuetudinary privileges, are so large that no Vice-Chancellor ever thinks of exercising them. On the other hand, the Hebdomadal Council inherits from the old Board of Heads, or does in fact exercise, inclusively of the Vice-Chancellor, or as his assessors, administrative powers which limit the powers vested by the words of the statute in the Vice-Chancellor solely. In other respects the statute " De auctoritate et officio Vice-Cancellarii " is very meagre. It is a part of our statute-book which has never yet been submitted to the revision which has swept away so much else that is no longer applicable. It remains as Laud left it, sufficiently betraying its authorship by its petty inquisitorial spirit. After a vague designation of the powers of the Vice-Chancellor, it is almost wholly occupied with arming him with powers against heretics and schismatics—powers which no Vice-Chancellor of this day could employ without exposing himself to the imputation of degrading his office to be the instrument of party spite. Notwithstanding the meagreness of the statute, the attributes of the Vice-Chancellor have become so multifarious, and depend to so great an extent on usage, that they may well have defied the sacrilegious approach of codification. In the presence of ancient privileges, which have come out what they are from the shaping hand of time, one is made to feel that a historical constitution contains a seed of life and vigour which no paper organiser can imitate. Even the enactment of the statute of 1636, which for the first time deprived the M.A.'s of their ancient right of electing their own Vice-Chancellor, did but incorporate into the written law the prevailing usage, which had been ratified by a usurpation of nearly a century. Under the year 1569 Wood mentions that the Earl of Leicester " took upon himself the right of naming the Vice-Chancellor sometimes without the consent of the Convocation, rarely or never done in former times."

The position and attributes of the Vice-Chancellor might be adapted to the requirements of our university without re-modelling the office. What is wanted is not to invest him with new powers, but to set him free to attend to what is important. The Vice-Chancellorship has been choked by an overgrowth of merely formal duties. Rather, as in the last century university education altogether became almost a formality, the Vice-Chancellor shared the general tendency. Now that other parts of our system are awaking into life, its presiding officer should undergo a corresponding revival. There has always been a sensitive anxiety to put the Vice-Chancellor forward in every business, till the attempt has defeated itself. He has now so much heaped upon him that, instead of being the guiding mind of the place, he is compelled to disperse his attention over details which can be better done by special subalterns. He should be set free from the drudgery of the desk, and from the transaction of purely formal business. The transfer of the finance of the university to proper officers will alone give considerable relief. The ceremonies attending degrees and presiding in Convocation might be delegated to deputies (pro-Vice-Chancellors). Instead of being an *ex officio* member of every delegacy, and so obliged to attend every sitting of every board or committee, it would be better that he should not be on any, but have reports made to him of the results arrived at when the work of detail had been accomplished. His higher energies would thus be set free for deliberation in Council, and his nominal presidency changed into a real one. His time would be more at liberty to cultivate the university relations with the world outside. For the purpose of entertaining strangers and foreigners, an official residence should be assigned him, with adequate appointments. The acting president of the National University should hold a position not below the highest officers of Church and State. This lofty station could excite no jealousy, as the existing usage might be confirmed by statute—viz. that the holder of the office should go out at the end of four years. The commissioners of 1850 did not propose any alteration in the mode of appointment, but wished Heads of Halls to be made eligible. I would leave the nomination with the Chancellor, but would extend his range of selection as widely as could safely be done. If proper security can be taken that the Chancellor shall no longer be a party man, and make party appointments, all limitations on his choice could be removed. At present the rotation among the Heads of Colleges, which rests partly on usagè partly on statute, seems a necessary safeguard against party selection.

When securities have been taken for the fitting selection of the Vice-Chancellor, I should propose to invest him, to a greater extent than is now done, with the delicate task of selecting the men to fill offices. This proposal will be developed further on.

Financial Administration.—I have been favoured by Professor Bartholomew Price with the following observations on the present system of university Finance :—

" The 'business' of the University is not essentially different to that of other corporations. As it possesses large and important privileges in reference to the city of Oxford, and to other external bodies, as well as to its own members, these require constant attention, and much injury has been received by the University through want of proper care during the last few years ; for while valuable privileges have been conceded, advantage has not been taken of the opportunity for obtaining just and reasonable compensation. The most extensive part of the business, however, is the financial. It consists mainly of—(1) The collection of the revenue ; (2) The distribution of the same ; (3) The keeping and supervision of the requisite accounts. A few words will be sufficient to show the importance of good management in each of these departments. The revenue is derived from rents of lands, tithes, dividends of the public funds ; from fees paid at matriculations, examinations, conferring of degrees ; from dues paid annually by all

members of the University, and from the Clarendon press.
The corporate revenue is derived from all these sources ; and
besides there are large properties held by the University in
trust, for charitable and academical uses. The revenue is
appropriated to the payment of University officers, of examiners, of certain professors ; to the general expenses of the University, the repair of public and other buildings ; to the
maintenance of the Bodleian Library, of the reading-rooms,
of the Randolph Galleries, of the museum, of the night-police,
of the public walks ; to the payment of preachers. The
accounts are such as are necessarily incidental to all these
items of revenue and disbursement, and require to be kept on
that system which has been found to be most efficient, and to
supply the most rigorous checks. A cash-book, a roll on the
principle of charge and discharge, ledgers, balance-sheets, etc.,
are such forms as the principle of double entry supplies,
and are what give the best security for accuracy and the
greatest facility for audit. Without entering into details as
to the sums, some notion of the extent of these accounts may
be formed from the fact that the fees have to be collected
from more than 2500 different persons, the annual dues (and
these are collected quarterly) from more than 7000, and payments made to more than 100. These are also exclusive of
the funds held in trust by the University. Of these separate
accounts are kept, which are also separately discharged and
audited ; and great care is needed in these accounts, as they
are exempted from the control of the charity commissioners.
Parliament has trusted the University in this matter, and the
University reciprocally has its trust to discharge.

" Although the business, as this meagre outline shows, is
large, yet there is in it nothing extraordinarily peculiar. The
accurate discharge of it requires only that plan which is
adopted elsewhere, and which alone affords the necessary
securities for accuracy and promptness. Corporations, lay and
ecclesiastical, guilds in the City of London, public institutions,

give instances of such a mode of conducting business. In these systems there are three departments—(1) A directing and controlling body; (2) An executive officer; (3) An examination or audit to test and certify the correctness of the accounts. Consequently the following organisation is required:—

" The superintendence and direction of all the business of the University should be vested in a finance committee or delegacy. All receipts should be accounted to them; and all payments made under their authority, with the securities against fraud or dishonesty which are usual with such bodies. This committee would meet at such intervals as the business required, would be large enough to give confidence, and not too large for the transaction of business or shifting of responsibility.

" They would require the services of an executive officer or secretary, who would be accountable to them and be their ' man of business,' for he would prepare all the business for their meetings, make minutes of their transactions, collect the revenue as it became due, pay the University officers, etc., keep the books, have the entries in the cash-book duly posted into the ledgers, prepare the balance-sheets and abstract of the accounts, prepare all the vouchers for the auditors, and keep, of course, all the trust-accounts. As the secretary would thus be brought into close and confidential relation with the executive of the University, he should also take charge of all the documents and papers which come into the hands of the executive, and especially of the Vice-Chancellor, so that they may be distributed and arranged for the purpose of subsequent reference. He would have an office, and be accessible at convenient times. He should manifestly be a gentleman of habits and taste for business, and if educated as a lawyer perhaps the better; of a methodical mind, and acquainted with the most approved mode of book-keeping; above all things, a man of good judgment and of prudence, as his work would be to conduct the business of the University and to protect its interests—such a person, in short, as the owner of large estates would select as a confidential adviser and manager of his business.

" The accounts should also be submitted, with the books and their vouchers, to competent auditors, who should certify to their correctness after comparing the items with their vouchers, and should also certify the correctness of the abstracts and balance-sheets which should be laid before Convocation. The number of such auditors should be small— perhaps there should be no more than two or three—and they might be advantageously assisted by a professional accountant.

" Such is a short outline of the mode in which the way of conducting business in similar institutions elsewhere may be applied to the University. Business of the magnitude and of the variety, which that of the University now has, cannot be properly conducted without adequate machinery, and the machinery above described is that which has been applied elsewhere, and offers more and greater guarantees for efficiency than any other. The adoption of it would be no violent innovation in the scheme detailed in the statutes of the University. The delegates of estates, to whom is now entrusted the management and letting of the estates, would become the finance delegacy ; and, strengthened by the finance secretary, who would be their man of business, they would administer as an executive, the revenue of the University. The delegates of accounts, who are the auditors—' Delegati pro rationibus computandis '—would continue the auditors, but the number would be diminished, and their efficiency, increased by the assistance of a professional auditor, would be augmented. The Vice-Chancellor, occupying an office of great dignity and honour, would be relieved of the burden and responsibility of the University accounts, which should not ever, as it appears by the statute, have been cast upon him ; and the members of the University resident in Oxford, the greater part of whom are devoted to education, learning, and science—pursuits eminently unfitting them for business—would have the assurance that their business and finance were managed in a way the most approved and least liable to miscarriage."

This suggestion of Professor Price I would extend in its scope. Why should not the colleges be relieved of the burden of management of their property, and throw their accounts into the same office, with proper provision for superintendence, in which the university business is to be conducted?

Proctors and Police.—The " watch and ward " is among the oldest of university privileges. When the students outnumbered the citizens, or were that part of the population from which riot and disorder had to be apprehended, the whole police was reasonably thrown upon the university. It was, indeed, rather a privilege than a burden, in times when, if you wished to be safe, it was necessary to protect yourself. Now, it is a burden unfairly distributed. The university alone, with a population of under 2000, bears the whole cost of the night-police, now about £1900 per annum. It is not an efficient force, and can never be made one, as the same constables must be out on duty every night. This arrangement, which is without parallel, it is believed, in any other town in the kingdom, is destructive of the health, and consequently of the morale, of the men. Even the liberal scale of wages, 21s. per week, is found insufficient to attract or retain efficient men in the force. All these evils have been long well known, and were dwelt upon in the evidence to the Royal Commission of 1850. No steps were taken by the university till 1862, when the matter was considered by the Hebdomadal Council. A committee of Council reported in favour of consolidation with the county police. This scheme would certainly provide an efficient force, under Government superintendence, by one experienced and well-paid officer of high social position. It would cost less than the present inefficient force. But it would still be open to the objection of separating between the day and the night service. The true remedy is the amalgamation of County, City, and university police into one corps, under an undivided authority. Even if the university were entitled to an exceptional position of independence, it would be greatly for its interest to waive its privilege. Partly from a conservative timidity on the part of the university, and partly from the interested opposition of the City, which dislikes being expected to bear its proportionate share of the expense, nothing has yet been possible. No arrangement can be satisfactory which does not explicitly resign the ancient claim of the university to an exclusive police. The gownsmen must be amenable to exactly the same police jurisdiction as the citizens. This will become more especially necessary as the students lodging out increase in number, and houses of refreshment on a large scale, such as exist at Padua, and in other foreign universities, are opened for their accommodation. A stipendiary magistrate to hear the cases would be imperatively required.

I have reprinted in the Appendix (A) a statement issued by the Council, which represents the grievance at present inflicted upon the university.

Sec. 3.—Of the Endowments.

From the general government of the university I pass to its Endowments.

In speaking of the endowments as university endowments, it is not forgotten that the university of the Chancellor, masters, and scholars, is one corporation, and each of the colleges distinct and independent societies, with their separate code of laws. But the common purpose which unites university and colleges into one comprehensive whole, requires to be kept in view in all consideration of the endowments. At the time of the last commission, in 1850, our disposition was to urge the distinction between the university and the colleges upon the Legislature and the public. Out of a just jealousy of their legal rights, the colleges resented the inclination which was shown to treat their property as equitably convertible to the uses of a distinct corporation. This was done notwithstanding; but, paralysed by our clamours and our undeniable right, the omnipotence of Parliament was only exerted to an extent which did not materially benefit the university, while it enabled the colleges to complain of confiscation. Since our rights are no longer invaded, we have had time for reflection. We have learned that there is no conflict of objects or interests between the colleges and the university—that they are, in fact, the same men under a different denomination. There was no point on which university reformers before 1850 had been more unanimous and decided than in the assertion that the usurpation of the colleges had been the destruction of Oxford. The same complaint necessarily held a prominent place in the blue-book of the commission. Even as late as 1856 we find Dr. Donaldson reflecting that "the subjection of the university to the colleges is the cause of all that is wrong in the practical working of the Cambridge system" (*Classical Learning*, p. 46). Hence the watchword of reform was the "Professorial system." The professor was the *university* officer, who had been supplanted by the tutor, a *college* officer. Parliament was invoked to restore the teaching to the university officer. The commission to which was entrusted the execution of the Act 17 and 18 Victoria, c. 81, dared not do this. The teaching still remains in the hands of the members of colleges. Yet we hear no more of the old complaint of the usurpation of university functions by the colleges. The explanation of this is that the reformers had seized upon the great evil of the place, but had assigned it to a wrong cause. One great and crying evil of old Oxford was the inefficiency of the teaching. But this inefficiency did not arise from the circumstance that the teacher was a tutor and not a professor, nor from the circumstance that he was a Fellow of a college, and not an unattached member of the university. I have always regarded the relation of tutor and pupil as being a relation more efficacious for instruction than the relation of professor and student. And I believe the soundest opinion among us inclines to the same side. The cause of the inefficiency of the teaching in Oxford in the old days was, as I have indicated elsewhere, to be sought in the low standard of attainment in the place, a standard common to the university and the colleges. Provided the teacher be competent—*i.e.*, provided he be a master in the science he professes to teach—he will gain in power by being brought into the close and confidential relation of tutor. And university professors are not always found to be at the level of existing knowledge in their special profession.

Even so far as conflict between university and college interests actually existed, it has been gradually ceasing to operate. " The members of the foundations of the colleges," says an anonymous observer, " are gradually losing their exclusive hold on the affairs of the university. The number of resident Fellows is diminishing ; the number of resident M.A.'s who are not Fellows is increasing. An important share in university business is now taken by men whose main connection is with the university itself. Some, indeed, are college tutors or lecturers ; but it is now not uncommon for a man to be a lecturer in a college of which he is not a member. Even in these cases the exclusive college connection and college feeling is very much shattered. Others of the resident graduates belong wholly to the university. They are simply professors and private tutors, whose whole connection is with the university, who are bound to their colleges by no tie beyond that which they share with their non-resident members " (*Saturday Review*, 2d February 1867).

The University *versus* the College, then, though it may heretofore have served the purpose of ascertaining our rights, and awakening us to our duties, is no longer a relevant issue. The question seems to have passed into a further stage, in which we are free to consider the whole of our endowments in reference to their national destination and utility.

It is obviously beyond the scope of this memoir to

enter on the abstract question of endowed establishments. Their expediency is one of those points which the progress of political experience is considered to have still left undecided. The fact of this indecision in the science of economics has an unhappy effect in practice which ought to be adverted to. A mass of opinion continues to exist among the public hostile to endowments, on principle. When, therefore, we have practically to deal with endowments we handle them as half ashamed of them, as if we must apologise for them, as if they could only be excused by being directed upon the most popular objects. We do not first propose to ourselves a social end, and then set about providing the means. We find a great national endowment, and we consider how we shall dispose of a sum which must be spent somehow. In this spirit the chapter property was treated in 1834, and the same feeling seems to have presided over the arrangements of the executive commission for Oxford in 1854. It is much to be desired that, when re-organisation of the university shall again be discussed, it shall not be under the paralysing influence of this impression.

We must not then assume the principle of endowment. This would be to beg the question, and to raise our whole superstructure on a disputable basis. Let it be that history has accumulated a weight of experience against endowments, which is a set-off against their obvious advantages. But whatever may be the case in a normal state of society, an imperfect stage of national life requires other aids. No one will dispute that we are now in a transitional period of society in this country—*i. e.*, society is not now organised for permanence. When it shall be so organised we may then do without endowments. The nation will then want nothing which it 'does not choose to pay for out of the annual taxes.

" If a government," says Mr. Mill, " is so wise, and if the people rely so implicitly on its wisdom as to find money out of the taxes for all purposes of utility to which they could have applied the endowment, it is of no consequence whether the endowment be alienated or not. . . . But all know how far the fact at present differs from any such supposition. It is impossible to be assured that the people will be willing to be taxed for every purpose of moral and intellectual improvement for which funds may be required. But if there were a fund specially set apart, which had never come from the people's pockets at all, which was given them in trust for the purpose of education, and which it was considered improper to divert to any other employment, while it could be usefully devoted to that, the people would probably be always willing to have it applied to that purpose. . . . If it be said that as the people grow more enlightened they will become more able to appreciate, and more willing to pay for, good instruction ; that the competition of the market will become more and more adequate to provide good education, and endowed establishments will be less and less nécessary ; we admit the fact. And it might be said, with equal truth, that as the people improve there will be less and less necessity for penal laws. But penal laws are among the indispensable means of bringing about this very improvement, and in like manner, if the people ever become sufficiently enlightened to be able to do without educational endowments, it will be because thóse endowments will have been preserved and prized, and made efficient for their purpose. It is only by a right use of endowments that a people can be raised above the need of them" (J. S. Mill, *Dissertations*, i. 31).

The question we have to ask is not, What shall we do

with our endowments? but, For a great national purpose which we have in view, how can we make the endowments go as far as possible in promoting it? A disposition is too prevalent to insist upon getting some work done for the money, but to care little what, provided it be only "work." The public are in that frame of mind with respect to endowments, in which indignation against their being "sinecures," is the predominant motive. They shall no longer be sinecures, everybody shall "do something." They shall even be made to learn (or to teach) the Greek grammar, if nothing better can be found for them to do. Little can be hoped from a university reform which is undertaken with no higher views of policy than a determination to put an end to sinecures. Full of a great and noble purpose to be effected, a statesman will at the same time not neglect to economise his resources. But no great or noble purpose can be answered by endowments when the national grantor allows them to subsist with a half suspicion that they are an abuse, and the grantee is compelled to vindicate his right to live by convulsive efforts to do something or other, merely as evidence of activity.

I have not information which would enable me to state the total revenue of the university and the colleges. The information does not exist at present in an accessible form. The report of the commission of 1852 was defective on this point. Their statement (*Report*, pp. 125-127) of the university income and expenditure is not accurate, and on the property and revenue of the colleges they have few data. Each college probably knows its own resources, but no college knows, except by casual rumour, anything of its neighbour's income. The decennial return of income to be made by each college, under the ordinances, has yet to be made for the first time. When made, it will be made to the visitor, and will not necessarily be before Parliament. Even if accessible, these returns, not being ordered to be made up on a uniform system, would probably require to be stated afresh before general totals could be calculated from them. When, in 1854, Parliament undertook to transfer a portion of the college revenues, it was not only robbing, but robbing in the dark. Before the Legislature again attempts a re-adjustment of the distribution of our income from endowments, it would surely be as well that it should be in possession of the exact figures. Respectful treatment of the university cannot require that its accounts should not be examined, while, at the same time, its property is being dealt with. A parliamentary return might be ordered on a uniform schedule of the estimated value of the realised property of the university and the colleges, of its annual proceeds, and of expenditure—such a return as is supplied to the Charity Commission by all trustees of charities. It is desirable even that such a return should be before the public as a guide in that public discussion which must in this country precede legislative action. If there be " danger" in this disclosure, surely discussion in ignorance, and therefore exaggeration of the actual amount, is still more " dangerous."

A statement was recently in circulation that the colleges would, in a given time, be in possession of £100,000 a year more than they could divide as personal income. (Each fellowship is limited, under the ordinances of the commission of 1854, to a maximum dividend of about £300 a-year). This statement was inquired into by Sub-committee I.; but the inquiry was made in a vague manner, which resulted in the vague reply that "the college would not in the next twenty years acquire any surplus which it would not need for its own purposes." With a view to the considerations and suggestions now to be offered, it is immaterial what is the precise amount of nett revenue of the colleges, be it £100,000, £150,000, or £200,000 a-year. I have not to arrange the details of a new scheme, but to consider the *general character* of the actual and possible appropriation of our resources.

First, as to the *actual* distribution of our income from endowments, considered as a national outlay for national purposes.

If we had before us the figures representing the gross income of the university and the colleges of Oxford in one sum, it might seem to many to be a large one. But we must remember that the gross revenue of these bodies is subject to very heavy deductions before it becomes the nett personal income of the individuals forming the corporation. The property of the colleges is almost wholly land or house property. That of the university is so in a great measure. After deducting from gross rental the cost of management and the ordinary burdens on land, the remainder becomes again the *gross* income of the corporations. This gross income is then again subjected to fresh burdens. These burdens are partly in the shape of oppressive local rates, partly in the shape of edifices costly to maintain, and partly wages and salaries of officers and servants required for the local and material existence of the various corporations. Under almost every one of the heads of local rate the university has gradually been fixed with an unfair proportion of the burden. Every one of these encroachments has a separate history of its own, forming to the historian a very curious sequel to the bloody Town and Gown battles of the thirteenth and fourteenth centuries. Of the police system, under which the university, for a population of 2000, is content to pay £1900 a-year, against £600 paid by the city for a population of 30,000, I have already spoken. The incidence of the poor-rate and of the paving-rate seems to be equally to our disadvantage. The rent of college-rooms has not been raised anything like in proportion to house-rent, yet college-rooms are valued to the poor-rate at a fancy valuation far beyond their actual return. Not only so, but though much university property is exempt from rate as "public buildings," it has been ruled by the Queen's Bench that all college buildings whatsoever are private property; and our chapels, halls, and libraries, producing us no revenue, and kept up at a great cost, stand in the rate-book at prodigiously high figures. In this case we have at least the satisfaction of being mulcted by the law of the land, and not by the city. The law has, of course, good grounds for the distinction drawn between university and college buildings. Yet reason cannot help suggesting that as the college buildings are for the exclusive enjoyment of the members of the college, so the university buildings are for that of the wider corporation of the Chancellor, masters, and scholars. None but *academici* have access to them except by courtesy. And how can college property be at one and the same time a public trust for national purposes and private dwellings for the purposes of taxation? The maintenance, again, of fabrics—ancient, and having an architectural character—forms a far heavier percentage on the income of the proprietor than the maintenance of an equal extent of ordinary house-property. Some part of this cost of maintenance being for tenantable rooms, or otherwise enjoyed by individuals resident, cannot be considered as a deduction from gross revenue, but forms part of the personal *beneficium.* Much as has been done of late years in the way of new, and re-, building in Oxford, far more remains to be done to arrest decay, or to fit the apartments to the purposes of modern civilised life. These demands must be borne in mind in making an estimate of our disposable means. As to the unequal apportionment of our other local rates, it has been a consequence of our local relations with the town. Our transactions with the city, instead of being conducted on a business footing, were for a long time managed as transactions between gentlemen and tradesmen. We were expected, and submitted, to pay a gentleman's price—*i.e.,* a little more than other people, and than the worth of the article. In return for this we obtained privileges from an unreformed House of Commons, an assembly of gentlemen whose sympathies were always with us. Things are now on the way to be put on a sounder footing. We obtain no privileges, and we want none; but we should decline any longer to pay a gentleman's price for our police—for our gas—for our water—for our local government. This class of *coulage* would be stopped at once if our finance, instead of being done by ourselves, was administered by an office like the income of any public company.

These deductions made, the distribution of the nett

residue of university and college revenues taken together may be considered as taking place in three channels :—

1. One portion, being the great bulk of our income, is laid out in subsidising education, in the shape of scholarships, exhibitions to students, and fellowships to graduates.

2. Another portion, of smaller amount, is expended in the payment of teachers—*i.e.*, professors, lecturers, chaplains, deans, or officers of discipline.

3. Lastly, a third, but inconsiderable, fraction of our income is appropriated to the maintenance and encouragement of science and learning, canonries, headships, libraries, museums, etc.

It will be observed that some of these institutions or persons serve more than one of the three purposes here distinguished. Five canons of Christ Church are also professors. A museum is often so arranged as to be useful in education, rather than scientifically ; and a professor may, if his statutes permit it, devote himself to the study of his science rather than to its teaching. This overlapping of functions, however, is incidental. With my present object of ascertaining what national purposes are actually realised through our endowments, it will be more convenient to discriminate the purposes, rather than the persons.

Sec. 4.—Actual Distribution of the Endowment Fund.

§ 1.—*Of Subsidies to Education.*

a. Scholarships.—Scholarships and exhibitions, being stipends enjoyed by students in the pupillary state, clearly fall under this head. The sum of £35,000 per annum, or thereabouts, may represent that part of our income which is absorbed by undergraduate students during their course of study, preliminary to the degrees.

This outlay upon students' pensions may, however, be made, according to the mode of its distribution, to answer three quite distinct purposes:—(1.) It may be given as prizes to merit, and so serve to stimulate industry. (2.) It may be given to poverty, and so serve to give the means of education to those who would be otherwise unable to pay for it. (3.) It may operate as a bounty on a particular kind of education—*i.e.*, it may be a mode of creating an artificial demand for classics, or mathematics, while the natural course of supply and demand would lead to the establishment of other kinds of education.

In which of these three directions does the sum expended on scholarships, etc., really act at present?

Of all the proposals of the Commission of 1850, none was more generally acceptable than the proposal to commute fellowships into scholarships—in other words, stipends to B.A.'s into stipends to undergraduates. For the complaint of the costliness of a university education is one of the oldest and most urgent complaints which has been standing against us. The reduction of college expenses was, at the time of the commission of 1850, a first object with the public. And an opinion was widely prevalent that exhibitions were a mode of meeting this costliness. In 1846 a petition praying for "the foundation of exhibitions, to be conferred, not upon grounds of literary merit, but of poverty, character, and economical habits," came before the (old) Hebdomadal Board. In compliance with the prayer of this petition, the board voted £20,000 out of the university chest for the purpose of helping poor scholars, but they afterwards rescinded the vote, and it never came before Convocation. When the commission of 1850 proposed a large creation of scholarships, the public, who thought they saw in this measure a means of lightening the burden of maintaining their sons at Oxford, welcomed the proposal, and that part of the reform movement hardly met with opposition from any quarter. It is true the commission had left no doubt as to their intentions in the large augmentation of open scholarships which they recommended. " What the State and the Church require is not poor men, but good and able men, whether poor or rich " (*O. U. C. Report*, p. 174). They meant scholarships to be so administered as to stimulate the industry of the able, not to aid parents in meeting the expenses of the place. The result of twelve years' experience is that the intentions of the commission have been carried out, and the expectations of the public have not been realised. Open scholarships have been multiplied on all sides with eager rivalry. The market is glutted. A scholarship open to competition is now, probably, within the reach of as low a grade of attainments as that which used to fill the old restricted scholarships. Yet university education is not cheapened. For what colleges have done in the way of reduction of their fees and charges with one hand, they have undone with the other, by lavish allowances to scholars. We have secretly supplied fuel to the fire we were engaged in extinguishing. Well-to-do parents continue to make their sons the usual allowance, and the scholar treats his £80 a-year as so much pocket-money, to be spent in procuring himself extra luxuries.

It may be said that the increase of the matriculations proves that a poorer class have reaped some of the benefit of the creation of scholarships. It is the case that the number of entries exceeds that of ten years ago by about 150 (Appendix B). But other causes are at work to increase the number of those who now seek admittance at the university. The rapid growth of general wealth, the rise of the middle class, the spread of the desire of cultivation, must ere this have shown themselves by a far larger augmentation of our numbers than has taken place, but for other powerful counter-motives. But even if our increased numbers be to a slight extent due to the increased number of open scholarships, this does not show that scholarships aid poor men. The question is not, Has the multiplication of scholarships drawn more men to Oxford? but, Has it brought the university within the reach of a class socially below the class who frequented it before? I think the answer must be that it has *not*. The class which enjoys the scholarships and exhibitions now is the very same class which monopolised them under the old system of close foundations. The difference is that the scholarship, instead of being a pension obtainable by interest, is now a reward for past industry and an obligation for the future.

The open scholarship fund, then, as now dispensed, does not act as an instrument of university extension. It acts as prize-money. Scholarships are educational prizes. The national outlay under the head " Scholarships and Exhibitions " is so much prize-money distributed among the grammar-schools, the university being merely the competent and impartial examiner. To effect this purpose, it is essential that all other considerations, such as family circumstances, should be rigidly excluded from the award, otherwise the whole effect is destroyed. Merit on the one hand, and impartiality on the other, are conditions of a prize system. Taking, as it did, this view of scholarships, the Commission of 1850 has been justified by the result. There can be no doubt that a most powerful impulse has been given to the grammar-schools by the opening of the scholarships. The same social class as before frequents the schools, but a direction and a motive have been supplied to their industry which were before wanting.

On the university itself the effect has been no less beneficial. Even if it has not increased the numbers, or the amount of talent, it has brought that talent forward in a way in which it was not before. It has awakened dormant energies, and stirred the stagnant waters. A class of young men has been brought within the range of intellectual ambition, who were never reached by it before—that large class who possess intelligence, but in whom intelligence is not a predominant faculty sufficiently powerful to urge to self-cultivation without extrinsic motive. The scholars constitute an order bound to study as much by the opinion of their fellows as by the tenure of their gown. The existence of such an order is beneficial beyond its own pale by influence and example. Study, from being the peculiarity of an exceptional minority, is becoming, let us say with thankfulness, more and more the tone of a large proportion of the students in many colleges, though in too many others the traditions of Eton still give the law to undergraduate opinion.

Such results must be admitted to be worth having. They are results cheaply purchased to the national university by a small sum in school prize-money, into the actual amount of which we must not minutely inquire. And, indeed, there appears to be no difference of opinion so far. All are agreed that scholarships may be usefully awarded as prizes. Even those who contend for the "claims of poverty" seem to acquiesce in the large appropriation of funds now made to competitive prizes. No one is proposing to alter the present scholarship system. But there are two opinions prevalent as to additions which may be made to the fund now distributed under the head of " Subsidies to Education."

1. There are many university reformers who wish to see a further and large creation of prize scholarships.

2. There is an influential section of opinion which would not call itself reforming, which is in favour of a large creation of exhibitions, which should not be awarded as prizes, but given to " poor men."

Each of these schemes requires a short consideration.

1. The fund from which it is demanded that more scholarships should be created is the fellowships. This opinion therefore is in part due to a growing feeling of the waste of endowment occasioned by the existing administration of fellowships. Here, it is said, is a channel ready provided into which the redundant waters of fellowship-endowments may be profitably directed. The scholarship system has proved its utility by experience. We have experimented with a small suppression of fellowships, and it has answered well. We have but to go on in the same direction to reap a more abundant harvest.

I am ready to admit that the fellowships as now

bestowed do not answer any proper purpose, and that the time has come when the destination of that fund should be reconsidered. But even if this fund was wanted for scholarships, it is, as will be argued further on, more urgently required in another direction. But it is not wanted for scholarships. There is in the nature of things a limit to the influence of prizes. A prize in education, whether honorary or pecuniary, is a stimulant applied to given faculties in the learner:—observation, attention, perseverance, etc. There must be in any congregation of boys enough of such prizes to operate through hope on all the individuals; not so many as to be attainable as a certainty by all who go through a given preparation. As soon as this limit has been reached, a further multiplication of prizes is not merely superfluous, it defeats their object. It requires to be carefully considered by those who are on the spot, and who have the means of knowing what is the average amount of attainment required to obtain a scholarship, if we have not already reached this limit. Some think that we have already passed it. The scholar's gown is too often to be found on youths who have no vocation for science or literature, and whom it was no kindness to have drawn away from their proper destination to active life. They have come here as a commercial speculation. High wages are given for learning Latin and Greek, and they are sent to enlist to earn the pay. In other words, we fear that the scholarships have been multiplied beyond the limit within which they act as an incentive to industry, and that they are become a bounty upon a privileged species of education. Such bounties, like the old bounty on agricultural produce, have but the effect of bringing under tillage land of a quality so inferior that it could not in the natural market have competed with more genial soils. When we consider, out of our 1700 students, how many are here chiefly because they are paid to come here, the reflection will arise, Can an education which requires so heavy a pecuniary premium to get itself accepted be really the excellent thing we profess it to be ?

I am compelled here to advance to a distinction which may be disputable, but which seems to me to touch the principle on which the distribution of our funds will have to be decided. Most educated men would probably agree in the opinion quoted above (p. 50) from Mr. Mill, to the effect that, in the highest culture the supply must precede the demand, and that, though in a perfect condition of society endowments would be superfluous, in a transition stage like ours they may be highly necessary. This is, in fact, to grant that education may be promoted by bounties. Granted ; but the distinction must come in between the elementary stages of education and those higher stages in which education becomes science and literature. Endowments being assumed, I contend that their proper objects are the later stages of education, or science and learning, not the elementary course fitted for youths under age. Science and learning are the luxuries, not the necessaries, of society. If you think proper to have them, you must create the conditions of their stable existence. They must be endowed. It is otherwise with so much of education as is a preparation for life. A good preparation for life will always be in demand—the best preparation in the most demand. If our education were, what we say it is, the best education to be had in the country, would it be necessary to bribe parents so heavily to let their children enjoy it ?

But it will be said, It may be the best, and yet parents below a certain grade of culture cannot see that it is so. Why not get the children here anyhow, so as you give them what is best for them ? This is an economical sophism which is well understood to be so in the lower grades of schooling. It is highly expedient that all children should learn to read, write, and cipher, yet no government would ever think of filling the national and parochial schools by paying wages to the children for attending them. There is no difference whatever in principle between paying wages for school attendance, and scholarships, when administered in such a way as to become an inducement to enter the university. It is quite an open question, and is even now under debate, how far it is the duty of a government to universalise elementary education by means of compulsion. Here too the analogy between the lowest and the highest grade of training youth, between the village school and the university, holds good. There are weighty arguments for and against compulsory primary education. The very same arguments—for and against—apply to the case of compulsory university education. A university degree is made compulsory on one profession, the clerical. It is quite an open question if a university degree might not with advantage be required, as in Prussia, for large departments of the Civil Service. If the question of compulsory university education has not yet been debated in this country, it is partly because of the expense, and partly because of the doubt which exists as to the real effect of the intellectual training given here. When the studies shall be put upon a satisfactory footing, and the extravagant habits of the place have been replaced by a spirit of self-denying economy, who can doubt that "compulsory education" will become a favourite form in which "university extension" will be advocated?

Care must be taken, then, that the scholarship fund is so administered by the university as to act as a stimulus to industry, and not to pass the point at which it becomes a premium on going to school, or staying there a longer time. But even within these limits, even as a prize system, we must remember that we are in danger of leaning too much upon it. These competitive examinations, even while they urge to work, have a fatal tendency to falsify education. Open scholarships have not been an unmixed good. They have stirred up the schools, but they have also stirred up an unwholesome system of training the competitors for the race. The youth comes up with a varnish of accomplishment beyond his real powers. He has caught the spirit of his professional trainers. He has learned to regard his classics, not as the portals of a real knowledge, but as the verbal material of an athletic conflict. It is useless for real genius to enter the lists of competition without this training. It is easy for mediocrity, by putting itself under training, to reach one of the prizes. Thus a life has been quickened among us, but it is not a thoroughly sound and healthy life.

Much remains to be done before the fund to be appropriated to prize scholarships will be in proper working order. I venture to offer the following suggestions:—

(1.) The whole number of such scholarships bears too large a proportion to the whole number of students, and might be diminished with advantage. Should the total of

F

students be materially increased—say to 2000—the number of prizes annually given might be increased in proportion.

(2.) The value of each scholarship is too large. This value has indeed reached its present dimensions by the accidental division of the university into independent, and, for this purpose, rival, houses. Every college is desirous to have its rooms full, and every college is desirous of showing as many university honours as it can. Consequently the colleges outbid each other in the general market for talent. If one college raises its scholarships to £100 a-year, the others must go as far in the same direction as their means will allow, except where, like Balliol, they can set off a prestige of long standing against a deficiency in the stipend.

(3.) Fewer scholarships, and of less money-value, would, I think, have fully as great effect as at present, if, instead of being given away for the convenience of each college, they were organised on a footing common to the whole university. A fixed number should be vacant every year, assignable among the colleges in the proportions of their respective contributions to the prize-fund. An examination might be held twice in the year. It should be conducted by boards of examiners, one for each of the subjects to which prizes were assigned —one-half of these examiners to be appointed by the Vice-Chancellor, the other half by the professors (in turns) of the several faculties to which the boards would belong. The examiners might be paid by a small fee taken from each candidate, or by a percentage upon the amount of prize-money distributed. These public scholarships, and these only, with the university scholarships, should entitle to the scholar's gown. The gown is not a mere badge of distinction, but is valuable as a token of an obligation. For the same reason, it seems better that the money-value, however small in amount, should be in the form of an allowance spread over the whole three years of residence than given in one sum. The head and tutors of the college should not merely have the power, but should be charged with the duty, to pronounce the scholarship vacant, upon failure of the scholar to present himself at the proper time for any of his public examinations, or on the ground of general in-attention to study. As the obligation to a course of study is a condition of the tenure of these prize-scholarships, there would be no hardship in enforcing resignation, even where ill-health or any other cause made study impossible.

2. There is an influential section of opinion which considers that the proper purpose of scholarships and exhibitions is to make the university accessible to the sons of parents whose incomes are too narrow for the scale of expenditure at present prevailing. The section of reformers who are desirous of converting fellowships into prize-scholarships are formidable from their influence rather than their numbers. The advocates of *Poor Men's Exhibitions* are numerous as well as influential. This latter scheme is probably, as a mode of " University Extension," that favoured by the largest number of those who usually interest themselves in our affairs. This always favourite scheme has been brought forward lately, strongly endorsed by one of the sub-committees on University Extension. This was Sub-committee II., consisting of the following names :—Provost of Worcester, Warden of All-Souls, Master of Pembroke, R. Michell, Professor Wall, J. Gilbertson, J. Rigaud, E. Palin, P. G. Medd. This

body reported that the best means of extending the university was " the foundation of Exhibitions for the assistance of such persons as cannot support, unaided, the expenses of a university education." A proposal so supported demands an attentive consideration.

We all understand by " University Extension," not merely an addition to the numbers attending Oxford, but the admission to its benefits of a class which has been hitherto excluded by social position or income; for these two things are not, in this investigation, quite the same. This diversity of the causes of exclusion had some share in the discrepancy of the reports of the various sub-committees. For, while some of the recommendations aimed at drawing to Oxford classes whom other circumstances rather than expense had kept aloof from the Universities, Subcommittee II. considered exclusively the case of small income. If there be a class which is excluded from superior education by its costliness, but is at the same time eager to obtain it, that class certainly must have our sympathies. Where our education is contemned or vilipended, we may be little disposed to recommend a trial of it. But where we see it prized and coveted, but placed out of reach by its price, it is a natural impulse to wish that some wealthy patron would come forward to aid talent in its struggle with the " *res angusta domi.*" Every one would desire to encourage any mode in which university extension should be made to reach this class. Had the proposal of Sub-committee II. been merely that such exhibitions should be founded by private subscription, it might have passed unchallenged. But when they call upon the university for a heavy contribution (£20,000) from its funds, and go on to absorb the surplus of the college revenues into the same, it is necessary that their scheme should be submitted to a close scrutiny.

Sub-committee II. ask for £20,000 from the university, to be met by contributions from college surplus—they do not say in what proportion. But their expectations are not immoderate. The sub-committee is aware " that the obligations imposed by the ordinances are in many cases unfulfilled; fellowships have not attained their maximum; professorships remain to be endowed, and open scholarships to be established. The expenses incident to the running out of beneficial leases are considerable; and if land has been let out on building-leases, the pecuniary benefit of the transaction will not be reaped by this generation or the next. . . . Certain statements propounded respecting the wealth of colleges we hold to be entirely unsusceptible of proof" (*Report of Sub-committee II.* p. 6).

In the first place, the university has not got £20,000 to give if it would. In the next, we see, from what the committee says, that much cannot be hoped from the colleges. Could £20,000, if obtainable from the university, be doubled out of college resources? Surely it could not. But let us suppose that from all sources a capital sum of £50,000 could be got together for such an object; out of this are to come the houses in which the exhibitioners are to live (*Report,* p. 10). There would have to be, if not as many houses as colleges contributing, at least several houses either rented or purchased out of the fund, and fitted and furnished also. £10,000 of the capital is the least that could be appropriated for these purposes. The remaining £40,000 would yield about £1600 a-year for stipends.

Something would have to be paid for " supervision," which is to be provided in each house. But let us suppose that as much as £1600 could be given away in exhibitions. The Sub-committee II. has not determined the value of their exhibitions. They are to be in aid of the students' maintenance, and not the whole of it. We might in this way obtain from twenty to twenty-five annual purses distributable to poor men. An excellent work of charity possibly, but scarcely deserving to be considered a scheme of " University Extension;" yet even this result is far beyond the means suggested in the report of Sub-committee II.

There are, however, sources from which much larger means for the foundation of poor men's exhibitions may be obtained. The sub-committee do not even hint at these means, but others will not be so conservative or so reserved. Fellowships might be appropriated on a large scale to the purpose. Fellowships and canonries have been converted into prize scholarships, why should not a further conversion of them be effected into poor men's exhibitions? There are, as it seems to me, other and more urgent demands on the fellowships which will leave at present little margin for such a purpose. But let us suppose that (say) 150 poor men's exhibitions were created at once by suppressing fellowships to the extent of £10,000 per annum—and it will probably be conceded that more than this could not be obtained from any source—we have to consider what would be the economical effect of such a measure. The exhibitions must be tenable for four years. This would give, allowing for casual vacancies, a supply of somewhere under forty to be filled each year. There must be every year more than forty unsuccessful candidates for the existing prize-scholarships

who• could bring satisfactory evidence that they are incapable, without aid, of supporting themselves at the University. If, subject to this proof, the examination is to be
competitive, it is clear that the forty new poor men's exhibitions will fall to the forty *proxime accessits* to the prize
scholarships. We shall thus but have increased the number
of the existing prizes, already too numerous, and failed in
bringing up a single representative of a new and poorer
class to Oxford. Instead of proof of inability to support,
it may be attempted to institute comparison of means.
But no practical person would dream of such an inquisitorial proceeding on the part of a board of trustees of an
academical charity. Any attempt of the kind must issue
in a system of solicitation, under which the most needy are
not the most urgent or successful applicants. We should
be thrown back on the old system of nominations, with all
its well-known abuses, so familiar to those who remember
Oxford before 1854.

The impracticability of any equitable gauge of poverty,
either by testimonial or by inquiry, has been felt by Dr.
Lowe—a warm advocate of poor exhibitions. He has
favoured me with some suggestions which indicate more
matured reflection on the difficulties of the question than
could perhaps be bestowed by a committee which was tied
to time for producing its report. Dr. Lowe writes :—

" I would fence in these exhibitions from the encroachments of the rich. . . . They should be limited in value
so far as neither to make them attractive to the rich, nor to
afford an entire maintenance to the poor. Not being prizes in
reward of eminent distinction, but granted as an encouragement to youth of promise, they should be given *in aid;* and
taking the minimum of what college expenses ought to be to a

man of humble means, reckoning as such the sons of gentlemen poor enough to compete openly for eleemosynary assistance, the exhibitions might be in proportion of a third—not more, I think, than the half of the whole. But to meet cases often likely to arise, needing further help than this salutary restriction would allow, college prizes for special essays, or other work, might be annually offered from these public funds, which to a poor man might often come with untold value, as deciding the question even of a term's residence. I hold it essential that these exhibitions should be known distinctly as eleemosynary. This would in itself help to keep back many applicants, who would present themselves if they were regarded as honorary distinctions also. But besides this, the exhibitioners should be known to be poor men, in order to protect them from the system of tradesmen's credit. It might further be well that the benefits of his exhibition should reach him in the form of reduced fees, in providing furniture or payment of a private tutor, rather than in actual cash. Battels above a certain amount should certainly involve censure, or, if necessary, the withholding of a term's *beneficium* " (*A Plea for Poor Scholars*, p. 10 : Parker & Co., 1867).

The scheme as thus presented by Dr. Lowe is freed from the glaring flaw of the proposals of Sub-committee II.— viz. the impossibility of ascertaining poverty. His exhibitions are to be open to all. But it is supposed that no one will seek them who is not driven by pecuniary necessities. The position is to be made sufficiently unpalatable to the taste of youth, so that no one will submit to it who can possibly do without £60 a-year. Dr. Lowe's proposal is, in fact, a proposal to restore the sizarships and servitorships of a past age. Indeed, it is only within the last 100 years that the scholar's gown, now a robe of honour, was a badge of social inferiority, and exposed the wearer to the

nickname of " charity-boy." It is not so much we that
have abolished servitorships, as time and manners that
have made the position untenable. The change has taken
place in the country, and the university has but conformed
in this respect to the state of things outside its walls.
This is a fact in which we must acquiesce even if we do
not like it. We *cannot* institute a social rank in the
University which shall be outwardly stamped as " poor."
For my own part I do not regret the abolition of the
graduation of rank. This is not from any preference of
the modern indefinite gradations of income to the old
defined hierarchy of rank from the " nobleman down to
the servitor," but because, whatever may be the feelings of
a commercial community out of doors, I think the university is the one spot where the material estimate of worth
should be redressed by a moral standard, and where no
gradations should be recognised but the academical graduation which is the summit of faculty and attainment. It
would be vain indeed to hope to isolate in the middle of
modern society a philosophic Utopia into which no considerations of wealth and its advantages should penetrate.
But we should at least abstain from stamping such in-
equalities of fortune with outward marks of our approval,
as was done under the old system of matriculation. By
the abolition of the rank of " nobleman," as proposed in the
recent award at Christ Church, the last remnant of the
caste system will be swept away. I cannot, therefore, think
with Dr. Lowe that it would be possible to begin again to
revive an order of poor men, under the idea that when
recognised as poor they would be respectable as such.
There seems to underlie this proposal a view of " poverty,"

which, whatever may be its justification in Middle-age theology, has no standing-ground in societies where it is known that labour is the one and only source of wealth. Dr. Lowe thinks that their status as poor men would protect them against the tradesmen. But all the most flagrant instances of abuse of credit of late years have been in the case of men who are relatively " poor."

Nothing, indeed, can be more respectable, nor does anything secure more profound respect among us, than the cases (would that they were more numerous!) where a youth of humble origin, from mere love of learning and intellectual aspirations, undergoes bodily privations, hardships, and, harder still to bear, the contumely of the world of flunkeys. It would be very desirable that there should be in each college a small reserve fund out of which subsidies could be granted to meet such cases when they occur. But it is quite a different thing to create a set of exhibitions which shall invite applicants on the ground of poverty. We may predict with certainty that such exhibitions would never reach the class of men for whom they were intended. The number of those who seek education by means of the university is very small compared with the number of those who seek the degree and the social status it confers. Poor men's exhibitions would be besieged by applicants of the latter character. The social position of clergymen of the Established Church is, it must not be forgotten, an object of ambition among families of small means. To obtain ordination as a literate is something, but it is more desirable to obtain it as a B.A. of the university. Exhibitions, awarded not for merit, but for poverty, would probably fall to this class of candidates for orders. Of the interests of the Established Church as involved in this question, this is not the place to speak. But it can hardly be maintained that academical funds can with propriety be applied in aid of a social ambition, at least when the social ambition is divorced from any intellectual aim.

The question of university extension has been debated much among us of late. The general authorities of the university have at length taken alarm at the fact, which has long been matter of remark by thoughtful observers, that the increase of the numbers of our students has not kept pace with population, with wealth, nor, what is most alarming of all, with the spread of the desire of cultivation. A searching inquiry into the causes of their deficiency—an inquiry which should not shrink from probing matters to the quick—is a necessary preliminary to a discovery of the remedy. We naturally wish to keep up our numbers. No scheme for the desired end seems to find favour but the crude scheme of bounties. Already, nearly one-third of the whole number of students within our walls is being paid for coming here. We have very much increased the number of our exhibitions in the last ten years, and we have increased our students in that proportion. And the cry still is for more exhibitions. Now it is certainly true that its expensiveness is *one* of the causes which limit admissions. Further, *one* of the modes of meeting the objection of expense is the endowment of exhibitions. But it is only *one* of the modes, and requires to be subjected to carefully-watched conditions, so as not to encourage indolence or foment extravagance. And it is a mode of meeting cost which, even when most lavishly employed, can only add to our numbers by tens. It can never "extend" the university to a new and lower class of English society. If this is to be done, the expensiveness must be itself attacked in its causes. Instead of subsidising the poor student up to the level of our expenses, we ought to bring down the expenses to the level of the poor. It is idle to say we cannot. We have never tried. For what we *have* tried to do is, to restrain those who have money to spend, from extravagance. Something, but not much, can be hoped in this way. Sumptuary laws will be evaded by the rich. We cannot much beat down what those will spend who can spend, though it is desirable, for example's sake, that extravagance should be discouraged in every possible way. But what we can do is to make it possible for those who choose to live here economically. There are in the London hospitals 1350 medical students. The whole cost of preparation for the profession averages about £150 to each. The cost of a student at Oxford, at the most economical college, is calculated at £120 a-year— *i.e.,* for his whole residence, a sum of £500. It is clear that the price of education is artificially enhanced. That this enhancement is due mainly to the college and tutorial system no one will deny. Let students be allowed to matriculate, not subject to that system, and there is no reason why an Oxford training should cost more than a medical training. It is true that the article purchased for, say, a sum of £200, will be a different article from that which now costs £600 or £800. For it is truly urged that the collegiate life and domestic discipline are what make Oxford what it is. What the B.A. at present carries away with him is made up of a small modicum of acquired learning, and a peculiar stamp which remains upon him through life, and which constitutes undoubtedly a relative social advantage, whatever its intrinsic worth may be. Let parents clearly understand that they may buy the degree for £200, but that they do not buy this social stamp along with it. The question of university extension will then be much simplified. The existing domestic system would then be continued, but as a social luxury, like the first-class carriage in a railway, for those whose fortune warrants their having the indulgence. But the lecture-rooms, examinations, and degrees of the university, should be as open to all comers as a London hospital. The true nature of the exhibition scheme would then stand out in a clear light. The effect of an exhibition would be to help the student whose own resources would enable him to have all the intellectual benefit of the university, to have, over and above these, the social benefit of the college—to help him out of the second-class carriage into the first. Will it be replied that the influence of collegiate discipline is not merely or mainly social, that it is also moral, and therefore a part of education in the highest sense of the word? In discussing the same subject in 1851, I endeavoured to show that the collegiate influence resolved itself into two parts—(1.) the tutorial, and (2.) the domestic influence. While the tutorial influence is one of the most powerful momenta of university life, the domestic influence cannot be rated highly as a moral agency.

" A college was (then) not divided into tutors and pupils, but, like a Lacedemonian regiment, πᾶν ἄρχοντες ἀρχόντων εἰσιν, all were students alike, only differing in being at a different stage of their progress. Hence their life was long a life in common, with a common direction and occupation, and subject to one law. The seniors were at once the instructors and example of the juniors, who shared the same plain food, simple life, and narrow economy, looking forward themselves to no other life. And in that mode was obtained that which constituted the truly invaluable element of the college system—the close action of the teacher on the pupil, of the matured character on the unformed, of the instructed on the learning mind, not without a very beneficial reaction of the young on the aging man—an influence not unknown to the great and experienced men who originated and promoted colleges. This insensible action of the teacher's character on the pupil's is the most valuable part of any education; and any scheme which involved the loss of this influence would be much to be deprecated. But it is contended that this influence is not now excited by the body of the fellows on the undergraduates. College-life has ceased to be the life in common, even for the fellows, that it once was. As between the fellows, as a body, and the student, it creates no society whatever. Our existing system of college habits so far separates the undergraduate from the fellow, that his merely being lodged under the same roof, makes him no real member of the family, brings him into no contact with his seniors. The young men associate with and form one another's character mainly. The habits and manners which gave the conventual system its good effects being changed, we must not think any virtue resides in its mere forms " (*Oxford University Commission. Evidence*, p. 43).

Many things have changed in Oxford in sixteen years. These relations have, unless I am deceived, not changed. The relation between tutor and pupil is not become less valuable. The domestic influence of the college is not more ascetic and purifying than it then was. I then ventured to urge, and stood almost alone among the residents in doing so (H. H. Vaughan, then Professor of Modern History, and Professor Wall, argued on the same side), the abrogation of compulsory residence within college-walls. Though the Royal Commission reported in favour of a modified form of the same proposal (lodging-houses under due superintendence), it was not adopted. Influential persons of all parties threw their weight into the scale against it—Archbishop Whately and Dr. Pusey, Dr. Temple and Mr. Hayward Cox. The system of private halls, of which I then said that it would prove " a slow, cumbrous, and inadequate means of university extension," was preferred, and has more than verified the prediction. We are now back again, after fifteen years' delay, face to face with the inevitable conclusion. *Compulsory* residence within college-walls must cease to be the law of the university. So certain indeed is it to come, that it is better to regard it already as a *fait accompli*, and to consider what the situation will carry with it.

One correction of the opinion which I gave in 1851, in favour of out-students, I desire to make, and to embody in these suggestions. What I contemplated in my recommendation, at that time, was out-students only as attached to some college or hall. But such legislation would be simply legislation in favour of the fashionable colleges. If every college could admit pupils without stint, and lodge them in the town, all the other colleges would be deserted in favour of the three or four which happened to be the fashion. This would be no evil, it would be a positive advantage, if resort to a college was governed by its repute for discipline and work, or by the presence in it of some distinguished tutor. In this way a small university in

Germany suddenly rises into notoriety by retaining one eminent professor. But with us in Oxford it is not so. The resort to a college is numerous in proportion to the social standing of, and the money spent by, the undergraduates frequenting the college. In other words, there is the greatest pressure for admittance upon the books of precisely the most expensive colleges. It follows that any measure which admitted lodging-out only in connection with a college, would be a measure of encouragement to the expensiveness of Oxford. It is therefore essential to any measure of university extension—meaning by the term the inclusion of a poorer and lower social class—that permission to lodge out in the town should not be fettered by any obligation to belong to a college.

1. Under a system of unrestricted lodging-out a student will have the opportunity of obtaining an M.A. degree at about half its present cost, say for about £250 or £200.

2. He will lose certain social privileges—the association with gentlemen, the opportunity of forming durable connections, the sense of common membership, and the other incidents of life within the same walls.

3. He ought not to lose tutorial guidance; and it will be proposed elsewhere that every student should enter under an M.A. as tutor.

This then appears to me to be the true direction of university extension. The erection of a new college, and the creation of exhibitions at the old colleges by private munificence, though on no account to be discouraged, will effect, and are perhaps intended to effect, other objects. The question remains, Will unrestricted lodging-out effect its object—that, namely, of opening the university to men

of smaller incomes ? In other words, will the middle-class
give three years of life and a sum of £200 for the M.A.
degree when that degree is shorn of its present social
distinction ?

Let us go on to say that in order to induce them to do
so, it must be made clear that it is worth their while to do
so. In plainer words, to cheapen the cost of a university
education is only one-half of university extension. The
education given must be better adapted to the wants of the
class intended to benefit by it. Let Oxford become, as
nothing but artificial legislation prevents it from becoming,
the first school of science and learning in the world, and at
the same time let it be accessible at the cost only of board
and lodging, and it will attract pupils enough. If what we
have to teach requires to be bolstered up by bounties to
the taught, that is evidence that what we have to teach is
not recognised as of intrinsic utility. If what the public is
calling for under the name of university extension means
certain social advantages, at the university and afterwards,
for their sons, let them understand that these advantages
cannot be had cheap, and if had, ought to be paid for by
those who get them. Exhibitions are a means of extending
to a small additional number—a favoured few—this privilege. But aristocratic society must always remain a
privilege, and always be costly. Social combinations apart,
the necessaries of life cost no more in Oxford than in other
towns of the South of England. The inducement to spend
three years here can only be found in improving the instruction. The true solution of the problem of university
extension is to be found at last not in expedients for
recruiting more students, but in raising the character and
reputation of the body of teachers.

It will be understood that those of us who advocate "lodging-out" do not do so as preferring it in itself to a conventual discipline. Lodging-out is to be permissive only. It is to be open to those who choose it. Probably most parents will continue to prefer a residence in a college to private lodgings. While I quite agree with those who think that much advantage is, or may be in a well-disciplined college, obtained by a life in common, I only urge that college residence should not be compulsory on those who do not choose to pay an enhanced price for these advantages. The education and the degree should be to be had not bound up with the social advantages. We are not proposing to substitute lodgings for colleges, but to leave the choice open. Let the experiment be at least tried. If the present college-life is really vastly superior to life apart in lodgings, it will maintain itself. I may repeat what I wrote in 1852 :—

" Instead of guessing in the dark at the probable effect of these plans, let us make the experiment. What is urged is not the creation of any new machinery, but that an oppressive restriction should be removed, and the field thrown open to private enterprise and energy. When free, this will speedily run into the best channels. Let us have halls and colleges, old and new, all with unlimited liberty of admission, to work together, and trust to the power of self-adjustment in things which will bring to the surface the capabilities of the several methods. It is incumbent, indeed, on a university to be cautious and deliberate in all its proceedings. But experiments are not necessarily rash—there are wise ones—there are even wise experiments in legislation which do not answer, and then to desist from them involves no disgrace. . . Untie our hands and open our gates, and let us at least try if we can attract here, and can usefully deal with, that larger circle of youth whom, we are told, we ought to have here. The ideal of a national university is that it should be co-extensive with the nation. It should be the common source of the whole of the higher and secondary instruction for the country. . If we can only draft in 500, say 300, students (additional) from a class whose education has hitherto terminated with the commercial school or the academy, ' the good that would be effected by acting even on this moderate scale cannot be represented by figures. It would be the beginning of a system by which the university would strike its roots freely into the subsoil of society, and draw from it new elements of life, and sustenance of mental and moral power!'" (*O. U. C. Report, Evidence,* p. 44).

All opinions to the effect that academical life within college walls is a more valuable moral and social discipline than a solitary lodging, however true, cannot prove that it should be made compulsory. Nothing would give us the right to coerce all the students within college walls but a proof that order and discipline could not be otherwise maintained. That a youth incurs peculiar dangers in an Oxford lodging, which do not equally beset him elsewhere, is an allegation which cannot deserve serious discussion. The 1350 medical students in London live where they like, and select their own lodgings according to their means, taste, or notions of convenience. When the student has entered them his landlady is the only person who can place any restriction on his choice of company. If it pleases him to do so, he may have a card-party every night in the week, and there is no human power to drive him to church or chapel against his will. Under these circumstances, it might be supposed that he would abuse his unrestricted freedom of action, and that, so far as morality and outward decorum are concerned, he could not be put in contrast with the undergraduate of Oxford or Cambridge, whose doings are under the control of proctors and the cognisance of college-deans. The case is quite otherwise. The orderliness, industry, professional zeal, and serious deportment of the medical students is sufficiently attested by those who know them. If black sheep are occasionally to be found among them, where is the college in the Universities which has not also its percentage of youthful sots and beardless boys with shattered nerves? (see Dr. Temple Wright, *Medical Students of the Period.* Blackwood, 1867). We may learn from this example how much more bracing and efficacious, as moral influences, are poverty, hard work, and an intelligent interest in the objects of study, than the surveillance and admonition which attend the wealthy, luxurious, indolent, and uninterested tenant of college-rooms.

When all has been done that can be done to raise the character of Oxford as a school, to lower its cost, and to make it accessible to all, we are not to look for any rapid and overwhelming influx of new pupils. Mr. Goldwin Smith has offered an opinion on this point :—

"It seems absurd," he says, "to go back to the days of Chaucer's scholar, and to expect that swarms of English youth of the middle and lower classes, will leave respectable and re-munerative callings and come up to Oxford to live an uncom-fortable and questionable sort of life in lodgings, merely for the sake of attending a few professors' lectures, when, by the help of books, newspapers, and the public lectures which are now abundant everywhere, they may enjoy almost as much intellectual pleasure and instruction in their own homes. We shall draw from a wider area both of population and of intellect, now that the tests on the lower degrees are abolished, and the system of studies enlarged ; but the difficulty of affording the time as well as the money will probably always confine within narrow limits the number of candidates for a long liberal education" (*Oxford Essays*, 1858, p. 284).

I should be sorry to think that one, whom the university is proud to put forward as her best representative, should seriously entertain no higher view of university teaching than that it administers a little intellectual pleasure and instruction such as may be enjoyed at home.   If a professor in this place is merely to give a few lectures "such as are now abundant everywhere," either the system of lecturing must be wrong, or the selection of men to fill the professors' chair must be improperly made.   It is possible that we may be suffering from both these evils.   But what we must contemplate the university as doing, is something different from lectures, " such as are abundant everywhere."   A methodical course of scientific teaching, under men each of whom is a master in his own branch of knowledge, is not only not abundant everywhere, but is not to be found anywhere at present concentrated in one locality.   It is the very purpose of these suggestions to urge the establishment for the first time in modern England of such a national centre.   When this shall be done, and not only the staple of a general culture, but specific instruction in the sciences which form the basis of the various professions shall be obtainable here, it seems likely that there will be pupils.   Most likely not in any overwhelming numbers.   But mere numbers cannot be an object.   Of our present 1700, how many are there whose presence here is unprofitable to themselves and to the community !   Deduct the rich, who are here for fashion sake, the candidates for ordination, from whom the B.A. is required by the Bishop, and those whom the premium of the scholarship and fellowship attracts, the small remainder will represent the number who are drawn here purely by the desire of education! We may look to improved conditions of study rather for an improvement in the intellectual tone of the students than for the influx of numbers. At the same time it may be fairly expected that the numbers will also be increased. The shallow literature and flashy lectures, " which are now so abundant everywhere," may have little intrinsic value, but they awake intellectual tastes and the desire of improvement. Young persons once brought within this influence begin to be aware of their deficiencies. Especially are such persons sensitive to the superiority of a systematic training. If too late to get it for themselves, they will desire it for their children. Newspapers and popular lectures may become in one generation the pioneers of a systematic culture in the next. They could not be expected to leave remunerative callings, but they might spare two or three years before entering upon them. With the growth in wealth grows the disposition to postpone the entrance upon business or active life till a later age. With the accumulation of capital the rate of profits sinks, and the counter temptation of fortunes rapidly accumulated is removed, while a larger number of persons are in the enjoyment of a moderate realised property.

b. Fellowships.—The number of fellowships, when the new ordinances have fully come into operation, will be somewhat over 300. As £300 a-year has been taken as the maximum dividend, this would give an annual distribution of £90,000. It may, perhaps, be objected that the fellowships cannot be placed under the present head of *Subsidies to Education*, that they belong to our third application of endowments—viz. to the *Promotion of Science and Learning*. We must, then, inquire what is the public purpose which is now promoted by the actual administration of the fellowship fund under the reformed statutes.

An endowment fund may be applied to encourage any direction of the powers of the understanding in one of two ways—(1), it may be bestowed as a stipend on condition of services to be rendered in the future, during its tenure; (2), it may be conferred as a pension, in recompense or acknowledgment of meritorious exertions in the past. This method of pension has this advantage, that successful activity of the intelligence being once ascertained to exist in any individual, we have a guarantee of its continuance, not only because his own antecedents constitute an obligation—*noblesse oblige*—but from the force of habit and spontaneous activity.

If we turn to the statutes of the colleges, as amended by the ordinances, to see on which of these two principles fellowships are bestowed, we find it is not upon the first of them. We find the ordinances in almost every college repealing the old obligations, and not substituting for them any new ones.

It is true that any assertion about what is, or is not, statutable in any college, must be made with diffidence. For the commission of 1854, instead of abrogating the old codes under which they found the colleges governed, and introducing new codes in their place, were content to issue general ordinances, leaving the old statutes in vigour, except in so far as they are repugnant to the ordinances. Hence no college can undertake to say what is or is not now statutable, without invoking a Visitor's decision, or a legal adviser's opinion. Three colleges only (Exeter, Lincoln, Corpus) possess new bodies of statutes, yet it would seem that in Corpus the old code is still in vigour, having been only repealed so far as it is repugnant to the new. Besides this, the ordinances in some cases entrust the society with the power of framing new regulations. Though the statutes and the ordinances are accessible in print, any new regulations so made are not. But I do not apprehend that the colleges received the power of attaching duties to fellowships as conditions of tenure; and I have no reason to believe that any regulation of this kind has been attempted in any college.

Subject to any doubt which there may be as to the interpretation of conflicting documents, it may be asserted that no duties are at present attached to fellowships. Now, the old statutes of foundation had in almost every instance imposed very strict conditions of tenure. For they had, in almost every instance, required the fellow to proceed to the superior degree in one of the faculties. Failure to do so was to forfeit the fellowship, *ipso facto*. The effect of this requirement, under the old university system, was to impose upon the fellow, as the condition of his tenure, a prolonged course of study, of from twenty to twenty-five years, in a special branch of knowledge—study not merely private and uncertificated, but evidenced by a regular appearance in the public schools for disputation, and by the performance of other public exercises. These exercises had been long disused by the university, and dispensed with for the degrees. The college fellow was unable to perform the public disputations, and was content to take the degree. In many of the larger foundations the college statutes had not merely imposed the faculty degree, with its necessary course of study, but had superadded private courses of study for the fellows, with extra disputations and exercises, as tests of proficiency to be given within the college walls. These had fallen into desuetude along with the public exercises. For the public university, and private collegiate, appearances and exercises no substitute had been provided. These exercises and disputations were, however, only the outward tokens, the tests, occasions, and evidence of the study, or continued pursuit of acquirement; they were not that study itself. Though the opportunity of publicly proving his proficiency was taken away from him, the fellow still remained under the same obligation to the study which had constituted the whole purpose of his foundation.

This was the statutable state of things when the Act of 1854 and the Commission intervened. According to the sufficiently defined mode of proceeding in a court of equity in dealing with a charity, either modern tests and evidences of continued pursuit of science, analogous to those prescribed by the founder, but now obsolete, should have been imposed on the fellowship; or if this was impossible, the endowment should have been diverted to an analogous use. The Commission did not adopt this course. The ordinances in every instance abolish the statutable regulations of studies and exercises, as well as the obligation to proceed to the superior degrees. In no instance do they attempt to substitute an equivalent. But though no duties are provided for him to perform, the fellow is maintained in the enjoyment of his stipend and emoluments. ‘In other words the ordinances of the Commission of 1854 converted the fellowships into sinecures. The Commissioners found an enormous abuse subsisting illegally, and they legalised it. The richest and grandest institution for the cultivation of science remaining in Europe was given into their hands for reform, for restoration to its original national and noble purpose—a purpose which, though forgotten in practice, still remained engrossed in the title-deeds of the colleges. The Commissioners took these title-deeds, erased the purpose, and returned the parchments smilingly to their owners. Was it ignorance of university history, or want of sympathy with science and knowledge, or timidity? With an irresolute hand they converted a small number of fellowships into professorships, and, it is whispered, would have done a little more in this way but for the senseless clamour that they were "taking college money for university purposes." A number of fellowships (and two canonries) were at the same time sacrificed for conversion into scholarships. This was an operation which happened to be popular, from the notion entertained that prize scholarships were a mode of correcting university expensiveness. Both operations had one character in common. They were a diversion of original endowments of science and learning into educational endowments. The scholarship is a school prize; and the professor, in the view of the Commission, is a teacher. The mass of the college endowments were left as fellowships, after being, by a stroke of the pen, converted into real sinecures. One or two feeble vestiges of a purpose may be found in the new regulations. In the statutes of Exeter College " all fellows shall be bound to promote the main designs of the college, especially by study, teaching, or aiding in the administration." A more vague suggestion in the statutes of Corpus is, that the fellow to be chosen shall be one whom the electors believe " ad profectum studii posse et velle proficere." These intimations of an object, unsustained by either test of performance or penalty for non-performance, occur in codes framed by the colleges themselves. The ordinances which emanated from the Commissioners content themselves with repealing the existing obligations, and replace them by no new ones.

It is true that the ordinances confer a discretionary power on each society of requiring the residence of fellows, and of enforcing their requirement by pecuniary penalty and even deprivation. This is understood to have been designed for the purpose of supplying men to hold the college offices connected with the education of youth. And it is probably generally believed that there is some connection between a fellowship and the work of tuition, or, in other words, that the income of a fellowship is part of the salary of a college tutor. This is not the case. The power given to enforce residence does not impose a duty on the non-resident fellow; it only creates a contingent liability to a duty. The liability is so remote, that it cannot be considered as infringing the security of the sinecure. It is well understood that a head and fellows would never vote an order to one of their colleagues already embarked in another profession to return to Oxford to become a bursar or a tutor, or mulct him in the proceeds of his fellowship if he did not. Indeed, such an act applied to one singled out from the whole number of non-residents, would be manifestly an act of arbitrary rigour.   If residence is to be compulsory, it must be equally compulsory.   A statute which entrusts to the majority of a college power to deny to one of their number a liberty which is enjoyed by all the rest, ought to remain a dead letter.   The person so selected would be in fact a scapegoat offered on the altar of justice by his fellows, to enable themselves to retain *their* fellowships unmolested.

But not only would no college act thus harshly—it never feels the necessity which might excuse harshness. The attractions of college tuition are sufficient in themselves to engage men in the service.   Classical studies yield to no other studies in intrinsic attractiveness.   Those, again, who are not within the reach of the genuine inspiration, easily prefer the occupation of teaching what they have just learnt, to engaging in a new and repulsive professional study, and going, as it were, to school again. And if the supply of tutors runs short in one college, it can be made up out of the abundance of its neighbour. Economically considered, the income of the fellowship is no more part of the payment for the tutor's services than it is part-payment for the services rendered by the young counsel to his client, or by the country curate in his parochial charge.   The £300 a-year was entirely at his disposal; he might have carried it to Calcutta or California, or amused himself with it in the picture-galleries of Italy. If he chooses to be a college-tutor it is because he finds his account in being so.   It suits his tastes, or his interests. Will it be said that the salary of a tutor would be insufficient if it were not eked out by the emoluments of a fellow-

ship? This is to confound together two very distinct
questions. The question, Can the amount of teaching required in the university be adequately paid for by fees
levied on the pupils, is one which will be considered elsewhere. The fact that the dividend of the fellow is no part
of the remuneration of the tutor's services is all I am now
concerned to point out. Endowments *may* be applied in
aid of fees, as payment of teachers, as in our endowed
schools. But the annual proceeds of his endowment are
only receivable by the master of a grammar-school on condition of services rendered. The income of a fellowship
transportable everywhere with the fellow, wherever he
moves, can form no part of the inducements which may
have led him to fix himself in Oxford. Tuition is a profession having its advantages and its drawbacks There is
no other tie between the fellowship and the profession of
tutor than the circumstance, that the qualifications required for election to the fellowship are partly the same
qualifications as are required in a tutor. Tuition is a
profession, and the only one, in which the fellow can engage at once, without fresh study, a new apprenticeship,
and additional expense. This would always insure there
being fellows ready to take the office of tutor. But the
income of this fellowship forms no part of the consideration paid for tuitional services. If fellowships did not
exist, tutors would be obtainable on the same terms as at
present. The average pay of a tutor (without the fellowship) is better pay than curacies, or than the expectancy
of briefs or fees. I am not arguing, it will be remembered,
that tutors are now "sufficiently" paid. In the scheme
proposed in these pages, the position held by the academi-

cal teacher is a very different one from that now occupied by the college tutor. All I am now concerned to point out is, that the fellowships are not part of the fund affected to the endowment of teachers.

Thus it appears that fellowships are not conferred on the first of the two principles above stated, as the only principles on which endowments can be applied to promote any given form of mental endeavour. They are found not to be stipends paid in return for services.

They are clearly bestowed on the second principle; they are pensions conferred in recompense or acknowledgment of meritorious exertions in the past. This is the ground on which the new provisions distinctly place them. The commissioners transferred the fellowships, whether intending it or not, from the first category to the second—from the category of benefices entailing duties, to that of sinecure benefices obtainable by qualification. The old qualification, viz., birth in a particular locality, had become a crying and intolerable evil. It was justly abolished by Parliament. The commission substitute for it "intellectual qualifications." We shall not find in the ordinances any definition of the " intellectual qualifications " to be required; but their nature is indicated by a provision that fellowships are to be accessible to " *excellence* in every branch of knowledge, for the time being, recognised in the schools of the University," (*Ordinances, passim*). In abolishing continued obligation, and making the conditions of a fellowship retrospective, more care might have been bestowed on ascertaining these conditions. Everything is intrusted to the honour and discretion of a self-electing board. As the statutes and ordinances do not

determine more precisely what " excellence " shall be sufficient qualification for a fellowship, we must turn to the
actual practice of the colleges to discover what it is at this
moment. The range of subjects is as ample and comprehensive as could be desired. It embraces, as far as words
go, all the subjects of all the four schools—classical literature; mathematical and physical studies; modern history
and jurisprudence; natural science. Pensions of £300
a-year awarded for " excellence " in each of these subjects,
might be a most powerful stimulus of science and learning.
Indeed, without the pension, the public honour attaching
to the possession of one of these national prizes might
alone make them objects of as eager competition as are
the chairs of the *Academie Française*. But when we come
to the actual practice, we find in it two circumstances
which limit the ample range seeming to be opened by the
words of the ordinances. 1. The competition is not between men of mature age and scientific reputation; nor is
it even between younger men, say from twenty-five to
thirty, who, though yet unknown, have been devoting some
effort to master some one of the greater " branches of
knowledge." The candidates are practically quite young
men of from twenty-one to twenty-five, who are fresh from
the schools, and have not yet entered upon the study of
any " branch of knowledge." It is a disadvantage to a
candidate to have devoted any time to special knowledge.
Even if an older man, say of from twenty-five to thirty,
should be among the candidates, he must, to give himself
a chance, have postponed the commencement of scientific
study, and remained in the practice of his school exercises.
For the competition is not an examination in acquirement,

but turns mainly on the performance of exercises. Electors generally prefer the younger competitors, or rather the examination is so arranged that the younger man has the best chance in it. Colleges contrive to fix their times of election so as to catch the men who are just out of the schools, as giving them a better field to select from. 2. As are the candidates, such are the awarders of the prize. The whole body of fellows are electors, who, if not mainly young men, are, as we have seen, men who, as fellows, have given no guarantee of excellence in any " branch of knowledge." They naturally examine in what they know, and the conduct of the examination usually falls into the hands of the youngest on the list, as himself most fresh from the performance of the exercises in which the competition chiefly consists. A fellowship examination is thus a mere repetition of the examination in the public schools, by a less competent board of examiners. It is entirely meaningless. It does not give opportunity for any advance in positive acquirement after the B.A. degree, even if it does not discourage it. A young B.A., when he has finished his liberal groundwork, his ἐγκύκλιος παιδεία— his humanities—may wish to devote, at his own expense, a year or two more to the study of positive knowledge in any direction—in moral science, in philology, in history. He may do so if he can find out how—but the University affords him no guidance, prescribes no path, holds out no rewards. He roams about the libraries at his will, and devours, as his curiosity prompts, much miscellaneous reading. He must go for instruction to Berlin or Bonn, or even to Catholic and *arrieré* Vienna; Oxford cannot give it him. But if he engages in the higher scientific study of any "branch of knowledge," in proportion as his insight deepens, in that proportion he sees his hopes of a fellowship vanish; he will be easily distanced in "Latin composition" by a junior competitor warm from his feats of boyish rhetoric, or ready with reams of speculative declamation on "philosophy."

These remarks it is hoped will not be misunderstood. So far from underrating the Oxford training, I believe it to be the best to be had at this time in Europe. When it is attacked by scientific men without culture, or positive philosophy which ignores the world of imagination, it is right to point out how much more complete our scholastic curriculum is than anything which is proposed in its place. But as *training*, as education merely; science it is not; knowledge it is not. It is but the instrument, the preparatory stage, the portal of knowledge. Merit in this preparatory stage is what the B.A. and the honours in the various schools are (or were) supposed to denote. The fellowships seem to be assigned by the ordinances to a further stage of intellectual growth, to excellence in some branch of knowledge. But the actual practice reverses this enactment, and perhaps it was not even the view of the framers of the ordinances. At any rate, present practice awards the fellowships, or the great majority of them, to the same merit, and the same stage of education, as that which the honours in the final schools are contrived to reward. No one can now obtain a fellowship unless he has gone through with some success the three years' honour course prescribed by the university. Speaking roughly, we may say that the twenty or thirty fellowships which become vacant every

H

year are filled up by as many of the most distinguished
of the students of that year.

It is then clear into which of the three channels, in
which our endowments are distributed, the fellowships
flow. They are not part payment of instruction; they
do not promote learning and science. They are educational prizes. The fellowships, as now administered, are
to the academical course what the scholarships are to the
grammar-school, so much prize-money offered for competition among the scholars.

Of their effect as prizes, the same must be said as was
said of the prize scholarships. As at the commencement
of the academical course, so at its close, the prizes are
too many in number, and too great in value. The prize
system is overdone. Prizes are multiplied beyond the
only end for which prizes are useful in education, that, viz.
of stimulating industry and awakening intellectual ambition.
Beyond this limit all the fellowships that are given act
as a bounty on a particular kind of education. A small
number of prize-fellowships, awarded after a vigorous
competition to the two or three best students of the
year, would, in combination with the honour lists, call
into play all the emulation which is necessary, and as
much as is stimulated under the existing system. All
that is beyond this serves only to draw students to the
universities, and creates an artificial demand for a drill,
the educative power of which is thus greatly impaired, inasmuch as its adaptation to the demands of life is distorted
or destroyed.

Here it is necessary to revert to a consideration which has
already been touched upon in speaking of the scholarships.

Scholarships, exhibitions, fellowships, every form of subsidy to education, over and above their stimulative effect as prizes, go to form an "avenue to life." They are steps in the broad road which leads from the cottage up to the highest employments in Church and State. A recent writer says :—

"The university might render a vast political service by bringing out the talent of the nation. At present there is no way upwards save by money-getting. The university might be to the nineteenth century what the priesthood was to the Middle-ages. In no country is the area from which men rise into public life so small as in our own. Compare France with England in this particular. Among us, without wealth no man has any hope of public life. The dislike of "adventurers" so general in Parliament, if probed to its real foundation, will be found to rest on a vulgar admiration of money. In no other country does such a dislike prevail ; and the consequence is, that in no country are politics so seldom studied as a profession as in ours. We are apt to think this an advantage. It is on the contrary a great evil. It restricts the supply. If we could extend the field of our choice over 100,000 of the middle and lower classes, should we find no available ability there wasted? And the area is narrowing every day. The times of patronage and small boroughs have passed away, and with them has gone many a chance to poor ability of an entrance into public life. Politics are now, as literature was in the days of Dr. Johnson ; patrons are gone by, and publishers are not yet. The Universities might be the publishers of political life" (*North British Review*, March 1867).

This is a function of endowments as "subsidies to education" which deserves the most watchful care. It is truly a national interest. The universities are eminently nurseries of talent for the public service. However else they may aim at ministering to general culture, it must not interfere with their being seminaries for public life. Will a vast diminution of the number of prize-fellowships interfere with this function? will it narrow the road, and lessen the opportunities now afforded to the poor man of competing with the rich in the path of honour and public service? I think not. And the writer just quoted is complaining that Oxford does not at present do what he is suggesting. The existing system by which twenty or thirty life pensions are given away to all the young men of promise every year, does not answer the purpose. We may, therefore, with safety to that purpose, divert these funds in another direction.

The truth is, that the fellowship has never been the direct and straight road to the public service, the path that leads from the Cumberland cottage to the woolsack, according to the popular belief. A few distinguished names can be pointed to in the Church, in law, in literature, and other walks of life, who, perhaps, would never have been heard of but for college endowments. But such cases have been the exceptions, and must always remain so. Were it not that a false notion of endowments is still so deeply rooted in large sections of society connected with our old Universities, it would be idle to keep on repeating, as we are obliged to do, that poverty, as such, constitutes no title to academical funds. Ability based on force of character, on tenacity, and industry, is what educational endowments seek to find and bring out. We must keep the fellowships as well as the scholarships free from the taint of a system which invites men to come to the universities, simply because they are poor, and because they see in them a way to a good pension on easy terms. To do this the prize-fellowships must be restricted in numbers, and rigidly bestowed so as to bring out the greatest amount of exertion. So administered, they might perhaps occasionally be a stage in the broad road of ambition, at once designating and aiding an aspirant for the highest political employments. The equal high-road for humble talent should lie through the universities, but not necessarily through a fellowship. The next stage to the scholarship should be a post in the public service, with prospect of promotion by merit. The fellowship endowment has surely other objects than to pension an ambitious man while he is trying to establish a Parliamentary or professional position !

Next to a regular connection between the public service and the university course, a re-establishment of the local grammar-schools would be necessary if we are to keep open this highway. The first step of the ladder is as essential as the last. The decay of the local grammar-schools had cut off the supply of men to the universities at its source. But that decay itself was only one of the minor symptoms of the social revolution in progress. The youth of the lower middle class left the grammar-school because it no longer taught them what it was their interest to learn. The commercial schools grew up, which taught nothing well, but which professed to teach the things they wished to learn. The public, which judges by profession, and not by performance, adopted the commercial academy. The local grammar-school decayed, or turned itself, in order to live, into a commercial school. Our middle-class youth passed into life without approaching the universities, without the faintest trace of the culture which still remained the traditional culture of the nation. The whole commercial and moneyed class—from the great capitalists

down to the point where it merges in the small retailer—
became separated by an impassable gulf of education from
the professional classes.

But mark well the reversal of social importance
which had accompanied the growth of this separation.
Down to the end of the wars of the French Revolution (1815), the aristocratical, political, professional,
and clerical sections of society had been everything in
social consideration. These classes had clung to the
traditions of liberal education. The career of English
life lay, accordingly, through the grammar-schools and
universities. But the enormous development of commerce and manufactures since 1815 has opened a new
world to energy. The career opened by commercial enterprise to the middle class is a far more tempting career to
ambition than those opened by the old road of the professions and public life. The thousands who tread this path
go without any education properly so called. Yet these
classes are in possession of great political power and social
consideration, which throws that of the professions into the
shade, and almost balances the power of the territorial
aristocracy. What is the consequence? It is that these
moneyed classes, containing the better half of the nation's
wealth and life, lie outside the pale of our educational
system. What they have not got they despise. Liberal
education confined to one half—and the least energetic
half—of the wealthy classes, is depreciated. The great
highway of successful life no longer lies through the universities. We wish to restore the road, and maintain one
broad-gauge line of refining education, along which all our
youth, the aspiring and enterprising, as well as the fanieant

aristocrat and the apathetic dullard, shall be willing to travel. It is impossible seriously to propose that this shall be done by pensions. What would £100,000 a-year distributed in pensions do, if tried as a set-off against the prizes that await skill and energy in business? Our endowment-fund is considerable, but I believe it is not equal to this task—that of buying up the best talent of the country. If we can succeed in making the education given meet the demands of all classes, all classes will desire to have it. If we want the old road to be travelled, we must repair it, not pay pilgrims so much a head, like a starving Swiss innkeeper, for going our route.

We have thus traced one—the most considerable— third of our endowment-fund to its destination as educational subsidy, expended upon or earned by students during their three years' course. An annual outlay of somewhere over £120,000 is applied—prospectively as scholarship, or retrospectively as fellowship—to extract from the pupil the amount of mental and moral exertion put forth by him in a three and a-half years' course. We have seen that, as now administered, this fund operates on education in three ways:—1. As a pecuniary aid to poor talent: 2. As a prize system stimulating industry: 3. And this is its chief effect, as a bounty, attracting within the scope of the education many who would not care to have it without a pecuniary inducement.

§ 2.—*Of Endowment for Instruction.*

In the tripartite division of the proceeds of our aggregate endowed fund, one-third share is employed in providing instruction. The endowed teachers are as follows:—

1. Divinity.

Regius divinity	£2300
Margaret do.	1700
Ecclesiastical history . . .	1700
Pastoral	1700
Hebrew	1700
Exegesis	300
Grinfield	45
Total . .	£9445

2. Mathematical, physical, and medical.

Savilian astronomy . . .	£600
Savilian geometry . . .	600
Sedleian reader	570
Experimental philosophy . .	500
Waynflete chemistry . . .	600
Linacre physiology . . .	800
Botany	300
Geology	400
Mineralogy	250
Hope zoology	300
Sibthorp rural economy . . .	200
Regius medicine	400
Clinical	200
Total . .	£5720

3. Law.

Regius civil law	£100
Vinerian	600
Indian law reader	200
Chichele International . . .	750
New chair at Corpus . . .	600
Total . .	£2250

3. History and philosophy.

Regius modern history	.	.	£600
Camden ancient do.	.	.	400
Chichele history	.	.	750
Waynflete metaphysics	.	.	600
White moral philosophy	.	.	400
Logic	.	.	400
Political economy	.	.	300
Poetry	.	.	140
Total	.	.	£3590

4. Philology.

Regius Greek	.	.	£500
Corpus Latin	.	.	600
Boden Sanskrit	.	.	1000
Arabic	.	.	300
Taylorian, modern	.	.	500
Anglo-Saxon	.	.	300
Teachers—French, German, Italian, Spanish	.	.	600
Teachers—Hindustani	.	.	150
Total	.	.	£3950

To obtain the total endowment of instruction we must add, besides one or two miscellaneous items (as, *e.g.*, the professor of music), small ancient endowments which each of the colleges possess for readers, lecturers, etc., and recent grants out of endowed funds for lecturers in science. The aggregate of such annual sums may be about £1500 per annum. Some of the above figures are not exact, but they are sufficiently so to give a general view of the distribution of the sums devoted to instruction out of endowments. The first thing which strikes us is the apparent disproportion of the outlay on the subject of divinity. This is so, however, only in appearance. The four or five great theological chairs are canonries more than they are professorships. As such they belong to the third class of endowment—that for the maintenance of learning. The regius professor of theology, who was once bound to lecture twice a week throughout the entire year, has been, by a modern statute (1839), released from the mere drudgery of teaching, and allowed to devote nearly all his time to the higher objects of sacred literature. The other divinity professors are indeed under more stringent, but not onerous, requirements to teach. But the whole of these chairs must be regarded as having a double position, a position in the Church as well as in the University. No one, who wishes to see the Church of England maintain its character in the country, will think an endowment of £9000 a-year an extravagant price to pay for the encouragement of sacred learning. It should be remembered, too, that the wealth of the chapters being now dispersed in dust over the face of the country, the theological chairs at the universities are the only preferment in the Church for which learning is a qualification. The dean of a cathedral may be, and sometimes is, a man of learning, but he may also owe his promotion to other considerations. The divinity professorships may thus be regarded as serving two purposes, and we might therefore deduct £600 a-year for " services " from each canonry, and consider the remainder as an endowment of learning. This would leave, as the teaching endowment of divinity, a total of only £3000. The distribution among the several branches of teaching is then at present as follows :—

Teachers of theology	. . .	£3,000
„ science, including medicine		5,420
„ law	. . . .	2,250
„ history and philosophy	.	3,590
„ philology	. . .	4,000
College lectureships	. . .	1,500
		£19,760

These figures represent, not accurately, but accurately enough for the purpose, the endowment of teaching, or the teaching that the university has the means of offering gratuitously. To ascertain the whole outlay upon instruction, we must add to this the sums levied by fees. The fees for college tuition have been estimated at £25,000 a-year. What is paid for private tuition is matter of conjecture. Dr. Peacock estimated what was paid to private tutors at Cambridge at £50,000 a-year (*O. U. C. Report*, p. 89). Nothing like this sum is spent here. It is probable that the expenditure on this item is still diminishing, as it is certainly less than it used to be. In putting it at £5000 a-year I shall be below the mark. Thus, the total outlay in the University on instruction from fees will reach the sum of £30,000 per annum. I may remark, by the way, the curious coincidence that the sum paid out of endowments to students exhibited, and the sum levied back from them in the shape of fees for tuition, public and private, nearly balance each other.

Scholarships, exhibitions, etc., to undergraduate		
students		£35,000
College tuition fees	. . .	£25,000
Private do.	. . .	5,000
Examiners' do.	. . .	2,000
Professors' do.	. . .	
		£32,000

Is this amount of gratuitous education little or much? This, again, is a question impossible to be answered. The sum paid for it is no indication either way. It might be argued that at least the wealthier classes of the public are tolerably satisfied with what is done, as they are content to meet an endowment of £35,000 a-year with voluntary fees to the amount of £32,000.

But, as before observed, it is vain to attempt to get at the value of the work done here by the amount spent upon it. Any sum, however small, is too much to pay for a bad education. If the opportunity of a really good education be given here, the largest outlay is, to a wealthy country, absolutely insignificant. The arrangements of the professoriate will be considered under its proper head. The subject of the incomes of professors and tutors will come before us again under the next section.

§ 3.—*Of Endowments of Science and Learning.*

Of our total endowment fund, one, and the smallest, third is affected to the promotion of science and learning. Under this head come the libraries, so much of the professorial endowment as is over and above what can be considered as payment for lecturing, and so much of the endowments of heads as remains after deducting services.

Of the professors there are only the canon professors, with, perhaps, the professor of Sanskrit, who have any margin, after deducting salary, which can be set down to this head.

The duties of the heads as gathered from the statutes are pretty much alike in all the colleges. They are, in general terms, the government of the society, its presidency, and general superintendence. The head is usually bound to residence during term (*i.e.*, seven months in the year). When not so tied by express enactment, an active discharge of his duties, and attendance at the college prayers, imply residence. There is, however, in all cases, a vice-gerent, who in the absence of the head exercises his powers. Even when the head is present the discipline of the undergraduate body is usually administered by the vicegerent, who must consult the head. As each college has one or more bursars who administer the finances, a head is able, if he chooses, to devolve the greater part of his administrative duties within his college upon his subordinate officers. The qualifications required for election to a headship are, the M.A. (or a superior) degree, and holy orders, two or three colleges excepted, where laymen may be chosen. The election of the head is by vote of majority of the fellows, who are required by the ordinances to choose the person " who shall be most fit for the government of the college as a place of religion and learning " (*Ordinances passim*). But the fitness thus vaguely described is left expressly to their judgment. In one college (Corpus) it is required that the head be " a man of ability and experience in all that relates to produce, rents, building, and the letting and leasing of property, etc.," and at the same time one who is " devoted to the study of the liberal arts and sciences " (*Statutes of Corpus Christi*, cap. 1), And in Exeter College he is to be of ability to promote " the literary, educational, and financial interests of the college " (*Statutes of Exeter College*, ii.) These are, I think, the only vestiges of purpose in respect of the office of heads to be found in the new ordinances.

There are no returns of the income of the headships. It will probably not be far from the mark to put the collective income of the nineteen heads of colleges at £23,000 a-year. Perhaps some deduction would have to be made from this in respect of outgoings and inconvenience arising from the nature of the endowments, consisting in annexed canonries or livings, in order to arrive at the nett amount. Of this nett income, a part being payment for services rendered in the management of the college, must be credited to our second division of the endowment fund, as an outlay on education. All that is over and above remuneration for superintendence appears, as far as the language of the statutes serves to determine, to be as much a sinecure pension as a fellowship. There are, however, purposes answered by the endowment of the head, which, though not enjoined by statute, are inevitable obligations of the position. The head is for the college what the Vice-Chancellor is for the university, its representative officer. All that is implied in representation constitutes his real duty far more than the details of administration. He is the sovereign of a constitutional state who reigns but does not govern. The suggestion that it is desirable that the Vice-Chancellor should be relieved from the drudgery of detail by which he is now oppressed, in order that he may the better represent the corporate body, is equally applicable to the head of a college. The requirement of the Exeter and Corpus codes, that he should be experienced in land-agency, may seem in itself not unreasonable. But where this requirement is coupled with a demand that he should be " devoted to the study of the liberal arts and sciences," the impossibility of such a union of qualifications in the same man becomes manifest. To compel the head by statute διακονεῖν τραπέζαις is at once to interfere with his proper function, and to have the bursarship ill administered. As colleges now are, with possibly a majority of non-residents, and certainly a majority of young fellows unacquainted with the antecedents of the estates, and even with the general nature and obligations of landed property, it is necessary that there should be one man of age and experience at their deliberations. But the scheme now offered provides a special office for estates and agency (see p. 44), and under it business qualities need no longer be demanded of a head. This would release the electors from the perplexity which a double qualification always occasions in choosing a man to fill an office.

Scientific and literary qualifications, are, as we have seen, exacted only in the codes of two colleges. If we look to the actual practice, it is necessary to remember that no headship in Oxford has yet been filled up by a body of electors who have themselves attained their fellow-ships under the system of open competition. And after making the deductions above enumerated, there remains no large part of the whole headship endowment-fund of £23,000 which has to be credited to the category of endowment of science and learning. The apology for bringing it in under this head is, that besides the two colleges, the statutes of which strictly require learning, in all the colleges the electors, even now, have the opportunity of giving this direction to this part of the endowment fund if they choose. If they have not so chosen, it has been in part that their freedom has been hampered by the requirement of business qualifications. The necessity for looking for that quality being removed, and the old traditions of election becoming extinct, as the body of electors is recruited on the present system, we cannot doubt that scientific and literary merit would be more regarded, and that these posts would be filled by more distinguished men, even if no change were made in the elections to fellowships. As, however, the present scheme proposes to convert the whole of the fellowship endowments from educational prizes into endowments for science and literature, so I would propose to include the endowments of the headships in the same category. Instead of being vaguely mentioned, eminence in science should be made the one statutable condition. In the cases of those colleges which are to be dedicated to the cultivation of one special faculty, the electors should be placed under as strict an obligation as can be drawn to choose the man best learned in their faculty.

As endowments of science and learning, it will be necessary to remove the limitation of these dignities to clergymen, in those colleges which still retain such a condition. In proposing this, I desire not to lose sight of the importance to the nation of maintaining a learned church. At that moment in our annals when we seem in greatest danger of foregoing this benefit, it may be said it would not be wise for the Church to give away what seems to be the last refuge for theological learning, which has been almost chased out of the cathedrals. It must be replied that the destruction of the canonries as the homes of learning, if a necessity, was a deplorable necessity. Something, however, was saved from the wreck; and by a better organisation of the chapters for the purpose, endowments may yet be obtained for theological science which will more than replace what it may lose in losing the headships of the colleges. But whether such a reorganisation of the cathedrals is attempted or not, the headships cannot, on the principles of academical management on which this scheme proceeds, be retained for the theological faculty. If the objection means not to claim them for theology, but only for learned clergymen, my scheme does not close them to clergymen, but only opens them to laymen. Clergymen, eminent in any learned pursuit, may still hope to fill these posts, as even in France a bishop may have a *fauteuil* in the *Academie*. The relation between the head of a college and the undergraduate student, again, will no longer be such as to imply the pastoral office. A notion has found supporters here, chiefly among the college-tutors, of making the head of the college into a sort of senior tutor for the undergraduates. This notion seems to originate in the desire to utilise somehow the endowments of the head, rather than in an enlarged view of the purposes of a college-foundation. It implies that the colleges are to be schools, and the University a locality in which twenty such schools happen to co-exist side by side. If this idea be carried out, which is not unlikely, the head would naturally become a head-master, and his duties would consist in the superintendence and instruction of young men. On this scheme the headship must remain restricted to clergymen. He must also be armed with despotic authority, not only over the pupils, but over the other teachers. The condition of a successful school is the concentration of authority and responsibility on one head. He must appoint and dismiss the other tutors, and

I

the college equality must be broken up. The present independence of the college fellow is the great impediment in the way of the success of a college as a school. Any college in Oxford might in a few years be made into a trade success by an energetic head, if he could override the resistance of the fellows. Nothing could be easier, at the present crisis and in the present temper of the public, than to give this direction to college endowments, and to confirm and complete by legislation the process which has long silently been going on, of the conversion of the college into a grammar-school, even if the conversion has not already taken place in fact.

If the position of a head of a college in Oxford, as it is, is unsatisfactory both to himself and to the world outside, it is owing to this, its ambiguous character. This ambiguity should be determined in one direction or in the other. He cannot at once be an active and successful master of a school, and also eminent in some branch of science. In the present " scheme " this equivocal character will be put an end to. For in our arrangement the colleges are divided into those which, ceasing to receive boarders, will be appropriated to one of the incorporated faculties, and into those which will remain boarding-houses. In the former, or colleges properly so called, the head will be the dean of his faculty, or the president of a learned body. In the other class of colleges, which would be more properly called hostels or *hospitia*, he will be the acting master and administrator. It may be a question whether he should also teach, as does the master in an English grammar-school, and the dean (*Decan*) in a German University, or whether he should only govern as a

French rector. He should be advised by a council of tutors, but not controlled by them in his decisions.

Libraries.—While nearly the whole of the endowments have been gradually withdrawn from the promotion of learning to which they were once devoted, one institution has been growing into an importance of the first rank in the learned world. The foundation of Sir Thomas Bodley, says Hallam (*Literature*, iii., 231), has been one main cause of the literary distinction of Oxford. A corporate body which has created such a collection must, it would seem, have been inspired by the love of letters. Yet the Vatican contains the largest accumulation of Greek MSS. in the world, though Rome has not for generations been able to show a scholar capable of editing a page of Greek. The riches of the imperial library at Paris, uncared for by their proprietors, are explored by the Germans. But the Vatican and the Paris are old collections, which are not now augmented, and are but monuments of bygone periods, when Italy and France respectively were the classical centres. The Bodleian has been in steady and continuous growth; a growth hardly interrupted even in the worst times, and which has even been most rapid during the last fifty years, a period during which the general movement in the university has been in a direction opposite to that of special attainment. All parties in Church and State have been contributors; Laud and Fairfax, Cromwell and Charles I. have helped to realise the confident prediction of the founder in 1604, that " the European world would never behold a repository more amply stored with all resources for the promotion of good learning "—" Quo Orbis iste Europeus nullum absolutius instructiusque ad bonas literas pro movendas, Deo auspicante, unquam visurus est "—(*Prefat. Statut. Bibl. Bodl.* 1610). Rome possesses her Vatican by inheritance. We not only possess, but have ourselves formed, our Bodleian. Here, however, our merit ends. Like the bees, we have gathered for others to use. A very small fraction of those who are in the enjoyment of the income of the endowments will be found among the frequenters of the library. It should indeed be said that the recent formation of a scientific library at the Museum—a library which, though on a very small scale, is a model of arrangement—has withdrawn from the Bodleian one considerable class of students.

The principal recommendations of the Royal Commission of 1850 were—

1. That books and MSS. should be allowed, under certain restrictions, to be taken out of the library.

2. That a reading-room should be annexed to the library, in which books might be read after the library was closed.

3. That by an arrangement among the managers the resources of the other libraries might be economised, and made to supplement, rather than to repeat, the Bodleian.

Of these recommendations the second has been since acted upon.

In the first recommendation I think a distinction ought to be drawn between books and MSS. MSS. may, without detriment, be lent out. The conditions, however, ought to be very precise, and strictly observed. The person applying ought to be required to show that it is impossible for him to come to Oxford himself to make his collation. Applications might be limited to those Universities or libraries which were willing to give reciprocity. The MS. should not be lent for use in a private dwelling-house, but in the precincts of the public library frequented by the borrower. Books ought not to be lent out of the library under any conditions.

Recommendation No. 3 has not been adopted, but I believe it is under consideration at the present time. The enormous increase of publication renders some such arrangement yearly more necessary, merely on the ground of space.

Since the report of the Royal Commission was issued new vigour has been given to every department of the library by the appointment of the present librarian. The arrangements of the Bodleian may now challenge comparison with those of any public library. In more than one point it is superior to any known to me. There is no other library of anything like the same extent in which the applicant is so quickly served with the volume demanded. If there yet remain desiderata in the management, we may be sure that there are insuperable difficulties which stand in the way. I may be permitted, perhaps, to express a wish—

1*st.* That the risk of fire arising from the heating apparatus may not merely be minimised but annihilated; when this has been effected, and not before, it might be considered if the MSS. collections of the separate colleges would not be better placed in the Bodleian building.

2*d.* That an assistant, qualified by professional bibliographical knowledge, be placed in the library at the service of readers. No system of cataloguing, or arrangement on the shelves, can supersede the necessity of such an officer. The principal librarian has far too much on his hands to give, as he now does, the bibliographical aid demanded by each student. How far the finances of the library could support additional burdens I do not know; but certainly the services of an accomplished bibliographer could not be expected to be secured for a salary of £300 a-year, which is all that the assistant-librarians at present receive. *Biblio-theks-wissenschaft* is one of the sciences which it would be desirable to naturalise in the University.

3*d*. Stillness and silence cannot be absolutely secured in any much-frequented library. In the Bodleian, the comparatively small number of readers would allow of our obtaining these desirable conditions of study in an unusual measure. We do not attain them. In spite of repeated prohibitions, the incessant stream of sight-seers continues to flow through the reading-room, the public business of the library to be transacted, and even the news of the day to be discussed, there. Some students may be able to overcome the distractions thus created. To those who cannot, the library is not now a place of study; and for them its use is limited to purposes of reference, collation, transcription, or such other work as is purely mechanical.

Sec. 5.—Of the Re-distribution of the Endowment Fund.

§ 1.—*General Considerations.*

We have now reviewed the actual distribution of our endowments into four portions :—

1. Costs of management, salaries of agents, college offices connected with property, law-expenses, University charges, extra rates, maintenance of fabric, etc.

I have not the means of ascertaining the aggregate amount of this burden on our gross revenue. It must always remain heavy, but its present amount may possibly be capable of reduction by a central system of management.

2. Prize-money distributed among the students, as earned by them during their school and college course, usually before æt. 24, £120,000 per annum.

3. Payments to provide the same students with instruction and supervision gratuitously (say), £29,000 per annum. This is thus computed :—

24 professors at £600 . . .	£14,400
Other professors and teachers .	2,000
College-endowed lectureships, etc. .	1,500
19 heads at £600 . . .	11,400
	£29,300

4. The remainder, being the surplus income of the professors and heads, endowments of libraries and museums, etc., may perhaps be considered as affected to the promotion of science and learning. The actual amount of this outlay is not easily stated, but it cannot be set down at more than one-half of the last head (No. 3), if we make, as it would seem we ought to do, a further deduction from the income of the headships for costs of "representation."

The figures given are, it may be repeated, offered as approximative only. They are sufficient for the purposes of this memoir, if they exhibit the proportions in which the distribution takes place.

To endeavour to arrive, *à priori*, at a rule of proportion for the distribution of any endowment-fund among its

possible objects would be futile. The consideration, however, which is the only one to which I wish to draw attention, is one which is forced upon us at the first view of the
figures as they stand. It involves the fundamental question
of what is a University ?

This consideration is that the great bulk of our endowments—so large a part that we may almost say the whole—
is expended on youths under the age of twenty-four—*i.e.*
that it has an educational effect. What is expended on
promoting science and learning is, by comparison, trifling
in amount, and, from the peculiar mode of its bestowal,
almost unproductive of any fruits. This is the actual
direction taken by the national endowment fund. And it
stands in direct contrast with the original destination of
that fund in that period of our history in which the institution of colleges had its birth. The endowments, in the
design of the founders, were endowments for men and not
for youth, and were not directed to education as a preparation for life, but to knowledge as a peculiar profession
which withdrew men from the ordinary professions, and all
those careers which are self-paying, and which could therefore only be supported by way of endowment.

It may be as well to preclude misunderstanding by
repeating that it is by no means to be assumed that the
destination given to these endowments by their founders
was, or would be now, wise and politic, and that the
actual reversal of that destination now prevailing is
unwise, merely because the one is ancient and the other
modern. Nor let us for one instant submit our minds to the
superstition of the law-courts that a man can exercise rights
of property after his death to all time, and that a use and

direction, once impressed upon property by a founder, must be obeyed for ever. Let the national trustee be considered to be entirely unfettered in the exercise of his trust. Let us address ourselves to the consideration of re-distribution as if the fund to be re-distributed had no lien upon it. I make no claim for the restoration of what once was, and has ceased to be, merely because it once was. I only seek to have the real issue clearly brought out before debate on university reform is the order of the day. No questions of detail can be entered on, or particular applications of funds determined till we have settled the relative claims of education *v.* science. Let it be understood that our endowment, once an endowment of knowledge, has become an endowment of education. The previous question will then be, Shall the existing application of the national fund be ratified, developed, and completed, and shall such anomalies as have arisen from the continued subsistence of fragments of another and older state of things in the middle of the new be removed?

An historical inquiry into what Oxford was is beyond the scope of this memoir. In recurring for a moment to the origin of colleges, the object is not the critical establishment of a fact, but only to enable us to realise the difference between an endowment for science and an endowment for education.

It is a vulgar error that colleges were in their origin establishments of priests to say masses for the souls of the founders in purgatory. The founders of the thirteen colleges which were erected before the Reformation were almost all of them exceptional men who shared indeed the religious ideas common to their age, but who were animated by views far too elevated to be common. The motive and design of college foundations is distinguishable chronologically into three periods :—

1. In the first period—thirteenth century—the motive is simple, and purely academical. Poor scholars, struggling with cold, and want, and nakedness, for the love of learning, begin to attract the attention of the char table wealthy. Of this type, the original statutes of BALLIOL (A.D. 1282) offer a pure specimen. The "scholars" of Devorguilla are not priests ; they are indigent students collected into a house (*domus*) and provided with a table of two meals a-day, while attending the University exercises. The college, if it can be called one, is subsidiary to the university. It is not an educational, but an eleemosynary, institute.

2. In the second period, of which NEW COLLEGE may be taken as the most developed form, this early motive is still present, but it is merged in a more comprehensive·aim. Colleges now become monastic institutions, but monastic institutions with a new aim superadded. Their statutes form, or imply, a rule of life. They are closely modelled on the best precedents of the regular orders. The difference is, that, instead of holding up pure contemplation as did the *regulæ* of the older orders, or evangelisation as those of the mendicant orders, they make the cultivation of knowledge the business of the life. The knowledge to be cultivated, too, is not ascetic divinity, not even exclusively theology, but such purely secular and technical studies as those of the Canon and Civil Law and of medicine. These establishments are complete in themselves, and not subordinate to the University, within which they are locally situated. Except, indeed, that the graduated progress

through the studies is arranged on the system then in practice in the University, these establishments may be compared
with the new direction given to monastic life by the Bene-
dictine rule of the congregation of St. Maur three centuries
later.

3. The Colleges of the *Rénaissance.* In these noble institutions, CORPUS CHRISTI (1516), CARDINAL COLLEGE
(1525), learning stands out as the supreme object of the
founders. The university curriculum had remained sta-
tionary, while for nearly two generations the mental activity
of the West had been taking a notable turn towards a newly-
discovered knowledge. Churchmen of enlarged mind and
modern experience had become imbued with the new ideas.
Fox and Wolsey sought in their rival establishments nothing
less than a reform of university studies, and to inoculate
Oxford from within with that classical spirit which could
not be forced upon it from without. They meant their
colleges to be for Oxford what the *Collége de France* was
intended by Francis I. to be for the university of Paris—a
rival establishment, where the new studies repulsed by the
old colleges might find an asylum, and by which the fashion
might be turned in their favour.

The statutes of all the three periods, even the latest,
contain, it is true, directions for prayers for the founder's
soul's health. This enactment, however, holds no principal
place, but generally comes in among the other regulations
in detail for the conduct of the chapel-service. In only
two instances, I believe, is prayer for souls in purgatory
recited in the preamble, or among the *objects* of the foundation. These two instances, All Souls' (1438), Lincoln
(1479), occur precisely at the time when learning in the

church had been reduced to the lowest ebb by the endeavour to suppress the movement of opinion by violence and cruelty. Even in these two codes, though purgatory is named among the motives in the preamble, the directions for the prayers do not occupy a greater proportion of space than they do in other statutes; and the preambles of these collegiate codes must not be taken, any more than the preamble of an Act of Parliament, as a sufficient account of their design, apart from the evidence afforded by the contents of the code itself.

In all of them, from the earliest (Balliol) to Cardinal College, study is with more or less emphasis set out as among the objects contemplated by the founder. In the early period it is only included as an assumed condition, but as experience of the utility of such foundations gathers, it grows to be the governing purpose of the legislator. The statutes of Devorguilla (1282) simply direct her scholars " diligenter scholas exerceant," and " studio intendant." The more ample code of New College (1400), afterwards (1479) copied for Magdalen, assigns as the purpose " ecclesiæ sanctæ profectum, divini cultus, liberaliumque artium, scientiarum, et facultatum augmentum." The life of prayer and praise was carried over from the monastic rules into the colleges, as the best, if not the only conceivable, condition of a life of learning.

The grade of study which the college was intended to promote is marked with precision. The university had laid out an ascending scale of knowledge and its public profession, commencing with the rudiments of grammar, and terminating in the apex of the Doctorate. To pass through the whole of this course, which was adjusted to a graduated scale, whose successive steps were called degrees (*gradus*), required at least twenty years. During the whole of this lengthened period, or till the Doctorate, the candidate was a student. Not that when he became Doctor he ceased to be a student. The statutes of Whitgift (1570), which relax the severity of the older practice, say, " After having undergone so great toil, so many perils and examinations, we are loth to impose more labour on the doctors than they are willing voluntarily to take upon themselves " (" Post tantum laboris susceptum, et tot pericula atque examina, nolumus plus laboris doctoribus imponere quam ipsi volunt sua sponte suscipere " *Cambridge Statutes. Heywood's Cambridge Transactions,* i. 9). After the Doctorate he was released from the compulsory exercises. Below the Doctor's degree his studies had not been merely private and voluntary, but tested by public appearances and indispensable exercises in the presence of severe seniors or of rivals. The twenty years of compulsory studentship fell into two periods :—1. That spent in the study of arts. 2. That given to the special studies of his faculty. The arts course, which answered to the elements of general literature and training, was common to all. When these had been acquired in a seven years' apprenticeship, the scholar was allowed to turn to the special studies of his faculty. In these studies he continued for nearly double the time of the preliminary course of arts.

If now it be inquired which of these two periods of the university curriculum it was the object of college endowments to assist, we shall find that it was the later period, or fourteen years of special study, and not the earlier seven years spent in arts. New College and Magdalen combined an endowment for both periods. But in the majority of the colleges, though fellowships might be conferred on B.A.'s, yet this practice was not favoured, and it gradually grew into a custom to prefer M.A.'s. Before adopting a clerk to enter on the study of law or theology, it was felt that there should be some knowledge of his disposition and ability.

The colleges thus were, in their origin, endowments not for the elements of a general liberal education, but for the prolonged study of special and professional faculties by men of riper age. The university embraced both these objects. The colleges, while they incidentally aided in elementary education, were specially devoted to the highest learning. They aided collaterally the art studies, by including sometimes junior students as a subordinate part of the foundation, and because the *Magister Artium*, while going on to his faculty degree, was at the same time perhaps a regent, or teacher, in the schools. But so far from it being the intention of a fellowship to support the Master of Arts as a *teacher*, it was rather its purpose to relieve him from the drudgery of teaching for a maintenance, and to set him free to give his whole time to the studies and exercises of his faculty. The arts course was sufficiently in request to support itself; the higher faculties demanded the aid of endowment.

This was the theory of the middle-age University, and the design of collegiate foundations in their origin. Time and circumstances have brought about a total change. The colleges no longer promote the researches of science, or direct professional study. Here and there college-walls

may shelter an occasional student, but not in larger proportions than may be found in private life. Elementary
teaching of youths under twenty-two is now the only
function performed by the university, and almost the only
object of college endowments. Colleges were homes for
the life-study of the highest and most abstruse parts of
knowledge. They have become boarding-schools in which
the elements of the learned languages are taught to youths.
Yet the legal identity of the corporation has been continued. Those who in 1854 declaimed against the
" spoliation " of the colleges, were able to base their
argument upon a legal footing, and talked glibly about
the designs of founders, without reflecting that time had
long ago repealed and reversed those designs far more
effectually than any Act of Parliament.

Time — not of course without the agency, the faults,
active or passive, of man. Who is in fault for the
renunciation by the university of her high vocation, and
her having taken up with the easier business of school-
keeping ? Not, most assuredly, the university itself. This
opinion is almost universal; but it is a historical error. It
is, indeed, an error of long standing, but perhaps the
articulate enunciation of it was not made before the
celebrated attacks on Oxford in the *Edinburgh Review*,
and particularly in an article " On the State of the English
Universities," in June 1831. At that time, the history, in
fact, of Oxford, and the theory of university education,
were all but unknown in this country. Sir W. Hamilton,
with an antiquarian learning on the subject which is still
unequalled, and with a firm grasp of the principles of
education, came forward, and in his masterly essays put

both the theory and the fact in a clear and striking light. But his righteous indignation at the degeneracy of his own university led him into one great and striking injustice. He argues throughout (Hamilton, *Discussions,* "Education," Art. iv.) that the higher courses of the professors were discouraged, and finally put down, by the heads of colleges, on system, from motives of self-interest, in order to give the monopoly to the fellow-tutor. This is certainly not the history of the sinking of the level of instruction in Oxford. The level of learning fell in the Universities because it first fell in the National Church. It fell in both, because the sovereign authority used its power over both Church and Universities for political ends. The proof of this assertion would require an examination of the ecclesiastical policy of Elizabeth and the Stuarts, for which this is not the time. It must be enough for the present to have drawn attention to the fact that there was an abundance of new life, and a promise of a glorious classical revival in Oxford, at the beginning of the sixteenth century, when Corpus and Cardinal Colleges were founded as homes for the new studies. Erasmus's words, in 1497, though the style is coloured with the warmth of young enthusiasm, point to an undoubted fact: — " Mirum est dictu quam hic passim (*i.e.* Oxford), quam dense, veterum literarum seges efflorescat. . . . tantum eruditionis, non illius protritæ ac trivialis, sed reconditæ, exactæ, antiquæ, Latinæ, Græcæque, ut jam Italiam, nisi visendi gratia, haud multum desiderem." (*Ep.* 14). These prospects of a new life were crushed in the next century, not by any *malfaisance* within, but by the violence of the ecclesiastical revolution without. So far from the death of learning in Oxford having been occasioned by the corrupting influence of over-endowment, it died hard, and yielded up its breath not without many a struggle. The grasp of ecclesiastical tyranny was on its throat; and the twenty-three years of Leicester's chancellorship (1565-1588) left it pretty much what it remained up to the present century, without independence, without the dignity of knowledge, without intellectual ambition, the mere tool of a political party. It may be that the statesmen of that day were not without excuse; that they were themselves the victims of a higher political necessity. This is a question for the historian. It is sufficient for us that it was the Government, and not the university itself, which crushed that academical freedom, without which learning cannot flourish. It was the Government which closed our gates to nonconformists, and compelled us to forget our proper duty, by occupying us as a spiritual police to maintain an arbitrary *juste milieu* of church government and doctrine. When Sir W. Hamilton pretends that it was the Board of Heads who in the seventeenth century silenced the professors, he forgets that, long before the Laudian statutes of 1636, the professors had ceased to have a class, because there were no longer any students sufficiently advanced to attend them. The standard of teaching is ruled by the standard already attained by the taught. Had the public lecturers of the university continued to teach, they must have lowered themselves to teach the rudiments. The very same taunts which were levelled by Sir W. Hamilton against the tutors of the colleges, would then have been equally applicable to the professors; for long before 1636 it was found impossible to retain any students in the university after the B.A. degree.

K

Passages referred to by Sir W. Hamilton himself sufficiently prove this. In 1539 the university thus addressed Sir Thomas More : —

"In old time we had each of us separate stipends, some from noblemen, some from the heads of convents, and a very large number from the incumbents of the rural parishes. Now these revenues are being cut off. Abbots are ordering their monks home, nobles taking away their sons, and priests their nephews and kinsmen. The number of scholars is decreasing, our halls are going to decay, and all liberal studies waxing cold. *The fellows of colleges are almost the only residents left.* They have only just enough to maintain themselves. If they are to be taxed, the colleges must go to the ground, or some fellowships must be declared vacant" (*A. Wood*, a. 1539, *ap. Hamilton Discussions*, p. 430).

For Cambridge, the interpretation of 1608, by which residence of the B.A. degree was made dispensable, is sufficient evidence. For though this interpretation was given by the Board of Heads, it was rendered necessary by the actual practice already existing, and is grounded by them upon the fact of that practice. It was, indeed, but legalising the abridgment of study which had taken place in usage, and which could no longer be prevented (Heywood's *Cambridge Transactions*, ii. 229). In this state of things the fellow-tutor came into fashion, as really better fitted to teach the only pupils that were forthcoming than the professor. The professor found himself without a class, unless he were to stoop, as the professor in a Scotch university is compelled, to do school-work. Of this condition of things in Scotland no one complained more than Sir W. Hamilton himself. Yet in Scotland the professors had neither been silenced by the heads, nor superseded by the fellow-tutors. In 1831, when Sir W. Hamilton came forward as the champion of learning, the heads in Oxford had already begun to attract to themselves that public odium which twenty-five years later overthrew them, and which would have overthrown them earlier but for the theological agitation which arose about that time, and drew attention away from educational reforms. Every evil felt in the university, even those of which they were innocent, was laid at their door. The extinction of superior education in the universities was a public calamity which had not been brought about by any academical rulers, or by incompetence of college tuition, but by circumstances and a policy operating on a much greater scale, and going back to a very early time. How would Whitgift, *e.g.*, have brooked a public handling by professors of Greek history or philosophy, when he doubted (1580) the expediency of printing being continued at Cambridge, and recommended that no books should be published there until they had first been allowed by lawful authority? (Heywood, *Cambridge Transactions*, i. 381).

The evil, indeed, is of so long standing that not only the public but we ourselves have tacitly acquiesced in its continuance, and have directed our efforts and our wishes for reform another way. We are content that Oxford should be a school, and we are laudably anxious to make it as good a school as we can. Our whole legislation, since the first enactment of the examination statute in 1800, has had this one object.

How entirely the idea of school-teaching has expelled every other conception of a university from among us may be instanced in the case of a foundation lying outside the line of the school examinations. In 1835 the university came into possession of a legacy from a munificent benefactor, Sir Robert Taylor, who died in 1788. The proceeds of this bequest were to be laid out in promoting the study of " the modern European languages." Here was an opportunity for naturalising in England the rising science of comparative philology, and acquiring for Oxford, without touching endowments already affected to older studies, a new literary celebrity which might have atoned for many years of disgrace and contumely. When this was found too " unpractical " for England, and when it was resolved to be content with a school of living languages, what languages would a learned university have thought of for endowment? A recent French writer, arguing for the establishment in Paris of. an *Ecole des Langues Vivantes*, says :—

" Bien entendu que cela signifie école des langues vivantes *rares et peu abordables*, car il ne saurait y etre question de ces langues courantes, usuelles, dont chacun peut se procurer des leçons pour son argent . . . . a coup sur personne ne songe à faire fonder là des chaires d'allemand, d'anglais, ou d'espagnol. Ce serait une moquerie. Mais tous les idiomes qu' il est chez nous ou impossible, ou du moins trés difficile de se faire enseigner." [He goes on to propose Tamul, Berber, Basque, Magyar, Finnish.] (Baron de Dumast, *Sur l'Enseignment Supérieur*, p. 39.)

What would be deemed an " absurdity " even in France, where all scientific institutions must be popular, was gravely committed by a university calling itself learned. We employed Sir Robert Taylor's bequest in providing gratuitous lessons in French, German, Italian, and Spanish, the languages of society and travel. The literature and the philological study of any one of these languages might have made by itself a very proper subject of a learned endowment. But this is not the design with which the Taylor statute endows those four languages. It distinctly intends to provide for the university students just those colloquial accomplishments which are provided by every school or lycée. As characteristic of the feeling prevailing among us at the time the original statute was made, it may be noticed that each teacher was to teach for four hours a-day, and for this he was awarded £150 a-year! The lowest grade of teaching, and as much of it for as low wages as possible—these seem to have been the principles of the framers of the statute. In 1857 it was the same. The mania for prize scholarships, then epidemic, infected the curators of the Taylor Institution, and they would have scholarships, of course for the languages learned in the institution. And they ordered an examination for these prizes, not critical and historical in the literature, nor philological and scientific in the language, taken as a whole from its birth to its extant form, but in the grammar and current idiom as spoken—an examination, in short, such as would be useful to a courier or a foreign clerk, or to a gentleman setting out on his first tour on the continent. That has happened which might have been certainly foretold, that the Taylor scholarships have always fallen to the lot of young men who had been born abroad, or whose parents had lived in Paris or Bonn, and who win their scholarships by what they had picked up in the nursery or the gymnasium. One service, indeed, the Taylor foundation has rendered to science:—It has made Oxford the home of the most eminent comparative philologist living. This may atone for much.

We have entirely ceased to consider ourselves as learners. Every resident looks upon himself, or wishes himself to be looked upon, as a teacher. Indeed, we have ceased to be anything more. The canons of Christ Church were all converted into professors by the Cathedral Act, 3 and 4 Victoria, c. 113, except three. Of these three two were suppressed as useless by the ordinance of 1858, and their revenues applied to augment the already overflowing fund of educational subsidy. No fellow of a college thinks of residing except those who are engaged in earning an income by tuition or by parochial cure. In the election of heads the disposition is to regard business qualifications. The heads of colleges are chiefly occupied in the conduct of university business, or in looking after college property. The heads of halls are engaged in the tuition of the students resident in the hall. We have created a few new professors—Logic, Latin, etc.; our idea of a professor's functions seems to be that he is a schoolmaster, and he continues the old Latin and Greek exercises, the practice of which was begun at Marlborough or Rugby, æt. 12, and the persevering reproduction of which will never cease till, at æt. 22 or 23, the B.A. is turned out of the final school with his education finished.

When we desire to know what the public thinks, where should we look but to the *Times*. There we find ourselves thus ticketed :—

" The other view regards the university as mainly a place of education for young men just before they enter upon life, and would confine its whole administration to this practical aim. These two views are directly contrary to each other. An atmosphere of discovery is not the best atmosphere for instruction. The men who are the most skilful and bold in speculation are not the best teachers. . . . We are confident that the latter of these antagonistic views, and not the former, is the one from which Englishmen in general regard the universities. They look upon them as places of education for their children, and if measures should be hastily passed which had the effect of subverting this character, *the universities would soon suffer by the withdrawal of undergraduates.* To some extent, it is to be feared, the universities have already experienced a change in this direction; and, at the same time, nothing is more common than to hear parents complaining that the education of their sons is not conducted with the care they expected. It is a growing subject of discontent among the public that the tutors and professors of both our universities are becoming more and more absorbed in their own scientific pursuits, etc." (*The Times*, 8th March 1867).

When we adopt, and acquiesce in, this view of ourselves, we cannot complain if the public take us at our own valuation. If you are a school, the public not unnaturally argues you are a very costly school. All those extensive buildings, those magnificent endowments, all those canons, heads, professors, fellows, tutors, to educate some 1700 pupils! The British soldier is said to be the most costly in the world, but we have the satisfaction of knowing that he is also one of the most efficient. Certainly the Oxford B.A. ought to be the most finished specimen of education in the world, if cost of production is the measure of value. £120,000 a-year applied as prize-money or bonus distributable among scholars, and another £50,000 a-year spent on teachers and masters out of endowments, besides nearly another £50,000 levied in fees by tutors private and public !

It is evident that a struggle is now at hand with public opinion on the application of our endowments. Of a resistance by the university to the popular will not a thought can be entertained for a moment. But in a contest with public opinion much will depend upon our having a good cause and a clear view of the right. When the central authority was strong it oppressed us, and bent us to purposes of government. The central authority in this country is in abeyance, and our danger now lies on the side of the popular will. Our lower middle class is now, for the first time, brought face to face with Oxford, such as the reforms of the last fifty years have made it. It has been determined that we are a school, and that we shall be nothing else. Tried by this standard, the public, as soon as it looks into our affairs thoroughly, will immediately discover two facts—1*st*, That we are not the right sort of school for its purposes; 2*d*, That such a school as it wants could be conducted for probably a fourth of the cost, and that the other three-fourths of the endowment are superfluous.

That we are not the sort of school the public demand, that we do not teach the things they think ought to be taught, is what we have been long in the habit of hearing. For the schooling hitherto given in the university has at least had one merit;—it has always involved the idea of culture for the sake of culture. It is therefore in direct opposition to the popular notion of education for success. It is founded on a totally different view of human life, and its relation to the external world. Besides the highest culture is, or is supposed to be, the privilege of the few. And the modern spirit abhors privilege; it will favour only that in which all can share. Culture requires fortune and leisure; it is a luxury of the rich; let them pay for it. The national university enjoying the national fund must furnish only such an article as shall be useful to the whole nation. Oxford has hitherto been monopolised by a small class—in its connections, if not in itself, aristocratic. Hence the learning in vogue there has been necessarily the learning which that small class favoured. Now that the nation is going to reclaim the universities for its own use, it will have such teaching as suits its purposes.

The classes now approaching us are not insensible to culture, but they esteem it for its bearing on social prosperity, not for its own sake. A very large part of the increasing desire for liberal education is only a desire for its material results. A better social position, access to the highest employments, a certain power and influence in deliberation and debate, and even a higher scale of remuneration for services, are seen to be necessary attendants on this education. These things are coveted, and therefore the education which gives them is desired. The universities, as soon as they are found to be generally accessible, will be conceived of as forming a bridge by which talent, born in lowliness and poverty, may make its way to an equality with rank and wealth. Probably the majority of the middle and lower classes would be content if our universities were remoulded in this sense. The fate which overtook the University of Paris in the storm of revolution is not likely to be our fate. It is not desired to destroy us, but to make us useful. If the public, which believes in newspapers, were to take us in hand now, it would no doubt try to set up a school of liberal education for its youth, in which the measure of attainment would be what will get him on in life. And the measure of life would be an empirical one—not life as it might be, but life as it is. Thus the type of our middle class, such as it now is, would be perpetuated. Education, instead of an elevating influence, would become, as in China, the stamp of a uniform pattern. At the same time, it is probable that the first result of such a principle of reform would be an increased efficiency of Oxford as a school. We should have a varied staff of masters, under whom every sort of accomplishment might be acquired in little time, or at little cost, and youth prepared to pass unnumbered competitive examinations in any subject. The hive would be purified; the drones would be driven out. The danger on which the *Times* dwells, that we are getting to know too much, and to do too little, would be abated. Every one would be doing a day's work, and receiving a salary in proportion.

Before this catastrophe overtakes us, can we do anything towards averting it ? We are, indeed, ourselves in a great measure responsible for the situation. In our dissatisfaction with ourselves, and the work we were doing, we have encouraged the agitation, and invited the interference of the outside public. We have thought it a more wholesome life to live under the surveillance of the press and Parliament, than wrapped in our aristocratic seclusion, and polishing our Latin verses. Now the press and Parliament are coming in upon us, and threatening to mould us to their own ideas. This indeed would be a disastrous consummation of our agitation for reform. Can we save the endowments, not for ourselves, but for our country? There is indeed a mode of "saving" the endowments, which we have practised once already, and might attempt again. We may fall in with the public conception, and turn ourselves at once into a good working school. By vigour in doing this, and by another grand holocaust of fellowships, we might perhaps purchase another respite, and retain the remaining emoluments on their present footing.

But would this be worth doing? Surely not. Many of us had rather that the endowments were not "saved," than that we should remain as we are. There remains only one thing to be tried:—we must engage in a grapple with public opinion, and endeavour to graft upon it, by discussion and by the reason of the thing, an idea of the purposes and possibilities of a university, which is at present wanting alike to its conception, and to our practice. We must do nothing less than ask that the college endowments be restored to their original purpose—that of the promotion of science and learning.

It will not be supposed that this proposal is offered without a consciousness of its unpopularity. It is an employment of endowments which will appear to the large mass of Englishmen of the middle class as a scheme proper only for Plato's Republic. And even scientific men, who might secretly be favourable to the measure, will probably consider it a Quixotic and hopeless proposal to be brought before a House of Commons elected by universal suffrage. From both points of view, it is liable to be condemned as unpractical. Before, therefore, explaining the mode in which it is now proposed to restore the endowments to their original purpose, a few reasons may be stated why it is not really so hopeless, as it may seem at first, to urge the suggestion.

(1.) In the first place, it is not a question of a new item in the budget, of paying for science out of the general taxes. Even were it this, I do not believe it would be hopeless. Sir Robert Peel persuaded the country (*i.e.* Great Britain) to tax itself to the amount of £30,000 a-year for an entirely novel institution, the Queen's Colleges in Ireland, because it was believed it would promote the civilisation of that island. It is true that the House of Commons of the future may possibly be an assembly of a more vulgar intelligence than it is at present. M. Rénan, who takes the most flattering view of democracy, confesses some misgiving as to how it might be possible to preserve a chair of the higher mathematics, *e.g.*, supposing it to be necessary to its preservation that the tax-payers should comprehend the bearing and utility of the science : — " Si un jour les contribuables, pour admettre l'utilité du cours de mathématiques transcendantes au Collége de France, devaient comprendre à quoi servent les spéculations qu'on y enseigne, cette chaire courrait de grands risques " (*Revue de deux Mondes,* 1864).

But this is not a question of a new tax to be levied. The college property indeed is national, and, as such, the nation, or its government, is under an obligation to lay it out to as much advantage as if it was a sum coming out of its own pocket. But it does not come out of its pocket.

It is already in hand, and has not to be voted. It must be disposed of, and cannot be disposed of by distributing it *viritim*. More than this: the annual revenue in question is not a tax on the industry of the country; it is in the form of rent. If the college estates were sold in small lots, somebody would be receiving the rent. They might become private property, and the rent would be spent in the purchase of enjoyment for a number of private individuals. Now, an endowment out of rent is not the subtraction of so much from the general wealth of the community. The expenditure has precisely the same economical effect, whether made by a private freeholder or by the members of an eleemosynary corporation. But whereas from the expenditure of the private landowner society reaps no moral benefit, the expenditure of an endowed corporation may have conditions attached to it which make it yield a moral and intellectual benefit for the general body. The gross annual value of real property assessed under schedule A is nearly £150,000,000. If of this gross value no more than £100,000,000 are net rental, what, by the side of this, is the £100,000 or £150,000 of our university endowments now under debate? £100,000,000 of rent are spent by private persons, under no condition or responsibility, but solely for their own individual enjoyment and benefit. To appropriate out of this sum, say £150,000, in such a way as to secure a public benefit for all — viz., the promotion of our social culture, instead of being munificence, seems a most penurious provision for the public. We are most jealous of the rights of individuals, and careless of the common welfare. Instead of seeming to be asking much in asking an endowment of science out of the rental of the kingdom to the extent of £150,000 a-year, one feels ashamed to be earnest in contending for what is so insignificant by the side of the vast accumulations of wealth in private hands.

(2.) In the next place, not only is the endowment in existence, and already expended, but, as I contend, the mode of its present expenditure is not merely useless, but actually hurtful. The greater part of the sum, as has been shown, is at present distributed in prizes to learners. Prizes to the learners, beyond the point up to which they serve to encourage diligence and stimulate exertion, have the effect of a premium on the thing taught. Adam Smith was, it may be granted, led by the social condition of Europe before the great revolution into an indiscriminate condemnation of endowments for any purpose. But the principle on which he reasoned can hardly be controverted. That principle is, that the endowments of schools and colleges diminish the necessity of application in the teachers, their subsistence being secured by a fund, independent of their success and reputation in their profession :—

" Whatever," he says, " forces a certain number of students to any college or university, independent of the merit and reputation of the teachers, tends more or less to diminish the necessity of that merit or reputation. . . Were there no public institutions for education, no system, no science would be taught for which there was not some demand, or which the circumstances of the time did not render it either necessary or convenient, or at least fashionable, to learn. A private teacher could never find his account in teaching either an exploded or antiquated system of a science acknowledged to be useful, or a science universally believed to be a mere useless and pedantic heap of sophistry and nonsense. Such systems, such sciences, can subsist nowhere but in those incorporated societies for education whose prosperity and revenue are in a great measure independent of their reputation, and altogether independent of their industry. Were there no public institutions for education, a gentleman, after going through, with application and abilities, the most complete course of education which the circumstances of the times were supposed to afford, could not come into the world completely ignorant of everything which is the common subject of conversation among gentlemen and men of the world" (*Wealth of Nations*, b. v. c. i. 3).

There is a weakness in this line of reasoning—that, viz., of assuming that the subjects of conversation among men of the world can be the criterion of the subject-matter of education. But I cite the passage for that in which it is strong, and not for that in which it is weak. The reasons assigned by Adam Smith against endowments in education bear with their full force only against endowing the teaching of given subject-matters on given methods. The payment of the teacher by endowment is not only allowable, but is necessary in all the higher branches of education. All that education, which has culture and not professional success for its end, must in an average state of society be supplied. The demand, though real, is not imperious enough to create the supply—to call the education into existence. We may, we must, endow the teacher; we ought not to annex the endowment to methods or matters to be taught. It must be conceded to Adam Smith's reasoning that, even in the endowment of the teacher, there is danger of inducing supineness and indifference to reputation. But this danger must be incurred, as without the endowment the article cannot be had at all. It is not a matter of choice as to which of two methods we shall adopt of supplying ourselves with the superior education—by that of endowment or that of free trade. The ordinary laws of supply and demand have never given it existence. But beyond the endowment of the teacher we cannot safely go. The risk of supineness on his part becomes a certainty when, besides providing him the whole or a part of his salary, we go on further to provide him with pupils by paying them to attend his school. To endow a professor in a university is as allowable, as necessary, as to endow a minister of religion. To attract pupils round the professor by largesses of money is as little allowable as to pay people for going to church.

We have, in our recent administration of our endowments, run exactly counter to this principle. As soon as we seriously took the alarm at the deficiency of our numbers—for not to have grown with the growth of wealth and population is to have fallen off—we set about to remedy it by recruiting and a system of bounties. This application of our revenues is useless and hurtful. It is useless, because our endowments, large as they may be when confined to certain purposes, are quite insignificant when used to compete for the purchase of talent in the market of enterprise. It is hurtful—to the learner, because to be paid for learning enfeebles the moral effect of the education; to the teacher, because an artificial supply of pupils deadens his sense of emulation; to the methods of teaching, because the uncertainty now reigning in Europe as to the relative merits of science deductive, science applied, and language, as instruments of training, requires for its settlement the free play of public experiment and the demands of civilised life.

(3.) Our middle classes, notwithstanding the prevailing want of refinement, the selfish and material interests, the worship of wealth, the weakness of ideas, and the denominational habits of judging which still enthral them, have undoubtedly made progress. They have reached that point where they are able to recognise a culture which they do not possess. The growing demand for education is a phrase in everyone's mouth, whatever it exactly intends. Now, it certainly is at present a demand for an education which fits for life, and for life as those classes in England conceive life—*i.e.* rising in the world. Still it is a demand for education; and the higher education, even when directed to a false ideal, has a tendency to purify itself. We have ourselves hitherto fallen in with the notion that we should educate for life, and for English life as it is, and have laboured to prove that our Latin and Greek were useful. We have pointed to Mr. Gladstone and Sir Roundell Palmer, and told with pride how one was Ireland scholar, and the other a double-first. This line of argument has misled the public, and done injustice to our cause. We shall have a better chance of a hearing, when we take our stand on the clear ground that the highest form of education is culture for culture's sake. It must stand not in opposition to professional life, but above it. The energy of a secular success is one only of the conditions of moral life, and not the whole of it. Refinement, if not actually a subtraction from public energy, is not a basis for it. Education is to be a preparation for life. Be it so. But then life is not all fighting. When

L

we shall dare to say these things, and can show an education which, while it fits for the struggle, yet leads up to a view of a life which is above the struggle, our position will not be confused by a cross issue, we shall not be coming before the world on false pretences.

(4.) It is ignorance, and not ill-will, that directs the popular discussions on the subject of the highest education. Men in general cannot imagine what they have seen no example of. When the British Association was first formed, it had to encounter a storm of vulgar raillery from our middle classes, not because they were against science, but because they were unable to conceive the use of organisation and concert in science. Like everything else in England, science had been the work of individual enterprise. That it could be promoted by association was a new idea, and as such not only false but ridiculous. A permanent organisation of science, a home where the cultivation of knowledge for its own sake shall be a profession, a life-business, will be also a new idea which a vast number of Englishmen will be loth to believe in at first. To them "college" has always meant a school which youths leave when they have finished their education, and of which heads, fellows, and tutors have been the machinery—a machinery cumbrous and expensive, but, after all, sanctioned by long usage, venerable from an ancient pedigree, and generally acquiesced in. To expect that the public should at once admit the idea of the universities becoming the intellectual and educational metropolis of the country, would be quite unreasonable. The public recognises results. In the last fifty years the physical sciences have filled the world with their marvels. Gas, steam, locomotion by land and water, telegraphy, needle-guns, the sun's rays employed in the service of art—these things strike not only the vulgar, but all, with admiration. It might not be impossible to bring home to the public conviction the real connection which exists between these striking conquests over the material world and the abstract study of the laws of that world. The idea of such a connection is one already familiar to all persons of education. To a perception of this connection is owing the pressure which exists for the introduction of physical science into schools and colleges. To have made this step is itself a grade in education. The uneducated man eats and breathes, and despises a statement of the laws of digestion and respiration as a superfluity. To get a general recognition by the middle-class public of the value of abstract exposition in any subject is to have gained a great point. Those who are ready to flout the popular disposition to (as they think) over-estimate physical science, hardly consider how much such an estimate implies. If it does implicate an undue attraction towards a special field of observation, it contains at least this precious germ, that it is a recognition of science—*i.e.* a recognition of the abstract, a recognition of the supremacy of mind. It is unphilosophical to talk of the materialist tendency of natural science—a superficial inference from the fact that what is known is matter. What is known in science is not matter, but the laws of matter; and law is ideal, is an abstract cognition.

" Undoubtedly the first thought which suggests itself to the mind is that a material force, and a moral and intellectual force, are essentially different. But such evidence as we have is all tending the other way. The conclusions forced upon us have been these—*First*, That the more we know of nature the more certain it appears that a multiplicity of separate forces does not exist, but that all her forces pass into each other, and are but modifications of some one force which is the source and centre of the rest. *Secondly*, That all of them are governed in their mutual relations by principles of arrangement which are purely mental. *Thirdly*, That of the ultimate seat of force in any form we know nothing directly. And *Fourthly*, That the nearest conception we can ever have of force is derived from our own consciousness of vital power " (Duke of Argyll, *Reign of Law*, p. 296).

This step may be considered gained. We have no longer the difficult task of justifying science in the eyes of the nation. It is willing to have schools in which an abstract teaching shall be given. But it inclines, naturally enough, to such science, and so far, as it sees pregnant with tangible results. What if it does ? Even in this demand the public is more than half right. We are all justly suspicious of what we do not quite understand. When a statement goes beyond my apprehension, how am I to know that it is not nonsense ? There has been in the world at various times so much idle speculation, so many frivolous applications of most keen intellect, so much superstitious veneration of fantastic combinations of thought, that some check on knowledge is highly necessary to prevent it from running riot in the wantonness of its own wealth. To keep our abstract tendencies to their bearings, their practical applications must be watched. On the side of character, too, the suspicions of the public are not entirely unfounded. A dilettante fastidiousness, an aimless inertia, an Oriental lassitude of habit, are not seldom seen to be the consequence of high philosophical training. The tendency of abstract thought and various knowledge to enervate the will is one of the real dangers of the highest education. It is a valuable element in the popular discernment that it has its eye strongly fixed on this danger. It is not a vulgar prejudice against knowledge, but a true though rough impression of one of the consequences of cultivation. M. Rénan thinks that scientific truths of a high order will be appreciated by the people when properly presented to them.

" The popular expounders of science," he says, " commonly err in attempting to lower themselves to the level of their public by the introduction of anecdotes, superficial analogies, telling experiments, trivial applications. They would have better success if they attacked the topmost summits of knowledge, the points where truths converge. I would not attempt to initiate the multitude into our subtleties and technical distinctions; but I maintain that there is no truth so fine and delicate as to be beyond the general apprehension. The process by which the results of philosophy are rendered popular is not one of attenuation but of translation. It is a capital error to treat the people as a child. They ought to be treated as a woman. An address delivered in the presence of women is better than one held where they are not; it is under stricter rules, and submitted to more severe exigencies. What is written for the people ought in like manner to be distinguished by greater care. One may say everything, but on condition of saying nothing that can be wrongly conceived " (*Révue des deux Mondes*, 1864).

Democracy has certainly not hitherto shown itself so favourable to science. The two countries which at this moment exhibit the most developed democratic feeling are France and America.

In America scientific culture has never been introduced. It has no universities, such as we understand by the term ; the institutions so called being merely places for granting titular degrees (Appendix C). Yet some of the Northern States have a system of popular education more complete than anywhere in the Old World, and which may well be envied by this country, where we have emerged from the feudal stage of serfdom only to land in the barbarism of a pauper proletariate.

In France, the revolution destroyed the university. The empire made an attempt to organise it on a new basis. But the Imperial University was only an association of the upper schools and colleges, and what little life it ever had animated only the schools. It had no department for the cultivation of any knowledge beyond the school level. This was not wholly owing to democratic tendencies. It was partly the jealous spirit of the imperial *regime.* A government, by preventing free association and competition, may prevent the organisation of knowledge. It cannot create it. It was in vain that Napoleon I. decreed the existence of a university in his grandest style : " The emperor wants a body whose teaching may be free from the influence of the passing gusts of fashion, a body that may keep moving, even though government be lethargic " (Arnold, *Education in France,* p. 35). To this day the "*fortes études*" are confessedly weak in France. That they are sustained in any degree is not owing to the university so much as to extraneous substitutes for a university. The traditions of learning are kept up in France, so far as they are kept up at all, by the *Institut,* by the *Collége de France,* in the *Cours* attached to the library, in the *Ecole des Chartes*, etc. It is by what may be called secondary intellectual interests, rather than by the highest intellectual tension, that the influence of France in Europe is maintained. The natural quickness and genial capacity of the people for ideas make them the readiest recipients of every discovery or suggestion made by others. " The habit of intelligence," says Mr. Arnold, " continues in the French people to be active, and to enlighten." M. Guizot says, " C'est la grandeur de notre pays que les esprits ont besoin d'être satisfaits en même temps que les interêts." These real and valuable intellectual influences at work in France cannot hide from us the fact that the highest development of scientific culture is not found in that country. It is weak on the side of its university, and that weakness distinctly affects the national character, the position of the country in the world, and its power as the leader of European civilisation. There is a superficiality about the products of French genius which marks the clever but second-rate mind. Clever writers, incomparable talkers, their assertion never carries with it the weight which is derived from known habits of patient and exhaustive investigation. To edit the thoughts of others is their business ; the real progress of knowledge is conducted elsewhere. The presence of single names, such as De Sacy and Villoison, Boissonade or Burnouf, proves nothing. They were isolated in their age and country. A free university, such as Napoleon I. wished for, in which might be seen an example of severer studies, of exact science, of profound learning, is now an object of desire for their country among thoughtful Frenchmen. M. Rénan, in the essay already referred to, endeavours to impress upon his countrymen the desirableness, nay the necessity, of such an institution, if France is to maintain its position, and continue to exercise the influence in Europe which it did in the seventeenth and eighteenth centuries. He would do this through the instrumentality of the *Collége de France.* He would revive in the *Collége,* which is now too much given over to popular *cours,* the spirit of Francis I. and Henri II., and call to it creative minds in the various sciences :—" Qu' aucune branche nouvelle d'etudes ne se manifeste en France sans qu' immediatement elle soit représentée au collége. Il n'est nullement necessaire que les chaires du Collége de France représentent le cadre encyclopédique de l'enseignement. Ce qui est essentiel, c'est qu'il représente l'état present du movement scientifique. A coté des établissements ou se garde le dépôt des connaissances acquises, il est nécessaire qu'il y ait des chaires independantes ou la grande originalité, qui dans l'enseignment proprement dit n'est pas une qualité indispensable, trouve sa juste place."

These aspirations of M. Rénan, prompted by the intellectual aspect of his own country in 1864, are identical with the wishes expressed by the Oxford Commission of 1850, after a survey of the position of the university. " It is generally acknowledged," they say, " that both Oxford and the country at large suffer greatly from the absence of a body of learned men devoting their lives to the cultivation of science, and to the direction of academical education. It is felt that the opening of such a career within the university would serve to call forth the knowledge and ability which are often buried or wasted for want of proper encouragement. It is evident that, for literary men, academical rather than ecclesiastical offices are the fittest rewards, and most useful positions. The fact that so few books of profound research emanate from the University of Oxford materially impairs its character as a seat of learning, and consequently its hold on the respect of the nation. The presence of men eminent in various departments of knowledge would impart a dignity and stability to the whole institution, far more effectual against attacks from without than the utmost amount of privilege and protection ; whilst from within it would tend above all other means to guard the university from being absorbed, as it has been of late years, by the agitations of theological controversy. If the professoriate could be placed in a proper condition, those fellows of colleges whose services the university would wish to retain, would be less tempted, and would never be compelled, to leave it for positions and duties for which their academical labours had in no way prepared them ; but would look forward to some sphere of usefulness within the university, for which they would have been fitted by their previous occupations. A professorship would then, in fact, become a recognised profession " (*O. U. C. Report*, p. 94).

So the commissioners argued, endeavouring apologetically to establish a broad ground of expediency for what they, in common with the public, believed to be a confiscation, or at least a diversion, of college endowments to the purposes of a professoriate. It had never occurred to them to ask the question, What purpose did college endowments originally serve ? What is their present effect ? Had they done so—had they read the statutes which they edited—they would have seen that they had before them in the college fellowships an endowment expressly destined by the founders to the maintenance " of a body of learned men, devoting their lives to the cultivation of science and to the direction of academical education." These endowments had, by time and the gradual lapse of things, been diverted into an overgrown and unhealthy system of prizes for school proficiency; and that, so far from its being necessary to apologise for asking that they should be restored to their original purpose, the conservative maintainers of the *status in quo* ought to have been called upon to justify by expediency the diversion of them from their purpose, which had actually taken place.

When I speak of the restoration of college endowments to their original purpose, it will be easily understood that this cannot be in the original form. The purpose is as desirable an object of national policy now as then. The forms which were the best in the fourteenth century are impossible in the nineteenth. A founder in the fourteenth century desired to organise an institution for the cultivation of science and learning. What form was he likely to give to his design? There was but one type known to him. He had never heard of the Museum at Alexandria, and would not have imitated it if he had. But he had before him the cœnobitical establishments of the West, all of one common type, but with every variety of specific application. With a very slight adaptation, this type was made to serve his purpose, and was grafted upon the Oxford schools. In conservative England these institutions have preserved their form through one religious, and more than one political, revolution. Only their purpose has been let slip.

But it is their purpose of which the nation is now greatly in need. Let us have back the purpose, and give up the old form for one fully adapted to modern habits of life. Let us have "a body of learned men devoting their lives to the cultivation of science and the direction of academical education." Let the colleges be once again what they were designed to be.

Supposing this to have been determined upon, the question arises, What form must the institution assume to give it a scope and influence proper to the time? Without going into details, three conditions of the success of such a body may be laid down. 1. It must be organised. 2. The persons composing it must be appointed for eminent merit, and not for other considerations. 3. There must be security taken that when appointed they devote themselves to the promotion of knowledge, and not either engage in other pursuits or subside into indifference.

1. It must be an organisation of science. College funds might be spent, and better spent than now, in giving pensions to men of science throughout the country, known to be engaged in independent researches. Individual pensions are a proper mode of promoting science and encouraging disinterested labour, and have often procured true glory to the country or the sovereign who conferred them. But neither in their bearing on science, nor in their influence upon the national life, are isolated life-pensions at all to be compared with an institution organised for perpetual succession. "The mere founding of a voluntary society for any given purpose evolves out of the primary elements of human character a latent force of the most powerful kind—the sentiment, the feeling, the passion,

as it often is, of the spirit of association. . . . When
the aim of any given association is a high aim, directed to
ends really good, and seeking the attainment of them by
just methods of procedure, the spirit it evokes becomes
itself a new law, a special force operating powerfully for
good on the mind of every individual subject to its influence.
Some pre-existing motives it modifies, some it neutralises,
some it suppresses altogether, and some it compels to work
in new directions" (Duke of Argyll, *Reign of Law*, p. 410).
The collegiate spirit is an essential element of such an
institution. " The bond of mind," says Dr. Döllinger,
" which ties together the members of a university into one
harmonious organism, consists not merely in a community of interests and a unity of endeavour, but in the
reciprocity of thought, the vital stimulus, the impulse to
ever-fresh activity, to push research, which the individual is
constantly receiving from the body. To the emulation
thus kindled, not only the living contribute, but the illustrious departed also. An association, such as is a university, lives and supports itself upon its past no less than
upon its present. Happy such a society, if bygone errors
and follies have ceased to cast their shadow and propagate
their baneful influence upon the minds and tempers of
successive generations!" (Döllinger, *Universitäten sonst und
jetzt*, p. 27). But all the advantages of the spirit of
association for an intellectual aim may probably be secured
without a common domestic life. The cœnobitic system is
now impossible, and has long ceased in colleges. But
without the cœnobitic system, celibacy in a Protestant
country falls to the ground at once. The *collegium*, in the
sense of the Civil Law, the incorporated society, having a

common purse and purpose, is still required; but the college, in the modern sense of the building, is not always fitted to be the home of the individual members of the corporation, who must be free to marry. In some instances the existing college buildings might be appropriated for the residence of the future married fellows. This would especially be desirable in the case of those foundations which were affected to the cultivation of particular studies. If it were proposed, *e.g.*, to amalgamate Merton with Corpus Christi College, and to dedicate the united college to the study of biology, chemistry, and the allied branches, the buildings might in this case be wholly appropriated to the use of the families of the fellows. In other cases, where no such special dedication took place, a college might remain fitted up in separate chambers as at present, and be let as lodgings to junior students.

2. A place in a reformed college will, of course, be much more worth having than a fellowship is now, and it will be of greater public concern that it should be properly filled. The question of appointment resolves itself into two—(1.) Who is to appoint? (2.) What test of merit is the appointing officer to employ? The present method of co-optation will no longer be applicable. For an examination-test is not to be thought of—first, because of the greater age of the possible candidates or nominees; and, secondly, because of the special character of the qualification. Each seat in the college will, as it becomes vacant, be dedicated to some particular branch of knowledge. There should be no fixed and statutable specification of qualities or acquirements. The statutes should only contain a very general designation of the studies to be pro-

moted by the college as a whole, and each seat in it should be left to be filled up by the most eminent man who may be available for those purposes, whatever may be the special direction which his researches have taken. "Il n'est nullement necessaire," says M. Rénan, "que les chaires représentent le cadre encyclopédique de l'enseignement. Ce qui est essentiel c'est qu'il représente l'etat présent du mouvement scientifique." The problem of university patronage is how to find an electoral body which shall be competent to look out for and to select true eminence in specialty, notwithstanding the misleading glare of popular reputation. The suggestions to be made on this head must be made in connection with the consideration of No. 3.

3. Security must be taken that, when appointed, the fellow shall devote himself to the pursuit of his science. This is undoubtedly a great difficulty, and yet the whole utility of an endowed body of learned men rests upon the possibility of obtaining such a guarantee. If this difficulty cannot be surmounted, it would not be worth while to propose a reapportionment of the fellowship fund, with the certainty that it would soon relapse into the same unproductive expenditure which it now is. We have seen how the college, in its original design, elaborately provided against the tendency of human infirmity to sink into indolent enjoyment.

(1.) The college was established within the limits of a university which rigorously exacted a long probation for its degrees, with public appearances in exercises and disputations. These exercises were no mere forms, but the serious occupation of keen-minded men, who were daily passing out into the world to take the most responsible business of political life or ecclesiastical government.

(2.) The statutes of each single college compelled its fellows to proceed to the higher degrees, and thus to continue in the practice of these public appearances before the university. But, besides this, they enacted an interior system of private exercises of the same kind subsidiary to the public appearances. It was the monastic common life and mutual surveillance brought to bear upon study, instead of upon ascetic mortification. Every fellow was a check upon every other. And the first duty of the head was to enforce diligence upon all. Both within and without the college all concurred to keep alive an intellectual rivalry, and sloth was shame.

(3.) If wealth be a temptation to indolence, the temptation did not exist for our collegiate predecessors. Their life was the life of the poor labourer. It was a life of self-renunciation for the sake of learning. The Oxford scholar came not from poverty and want to fulness and ease, but to prolonged poverty. For it is a historical misconception on the part of those persons who contend for " the claims of poverty " to imagine that they would be fulfilling the founder's intentions by electing " poor men " to fellowships. The expression " indigentes scholares " of college statutes implicated not only the antecedents of the fellow, but his life after his fellowship was obtained. He is, in view of the founder, to be as poor after election as before it. The indigence contemplated by the statutes is not indigence with £300 a-year pocket-money. If the advocates of the " claims of poverty " really wish to restore the state of things in this respect as designed by founders, they must keep down both sides of the account. They must not merely ascertain that the *candidate* for a fellowship is " indigent," but they must keep him " indigent " after he has become fellow, and give him only his chamber, his clothes, and two scanty meals per day.

This was the system of safeguards against inactivity which was provided in the Middle-age endowment of science and learning. These securities are not only obsolete, but impossible now. It is not a question of what we may wish, but of what can be. A fellowship *cannot* be a cœnobitic life under a vow of perpetual continence. The university has ceased to enforce any public test of proficiency after the B.A. degree. The miserable forms which were long kept up, of " dispensing " with exercises, are now abandoned in the case of all the faculties, except the theological faculty, which reform has not yet reached. No one could seriously propose to revive public exercises for the higher degrees. Proposals and attempts have indeed been made for imposing an examination-test for the higher degrees in the various faculties. But all such attempts have inevitably failed. An examination is not possible where the proficiency is great, for who is to examine ? " The relation of examiner and examinee is always offensive and unnatural where it is not characterised by great differences of age or of attainments " (Peacock, *Statutes of Cambridge*, p. 148). The commission of 1850 therefore rejected all examination-tests for the superior degrees, but recommended that they should remain as titles to designate academical standing (*O. U. C. Report*, p. 85). This was in effect to give their high sanction to one of the greatest scandals of the English universities, the sale—no other word describes the trans-action—the sale of our degrees.

Neither a revival, then, of the old system of disputation, nor an extension of the modern system of examination, are possible as means of exacting continued application from men of mature age. A " certificate " of study was pro-posed in 1854, as a qualification for a vote in Congrega-tion. But it was laughed out of court as soon as men-tioned. It was asserted that the habitual " study " of the *Times* newspaper in the common-room would be a ground for applying for, and receiving, the necessary certificate. The exaction of a written dissertation on a given thesis, as is done for the degree of M.D., seems likely to be effica-cious only where the writer's reputation in a practical pro-fession is at stake. As a condition, or test, of the tenure of an endowment, it is defective as not being continuous pressure.

To pension men of science, again, when advanced in life, would be safe, because their work would be already done. But it is not what is wanted. What is wanted is to enable men to devote their youth, and the meridian of their powers, uninterruptedly to knowledge, to take them up as early as possible, and to open a career to theoretical science, which shall be as well defined as those now open to the practical professions, and, at the same time, make an equal demand for energy and exertion.

There remains but one possible pattern on which a university, as an establishment for science, can be con-structed, and that is the graduated professoriate. This is sometimes called the German type, because Germany is the country in which the system has most recently borne

M

the most signal fruits. The education given in German schools and universities is not superior, even if it be equal, to what is attainable in England or France. As teaching institutions, their universities have great merits and equally great defects. But as establishments for the cultivation and encouragement of the highest learning, the German universities have left everything of the kind at this moment existing in Europe behind them. Though known to us as the German system, there is, however, nothing peculiarly Germanic in the arrangements of their universities, so far as their commanding reputation is due to those arrangements. The only peculiarity which they derive from country is one which may possibly be lost to them before long. The rivalry between a number of petty states, ambitious to compensate for their political insignificance by distinction in science, has been at least one cause of the eminence which the German university system has now attained. However this may be, it is not as schools, but as centres of mental activity in science, that these institutions command the attention of Europe, and have become the referees to whose verdict every product of mind must be unconditionally submitted. The German university, Dr. Döllinger goes so far as to say, has nothing but the name in common with the university of France, or the universities of England. It is an association of men of learning and science, under the title of professors. The position created for them is such as to place them under the most powerful inducements to devote their whole mind and energies to the cultivation of some special branch of knowledge. In a large university, such as Berlin, every science, and almost every subdivision of science, is represented. Of teachers of various grades, Berlin numbers now about 170. These are not endowed out of Church property, or out of rent of land in any shape, but are paid out of the annual taxation. This is not certainly an advantage either to themselves or to the country, but is mentioned to show what sacrifices other countries, not so rich as ourselves, are willing to make for an object which we have not yet come in sight of as a desideratum. The reputation of Berlin rests not upon any education given to its 2000 students, but upon the scientific industry of its professors. "The life of a professor" (Professor Ritschl is reported to have said) "would be a very pleasant one if it was not for the lecturing."

Such an institute has nothing new about it except the name "professor." The principle of the graduated professoriate was already matured in the fourteenth century. Two centuries of experience of high schools had led to the collegiate system. The unendowed regent master, who was paid by fees, and taught only as long as he could attract pupils, gave way to the endowed clerk, who was to combine the functions of student and teacher in his faculty.

In proposing the German University as the model to which we must look in making any alterations in our own, I wish to confine myself entirely to this single point of view — viz. of a central association of men of science. No comparison is intended between English and German education, between the effect of the respective systems upon the students who pass through them. So far from trying a university system by this test, the aim of the present writer is to insist that we shall never place our university on a sure footing as long as we regard the undergraduate alone as the end and purpose of the institution. A professor in an English, and still more in a Scotch university, is apt to make it his ground of complaint that he has to teach the rudiments, and to think that if he had but more advanced pupils all would be well. What I wish to contend is, that the professor of a modern university ought to regard' himself as primarily a learner, and a 'teacher only secondarily. His first obligation is to the faculty he represents; he must consider that he is there on his own account, and not for the sake of his pupils. The pupils, indeed, are useful to him, as urging him to activity of mind, to clearness of expression, to definiteness of conception, to be perpetually turning over and verifying the thoughts and truths which occupy him. " The words of Pyrrhus to his Epirotes, ' Ye are my wings,' express the feeling of a zealous teacher toward hearers whom he loves, and whose whole souls take part in his discourse " (Niebühr, *Rom. Hist.* i. p. 11).

But we must go further than this: Even merely to be efficient as teacher, the university teacher must hold up to himself a higher standard of attainment than the possession of so much as has to be communicated to the pupil. There is a vast difference here between the elementary stages of education and that highest development which a university education aims to accomplish. A teacher of the elements of anything — language, mathematics, science, drawing — may be an excellent teacher without possessing more knowledge than what he is actually required to communicate; but it is no longer so in those higher regions of instruction which lie beyond the acquisition of knowledge, or the practice of an art. Here it is not the substance of what is communicated, but the act of communication between the older and the younger mind, which is the important matter. It is an influence which passes, and not a fact or a truth. The *mind* of the learner can be acted on only on the condition that the mind of the teacher is itself active. This is the explanation of a fact which, to some persons, seems paradoxical : that investigations, the positive results of which have turned out to be false, have been most efficacious agents of exciting and directing the zeal and research of younger students. The theories of Wolf on poetry, of Niebühr on Roman history, of Baur on the composition of the New Testament, are cited as telling against a professoriate, as evidence of a temptation to which professors are supposed to be liable to broach untenable hypotheses. But a fertility of ingenious hypothesis is a well-known condition of any period of scientific activity. The influence exerted by Wolf on philological studies, by Niebühr on historical, and by Baur on theological, was quite independent of the truth or falsehood of any hypothesis started by them. The effect of the lectures of these great men is traceable to one cause —viz. that what they said proceeded from fresh investigation, from a mind filled with the subject, with a belief in it, and a zeal for it. No teacher who is a teacher only, and not also himself a daily student, who does not speak from the love and faith of a habitual intuition, can be competent to treat any of the higher parts of any moral or speculative science. It is not originality, but complete mastery of all the proper conceptions, which is here required. Nay, it is not so necessary for a teacher that his knowledge should be complete as that it should be real. A growing mind is often a more serviceable instructor to a learner than a formed mind; hence the well-known fact that the young often learn more from a young tutor, just a little their senior, than from an accomplished man of science. " Pectus est quod disertos facit," Quintilian's (x. 7) oratorical maxim, transferred by Schleiermacher to theology, must be extended at least to all historical and moral science.

For teaching, there is required a persuasion, as well as for advocacy, though of a different kind. The highest education cannot be given through a literature or a science which has no other than an educational value. Classical learning, or Greek and Latin, is often spoken of by its advocates in this country as if it had no intrinsic value, as if it was an instrument of training and nothing more. If this were the case, Greek and Latin, however proper a matter for school discipline, would not be an adequate subject of the superior education. The university is hereby distinguished from the school, that the pupil here takes leave of disciplinal studies, and enters upon real knowledge. The further consideration of this distinction belongs to the section on " Studies; " it only concerns us here as it points to a difference between the school teacher and the university teacher. The student comes to the university to enter upon the studies of men, to grapple with those thoughts which are occupying the men of the time. He is the apprentice of a faculty which is to introduce him into the real business of life. The teacher here cannot be content with knowing a little more than his pupil, with reading ahead of him; he must be a master in the faculty. Our weakness of late years has been that we have not felt this;—we have known no higher level of knowledge than so much as sufficed for teaching. Hence, education among us has sunk into a trade, and, like trading sophists, we have not cared to keep on hand a larger stock than we could dispose of in the season. Our Faculties have dried up, have become dissociated from professional practice at one end, and from scientific investigation on the other, and degrees in them have lost all value but a social one. The intrinsic value of knowledge being thus lost sight of, and its pursuit being no longer a recognised profession, it is easy to see how the true relations of teacher and learner have become distorted or inverted. The masters of arts, the heads and fellows of the colleges, who constituted the university, and who were maintained here " to godliness and good learning," have become subordinate to the uses of the students, for whom alone all our arrangements are now made. It is because our own life here is wanting in scientific dignity, in intellectual purpose, in the ennobling influences of the pursuit of knowledge, that it is owing that our action upon the young is so feeble. The trading teacher, whatever disguise he may assume—whether he call himself professor or tutor—is the mere servant of his young master. But true education is the moulding of the mind and character of the rising generation by the generation that now is. We cannot communicate that which we have not got. To make others anything, we must first be it ourselves.

Casting our eyes for a moment over a wider sphere than that of the university and of the highest education, we find a source of weakness of modern society at large, in this very circumstance. The prominence of the young in our family life, their growing importance, the tyranny of the children over the household, the devotion of fathers and mothers to the one absorbing object of bringing up their sons and daughters—how is this characteristic of our modern life to be explained? We find it often attributed to the democratic spirit of our century. It is said that where, as in America, the children can at an early age support themselves, they become of course independent. Doubtless this is true, but it is a very partial account of the fact now stated. The subordination of the younger part of society to the older part is not a matter of dependence, or discipline, or police, but of force of character and mental superiority. In an age or country where the life of the citizen is intense and noble, animated by lofty aims, by adequate scientific conceptions of the present state of being, or by the anticipations which religious faith forms of the future, there will result, as of course, an education by the mere action of society itself. Life becomes an education. In the Puritan communities of the sixteenth century it was not so much any peculiar discipline which created the stern despotism of parental authority, as it was that life itself was, to the man, full of serious employment and lofty duties. In our age, on the other hand, it is our feebleness of moral purpose, the absence of great conceptions and aims from our own personal life, which makes us so ready to fall into a false relation towards our children.

It is requisite, then, that the university teacher should be first himself a man of science; that science should be his own pursuit, and the object of his own life, with its own ends and rewards, and that it should not be merely taken up that he may teach it again to others. In the words of Bacon, " Readers should be of the most able and efficient men, as those which are ordained for generating and transmitting sciences, and not for transitory use. This cannot be except their condition and endowment be such as may content the ablest man to appropriate his whole labour, and sometimes his whole age, in that function and attendance ; and therefore must have a proportion answerable to that mediocrity or competency of advancement which may be expected from a profession, or the practice of a profession" (*Advancement of Learning*, p. 111). This is what we, in Oxford, are wanting in at present. Our teachers are, perhaps, better than they have ever been, but we are still only professors of teaching. It is partly due to this sophistic teaching that the name of " professor" has acquired its ill odour among us. It will never lose its disfavour until it has become associated among us with the dignity of a life devoted to science. I should have been glad to have avoided, for the purpose of these Suggestions, the use of the title altogether, had it been possible. But those who have followed the course of these remarks will understand that I have not been advocating the substitution of professors for tutors, as of one kind of teacher for another, but the abolition of trading teaching of any kind. The controversy about the " professorial system " is quite another matter. It cannot be repeated too often that the drift of these Suggestions is the conversion, or restoration, of college endowments to the maintenance of a professional class of learned and scientific men. It so happens that the best extant type of such an institution is the German professor—two words which are, even taken separately, not calculated to recommend anything to general acceptance in this country, and the combination of which is doubly unfortunate. But there is, as has been already said, nothing peculiarly German in the thing itself. Such an order of men has existed at various periods of history, and in different countries—in Athens, in Alexandria, in various cities of the Empire, in modern Italy, in France, in Holland. If it is to the German universities that we must at this moment look, it is only because they have lately acquired that which we have long ago lost.

" I am aware," Mr. Grant Duff says, " there is much in the German universities which is not worth imitating, and much that is susceptible of improvement. All sensible Germans will admit that. But the fact remains that, after making every deduction demanded by the strictest criticism, they are at this moment, in all that constitutes real efficiency, far ahead of all similar establishments. There are many who say that the excellence of the German universities depends on a peculiar aptitude for learning in the German people. . . . But the reputation of the Germans as students is altogether modern. At the beginning of the last century the state of the German universities was below contempt. It does not seem ever to have occurred to Leibnitz that the German universities could be made of any use whatever in raising the intellectual standard of his countrymen. The reputation of the Germans as scholars is as modern and *parvenu* as that of the Scots is ancient and venerable. It was only during the last, and still more during the present century, that the intellectual fame of Germany began to rise steadily and swiftly. . . . In this world of change the intellectual rank of nations, like their material prosperity, never continues in one stage ; it is ' hodie mihi, cras tibi.' A people which relaxes its efforts in any one department soon falls in that particular department behind its neighbours. How we fell behind our neighbours in the matter of learning, it is not for the moment material to inquire. How the Germans got before others in learning, and in the highest kind of intellectual cultivation, can be told in a sentence. It was borne in upon them that they were deficient in learning and cultivation, and they made a fierce, sustained, and of course successful effort, to wipe away the reproach. Never let it be forgotten, to the honour of Prussia and of William von Humboldt, that it was in the deepest agony of her political degradation, when she was crushed under the foot of Napoleon, that she founded that noble University of Berlin which has done so much for Germany" (*Inaugural Address at Aberdeen*, p. 33).

In order, then, to make Oxford a seat of education, it must first be made a seat of science and learning. All attempts to stimulate its *teaching* activity, without adding to its solid possession of the field of science, will only feed the unwholesome system of examination which is now undermining the educational value of the work we actually do.

It may be necessary to guard the suggestion of this principle against misconception on another side. The university is to be an association of men of science. But it is not for the sake of science that they are associated. Whether or no the State should patronise science, or promote discovery, is another question. Even if it should, a university is not the organ for this purpose. A professoriate has for its duty to maintain, cultivate, and diffuse extant knowledge. This is an everyday function which should not be confounded with the very exceptional pursuit of prosecuting researches or conducting experiments

with a view to new discoveries. The professoriate is
" to know what is known and definitely acquired for humanity on the most important human concerns " (Grant Duff,
Inaugural Address, p. 27). Dr. Newman has pointed out
the difference between the objects of " academies, and the
uses of a university in this respect." "There are other institutions," he says, " far more suited to act as instruments
of stimulating philosophical inquiry, and extending the
boundaries of our knowledge, than a university. Such, for
instance, are the literary and scientific academies, which
are so celebrated in Italy and France, and which have
frequently been connected with universities as committees,
or as it were, congregations or delegacies, subordinate to
them. Thus the present Royal Society, originated in
Charles II.'s time, in Oxford. Such just now are the
Ashmolean and Architectural Societies in the same seat
of learning, which have arisen in our time. . . Such is
the sort of institution which primarily contemplates science
itself, and not students. . . The nature of the case
and the history of philosophy combine to recommend to
us this division of intellectual labour between academies
and universities. To discover and to teach are distinct
functions. They are also distinct gifts, and are not
commonly found united in the same person. He who
spends his day in dispensing his existing knowledge to all
comers is unlikely to have either leisure or energy to
acquire new" (*Discourses on University Education*, p. x.)
And Crevier long ago affirmed the same distinction:
" J'ose dire, que de tous les établissemens littéraires, celui
des universités est le mieux entendu. Il vise tout entier
à l'utile; et le brillant ne s'y joint que comme l'accom-

pagnement inseparable du bon usage des talens de l'esprit "
(*Hist. de l'Universite de Paris,* liv. 1).

§ 2. *Outline of a Scheme.*

The distinction, just adverted to, between the dissemination of knowledge and discovery, becomes important when we engage in an attempt to discover, *what* branches of knowledge ought to be professed in a university. Were a university an institution for the promotion of science, its organisation would have to follow some approved scheme of arrangement of the sciences in rational order. But as it has not in view the interests of science, but the interests of the community in transmitting the traditions of knowledge from the generation which is passing away to the generation which is succeeding it, we must look for some other principle by which to determine what knowledge shall be professed.

Were, again, the university a merely educating body, in the limited sense of the term education, then we should only have to discover what disciplinal exercises experience had shewn to yield the best training for the young mind, and to take care that courses of lessons were established in them. But we have rejected this also as too restricted a conception of a university. It would seem to remain that no branch of human knowledge should be excluded, but that every subject, which it is for the interest of the community to have preserved and diffused, should be professed here. Dr. Chalmers has expressed this idea: " Is it not better for the country," he says, " that at the great fountainheads of its literature there should be rendered a supply of human knowledge in all its branches ; and that there should in the wide range of its professorships be as many affinities provided as might suit the peculiar aptitude and disposition of every genius ?   In this way each master-spirit is furnished with its own proper science, and each science in the encyclopædia of human learning acts by its own magnetic charm on every spirit that is kindred to itself" (*On Endowments*, p. 96).

The corrective to the seeming infinity of this cadre is supplied by the old classification of faculties, which is still known in Oxford sufficiently well to be capable of resuscitation.   All that is required is to adopt the old arrangement of the four Parisian faculties to the modern condition of knowledge to make it sufficiently useful for our purpose :—

> Theology.
> Law.
> Medicine.
> Classics.
> Philology and Language.
> Historical and Moral Sciences.
> Mathematical and Physical Sciences.

This will be a division sufficient for our purposes, and will have the great advantage of being scarcely at all a departure from existing arrangements.

It is neither possible nor desirable to determine *à priori* how many, and what, subjects shall be professed under each head.   Nor need any permanent assignment of chairs be made.   Each faculty will be organised as a deliberative body on its own arrangements, and will recommend to the

Hebdomadal Council, from time to time, such modifications in the material and number of its professorships as occasion shall require. An eminent investigator often creates a new subject, and a generation or two exhausts its interest. And it might be desirable just at first, till the standard of theological and philological learning among us shall be brought up more nearly to that which prevails in the inductive sciences, to invite one or more distinguished men from the continent to settle among us, and to create for them exceptional positions.

The collective professors of each faculty, whether associated in one or more colleges, would form a general board or collegium, competent to make, subject to the organic statute (see p. 28), from time to time, regulations for the conduct of the studies, lectures, and examinations in their faculty. The senior professor, as dean of the faculty, would be chairman of the board. If the number of the professors in any of the faculties should be inconveniently large for meeting together, a standing committee should be formed, on which each professor should sit by rotation.

From Germany we may learn the possibility of maintaining a body of men brought up to the life-profession of science. If a foreign country can lend to us an idea which we once possessed, but have lost, we, on the other hand, have retained a form for such an establishment, which is greatly superior to any they possess. Independent colleges, incorporated by charters, and possessing property of their own, could not be tolerated in an absolute or bureaucratic government. Such corporations exist in this country. They are located in the precincts of the university. They have at present no occupation. On looking into the statutes of these bodies, it is found that they were actually founded for the promotion of science and learning. What is simpler and more natural than that they should be restored to their original purpose? The colleges can be with the least change possible adapted to the faculties, and their subdivisions.

1. The theological faculty in Oxford at present is represented by five professors :—

> Regius.
> Lady Margaret's.
> Pastoral.
> Ecclesiastical History.
> Exegetical.
> Hebrew.

The Hebrew chair is classed in this faculty, because the function of a professor of Hebrew seems inseparable from that of biblical interpretation.

Could the theological faculty here be regarded from an academical point of view, there are many suggestions which it would be obvious to make. The question, if some of these chairs should not be open to laymen, is a very weighty one. The creation of junior lectureships in the faculty, and the better demarcation of the matters assigned to each chair, might be touched upon. But, as the university is at present also a seminary for the professional education of the clergy, the theological faculty in Oxford holds a double position. The average level of theological instruction which can be attained for a numerous profession like that of the clergy of the Established Church, is necessarily much lower than that which would be reached by the professors of the faculty, could they regard themselves as lecturing to a select class of pupils. As it is of the highest consequence to the welfare of society that the clergy should continue to receive their education in common with the rest of the community, and not in clerical seminaries apart, the university is powerless to remodel its theological faculty upon merely scientific considerations. It can only act at all here in concert with the heads of the church. The authorities of the church, being themselves also academical men, cannot but share in the desire entertained in the university to raise the tone of theological instruction, and with it that of theological literature in England. The difficulty of touching this matter at all can hardly be over-estimated. The present memoir being confined to university objects, I am glad to be dispensed from entering into further detail by finding myself on ground which is not purely academical

I will only add here a list of the courses which are given in this faculty, in one semester, in the University of Berlin, where the number of students is somewhat over 2000 :—

1. Encyclopædia of Theology.
2. History of Dogma.
3. Introduction to Old Testament (Prof. Uhlemann).
4. The Psalms.
5. Syriac Version of New Testament, select portions.
6. Introduction to Old Testament (Prof. Vatke).
7. Prophecies of Isaiah.
8. Select Doctrines.
9. Introduction to Old Testament (Prof. Hengstenberg).
10. Explanation of Isaiah.
11. History of the Passion.
12. Exegesis of Genesis.
13. Do.   2 Samuel.
14. Do.   Genesis.
15. Grammatical Explanation of 1 & 2 Kings.
16. Gospel of St. Luke.
17. Christology of the Old and New Testament.
18. Gospel of St. John.
19. Homiletics.
20. Epistle to the Romans.
21. Patristic.
22. St. Augustine *Manuale*.
23. 1 & 2 Corinthians.
24. Apocalypse.

N

25. Galatians, Ephesians, etc.
26. Evangelical Faith.
27. Inspiration of Gospels.
28. Biblical Geography.
29. History of Missions.
30. Criticism of the Gospels.
31. Ecclesiastical History, 1st part.

32. Relation of Philosophy and Theology.
33. Christian Morals.
34. Practical Theology.
35, 36, 37, 38. Various courses of " exercises," written essays, prepared discussions, construing, etc.

2. Law, history, moral and social science, etc.

The professorships at present existing in Oxford in this faculty are :—

> Regius Civil Law.
> Vinerian Common Law.
> Chichele International Law and Diplomacy.
> Corpus Professor of Jurisprudence [proposed].
> Regius Modern History.
> Chichele do.   do.
> White's Moral Philosophy.
> Waynflete Moral Philosophy and Metaphysics.
> Logic.
> Political Economy.

We are met in this faculty, in respect of the technical law-studies, by the same difficulty as in the theological faculty—viz. that the university is not competent to make its own regulations with a simple regard to academical interests. Legal education has been wholly withdrawn from the English universities. It is subject to the exigencies of a practical profession, and it would be mere quixotism to propose a law-establishment on the scale of the law school of Berlin, with its sixty-three courses of law-lectures, by twenty-three professors and lecturers. Whatever the university may be able to do in the way of direct preparation of the legal practitioner must necessarily be concerted with the authorities of the Inns of Court. It would seem that the difficulties to be surmounted here are not less great than in the theological faculty—difficulties created partly by coarse professional instincts of the English lawyer, and partly by the exigencies of practice. All the more liberal minds in the profession seem to be agreed in desiring to get some short course of scientific and theoretical instruction before entering the conveyancer's chambers. Some few even dare to hint that there is such a science as jurisprudence, and are aware that for want of this science our statute-book is the " opprobrium jurisperitorum." The Roman jurisprudence, says Dr. Maine, has its place between classical literature and English law. " It would bridge over that strange intellectual gulf which separates the habits of thought which are laboriously created at our schools and universities from the habits of thought which are necessarily produced by preparation for the bar—a chasm which, say what we will, costs the legal profession some of the finest faculties of the minds which do surmount it, and the whole strength of the perhaps not inferior intellects which never succeed in getting across (*Cambridge Essays*, 1857, p. 26). In what way law, as a scientific study, can be naturalised in Oxford, cannot be determined without the aid of the authorities of the law. Mr. Grant Duff, who has made more than one zealous effort in this cause, writes to me :—

" If Oxford were engaged in reforming herself, with a view to take that position amongst the learned bodies of the world to which she is entitled by her wealth and her prestige, there can, I suppose, be no doubt that she would establish a complete faculty of law, such as exists, for example, in the University of Berlin. Of course, however, nothing of this kind is in contemplation; and, indeed, there is so much good work to be done, which lies close to the hands of Oxford reformers, that they will, I trust, for many a day to come, forbear from expending their strength upon schemes so large and difficult.

" What is wanted is, I presume, merely a slight improvement; and, in making that improvement, the university will no doubt have regard to other institutions, which it can make useful for its own purposes.

" Much may be said in favour of a great law-school forming part of a vast educational institution, which occupies itself with the whole circle of human knowledge. The accidents of history have, however, placed *our* great law-school in London, and have divorced law from all other branches of learning.

" Oxford must for the present accept this state of things, and be satisfied with sending up to the Inns of Court young men as well prepared as possible for making use of the opportunities which they may find or make there.

" If the Inns of Court were doing their duty, if they were to England what the *Ecole de Droit* is to France, this task would be an easy one; but although committees and commissions have reported against the existing abuses, and members of both Houses have not been slow to call the attention of the legislature to them, the pecuniary interest and the professional prejudices of large numbers of men have hitherto been strong enough to prevent any effectual reform.

" True it is, that in the year 1853 a system of lectures and examinations was introduced; but it is very slight and inadequate—so slight and inadequate that many contrive to pass through it without getting any good at all.

" Till, then, the Inns of Court are put upon a proper footing, Oxford may as well consider that her alumni will have no legal teaching at all, except what she gives them, before they find themselves in the chambers of a conveyancer or some other practising lawyer in London.

" She will have done her part for them sufficiently well, if she puts them in a position to do without any further elementary teaching.

" Her elementary teaching should be, I think, confined to instruction in Roman law, in constitutional law, and legal history, and in what I may call the principles of legislation. If, in the first of these departments, a young man could pass a good examination in the Institutes of Gaius and of Justinian, together with such accessory books, or parts of books, as any competent lecturer would point out ; if, in the second, he had studied Hallam and May, with Stephen's *Commentaries ;* if, in the third, he had mastered Bentham's *Principles of Legislation, Principles of a Civil Code,* and *Principles of a Criminal Code ;* had read Austin and Maine, of course, as before, with the assistance and illustrations of a good lecturer ; he would have laid a very good foundation for his London reading.

" Supposing that an elementary law - school were once fairly established in Oxford, I do not think that even the most sweeping reforms at the Inns of Court would cut the ground from under its feet. It would, probably, if the Inns of Court were made into an *Ecole de Droit,* develop into a school for public life — a school through which all sensible fathers who destined their sons for Parliament, for diplomacy, or even for the life of an intelligent country gentleman, would insist upon their going.

*   *   *   *   *

" A greater amount of study given to Roman law at Oxford could hardly be without effect upon the historical teaching of the place. It would lead to greater attention being paid to the later history of Rome—to the last 100 years of the Republic, and to the Empire. It is intelligible enough, that when Niebuhr's researches first became known in England they should have caused an extraordinary amount of attention to be given to the first decade of Livy; but now that those researches have taken their proper place amid other contributions to human knowledge, it is surely fitting that the first decade of Livy should fall back into a very subordinate position. It seems to me that Mommsen, and Merivale, and Gibbon, should now form the staple of the Oxford teaching of Roman history; that in all colleges which laid themselves out for historical teaching, lectures should be delivered with an express view to supplementing that course of reading according to the notions which happened to be approved in the university; and that candidates for honours should be expected to show a reasonable acquaintance with the original writers to whom the lecturer would necessarily refer. If some plan of this kind were followed, the Institutes of Gaius would not open altogether a new world to men who had gone through the amount of historical reading which is usual in Oxford, or was usual a few years ago."

Apart from its professional bearings, the remains of Roman law are too important a department of classical study to be allowed any longer to remain in the oblivion to which our present system condemns them. The history of Rome, without Roman law, is a dead letter; and the text of the Corpus Juris is one of the most important monuments of the language. As such it became, on the revival of learning, as much an object of attention on the part of scholars, as it had been of jurists. Sir W. Hamilton remarks :—

" In most countries of Europe ancient literature and the Roman law have prospered and declined together; the most successful cultivators of either department have indeed been almost uniformly cultivators of both. In Italy, Roman law and ancient literature revived together, and Alciatus was not vainer of his Latin poetry than Politian of his interpretation of the Pandects. In France, the critical study of Roman jurisprudence was opened by Budæus, who died the most accomplished Grecian of his age; and in the following generation, Cujacius and Joseph Scaliger were only the leaders of an illustrious band, who combined, in almost equal proportions, law with literature and literature with law. To Holland the two studies migrated in company; and the high and permanent prosperity of the Dutch schools of jurisprudence has been at once the effect and the cause of the long celebrity of the Dutch schools of classical philology. In Germany, the great scholars and civilians who illustrated the sixteenth century disappeared together, and, with a few partial exceptions, they were not replaced till the middle of the eighteenth, when the kindred studies began and have continued to flourish in reciprocal luxuriance" (Hamilton, *Discussions*, p. 331).

Sir W. Hamilton lived to see the history of Rome reconstituted by a German professor, by aid of those documents of Roman law, the contents of which were wholly unknown in the classical university of Oxford. The history, literature, and archæology of Roman law might usefully employ two or three professor-fellows. Though the subject strictly belongs to the faculty of philology, its professors would rank in the law faculty, as they must of necessity be professional lawyers or law graduates.

The necessity for some theoretical training, preparatory to the conveyancer's chambers, has received the sanction of the profession. The commissioners appointed to inquire into the arrangements of the Inns of Court in 1854 made the following recommendation. (The commissioners were Sir W. Page Wood, Sir John Taylor Coleridge, Sir Joseph Napier, Sir Alexander Cockburn, Lord Westbury, Sir Thomas Erskine Perry, John Shaw Lefevre, Henry S.

Keating, Thomas Greenwood, James Stewart, and Germain Lavie) :—

"We deem it advisable that there shall be established a preliminary examination for admission to the Inns of Court of persons who have not taken a university degree, and that there shall be examinations, the passing of which shall be requisite for the call to the Bar; and that the four Inns of Court shall be united in one university for the purpose of these examinations, and of conferring degrees" (*Report, etc.*)

The only part of this recommendation which has been adopted is that part which is of no importance—namely, a preliminary examination for admission to the Inn of persons who have not taken a university degree. This is as futile as all entrance-examinations, merely putting the candidate upon wasting six months in cramming up a minimum of forgetable matter. The important part of the commissioners' recommendation, that there shall be examinations and degrees required for the call to the Bar, has slept. What might be done at Oxford in this direction does not depend entirely upon ourselves. But no course of studies can be thought of unless there is a largely increased body of professors in the faculty resident here. The due encouragement of the science of jurisprudence, and the critical study of the monuments of Roman and Feudal Law may justly claim no inconsiderable share in our endowments. Ten or twelve professor-fellows of recognised eminence in various departments, incorporated in a law-college, would give a very different aspect to the question of a university law-degree as a qualification for a call to the Bar. A good beginning has already been made at All Souls'. The gross corporate revenue of the college was returned for 1850 as £9622.

Deducting charges (say £2000 a-year) this could scarcely suffice for the endowment of a complete law-college. It is possible that the rental may be capable of some increase by running out leases, and something would be realised by the sale of the advowsons, which are valuable.

For history, the commission of 1850 contented themselves with the recommendation that "there should be at least two professors in the wide field of Modern History, one for the History of England only." This was surely inadequate, even for the purposes of teaching. But for an endowment which is to sustain and encourage historical studies, we must contemplate a much larger application of our fellowship fund. In what are called the "Historical, Political, and Administrative Sciences," the following courses were given in the University of Berlin in the winter semester of 1861 :—

Philosophy of History.

Encyclopædia of History.

Synoptical Review of Ancient History [Prof. v. Raumer].

Middle Age [Prof. Ranke].

History of Germany.

Modern History from 16th century.

Modern History from 18th century.

Ethnography of Europe.

History, Geography, and Political Principles of New World.

Geography and Political History of Germany.

Political Economy.

Principles of Administrative Science.

Science of Finance.

Administration of Prussia.

General Statistics in connection with the administrative system of Prussia.

> Historical View of Economical Systems.
> Administration of Prussia.
> Saṅitary Police.

These courses are exclusive of courses on ancient history, a subject which is classified in the German universities under the faculty of " Philosophy," along with modern history. This is undoubtedly its proper place in a strictly philosophical arrangement of sciences. There is no break in the continuity of historical cause and effect. But as all professors of Greek and Roman history must necessarily be philologians, I have preferred to place them in the faculty of Language.

To the ground thus covered by the University of Berlin, our connections with every part of the globe, our Indian and Colonial Empire, our relations with the East and with America, seem to require us to add largely. Nor can a nation, which at this moment conducts and reaps the profit of the commerce of the world, think that one professor of political economy is a sufficient representation of those vast and important subjects. The phenomena of capital and labour, of currency and exchange, not only involve practical questions of the highest moment, but questions which even the public see cannot be elucidated without science and theory. It is impossible, without an apprehension of the laws of these phenomena, to form any adequate conception of the world we live in. We can no more understand the body politic and its history without political economy, than we can understand the natural body without physiology.

Oriel, which under the ordinances is charged with a pension to the Regius Professor of Modern History, might be thought of for appropriation to these studies. But its available funds would hardly suffice for the endowment of a subject having so many ramifications as history. And the former reputation of Oriel—Arnold is hardly an exception—connects it rather with the moral and speculative sciences. Queen's would be more nearly equal to the requirements of this science; the new professor of modern history being transferred thither from Chichele's foundation, and Oriel being relieved of the Regius Professor.

The college of Bishop Butler would provide a home for moral and mental science, merging in its foundation the present Logic, White's, and the Waynflete chairs, and extending over a wide field, which is at present wholly unrepresented in the university—the *Staatswissenschaft* of German universities.

3. Most persons seem to be agreed in thinking with Dr. Daubeny that much might be done for medical education in Oxford without attempting to make it a place of clinical instruction. In medicine, as in law, our efforts must be confined to the preparatory courses—chemistry, anatomy, physiology. Much has been done since the report of the Royal Commission in this direction. We have now, Dr. Daubeny said at the British Association in 1866, " a staff of professors as efficient, and means and appliances for the prosecution of chemistry, anatomy, and the like, as ample as are to be found in any other rival institution " (*Report of British Association, Nottingham,* 1866). This provision for the instruction of medical students has been made partly by the appropriation of collegiate endowments, but mainly by capital sums raised

by the university out of casual profits made by its establishments for printing Bibles.

It has, however, been felt all along that the inductive sciences were entitled, on their own merits, and not merely as preparatory to a profession, to a home in the university. It is further evident that they will never become so naturalised until they participate, in a fair proportion, in the endowments provided for the encouragement of learning. The Royal Commission of 1850, accordingly, recommended that some fellowships should be set apart for merit in the " new studies," as they were called. This has been done partially at Magdalen and at Christ Church. At Magdalen every fifth fellowship is to be filled up by " an examination alternately in subjects recognised in the school of mathematics and in that of physical science." At Christ Church, studentships have been filled up by science examination. The beginning thus made should be carried further, and the vicious principle on which these, as all other, fellowships are now awarded should be corrected. That is, instead of being bestowed as a prize for past " merit," the fellowship should convey a prospective obligation to the prosecution of the studies intended to be promoted by the endowment.

We have at present a total of twelve professors for mathematics, natural science, and medicine. They are :—

> Savilian Astronomy.
>   Do.   Geometry.
> Sedleian Natural Philosophy.
> Experimental Philosophy.
> Waynflete Chemistry.
> Linacre Physiology.

Geology.
Mineralogy.
Botany.
Hope Zoology.
Regius Medicine.
Clinical.
Lee's Readers $\begin{cases} \text{Anatomy.} \\ \text{Chemistry.} \end{cases}$

Against this meagre list of poorly-endowed professors of science, the University of Berlin could set in 1861 nearly forty names of teachers engaged on these subjects. And the following courses of lectures were being delivered by them :—

1. Higher Algebra, and Calculus of Finite Differences.
2. Experimental Physics.
3. Meteorology.
4. Botany.
5. Botanical Meetings.
6. Experimental Chemistry.
7. Organic Chemistry (select parts).
8. Experimental Physics.
9. Physical Conferences (*i.e.,* Lectures *sine ulla solennitate*).
10. Theory of Numbers.
11. Systems of Rays.
12. Analytical Statics and Dynamics.
13. Theory of Elliptic Functions.
14. On the employment of Algebraical methods in Geometry.
15. Differential Calculus.
16. Algebra.
17. Continued Fractions.
18. Interpolation and Mechanical Quadratures.
19. Mathematical Physics.
20. Integration of Differential Equations.
21. Integral Calculus.
22. Analytical Geometry.
23. Mathematical Physics.
24. Solution of Physical Problems (Optics, Electricity).
25. Mechanics of the Heavens.
26. Electricity.
27. Physical Geography.
28. History of Physics since Galileo.
29. Mineralogy.
30. Crystallography.
31. Chemical part of Metallurgy.
32. Organic Chemistry.
33. Introduction to Theoretical Chemistry.

34. Of the Organic Bases.
35. Organic Chemistry.
36. Physiology of Plants.
37. Special Botany.
38. Zoology, with Demonstrations.
39. Zoology and Zootomy (Practical instruction in).
40. Entomology, General and Specific.
41. Special Botany.
42. Pharmacognosis.
43. Inorganic Pharmacy.
44. Agricultural Botany, and Diseases of Plants.
45. Entomology of the Farm.
46. Œconomics of Agriculture.
47. Breeding and Management of Cattle.
48. Farm-management.
49. Popular Organic Chemistry.
50. Analytical Chemistry.
51. Organic Chemistry.
52. History of Chemistry.
53. Chemical Investigations.
54. Chemical Conferences.
55. Juridical Chemistry.
56. General Geology.
57. Natural Philosophy of the Ancients (Aristotle).

N.B.—The above list is exclusive of practical courses, laboratory instruction, etc. It is also exclusive of the lectures of the Medical Faculty. Where the same subject occurs twice, the course is given by a different professor in each case, and is probably adapted to students at a different stage of their career. But concurrent courses by two, or even more, professors, are not prohibited.

Law already forms a separate faculty, and I have proposed that this faculty shall be localised in an endowed corporation in the existing foundation of All Souls' College. It is surely time that the inductive sciences should have a substantial recognition. Instead of a few fellowships and scholarships scattered up and down the colleges as they are, science has a right to a substantive part of our endowments. A new faculty of science is required, qualified to confer degrees. The professor-fellows of this faculty should be incorporated in a college, or the principal subdivisions of science in separate colleges. Corpus and Merton, as has been already suggested, might furnish the home for the biological sciences. If to Corpus and Merton were added the splendid endowments of Magdalen, the mathematical and experimental sciences would not be occupying a larger space in our establishment than their importance entitles them to. We must remember that it is in respect of these branches of knowledge that we have the heaviest arrears of neglect to make good. " Naturalis Philosophia," as late as the statutes of 1636, formed a substantive part of the requirements for the M.A. degree. Since that time, while the sciences have attained an enormous development both in number and magnitude, we have all but ignored their existence. So infinite are the subdivisions of science, that it will not be easy to find room for them all, especially if, as it seems fit in a place of education, we are to include practical applications of science, such as mining and civil engineering, which may fairly claim to be represented here.

5. In Oxford, as in all the universities of the Parisian form, degrees in arts were not final or consummate degrees, but steps on the road which must be travelled in order to arrive at the " apex doctoralis," or doctor's degree, in one of the superior faculties. The first seven years of the whole period of study were employed on studies, which, varying in their nature in various periods of the university history, went under the common name of " Arts." The term denoted the contrast, fundamental in Greek habits of thought, between art and science. From Greek civilisation the distinction was transmitted to the Middle-age university, which grounded upon it its arrangement of the curriculum of study, and the steps (*gradus*) of intellectual ascent. The degree of Magister Artium must be attained

before the study of one of the sciences could be commenced. The two terms art and science have, in modern
English, lost that signification of contrast, and assumed
another relation to each other. But the distinction
formerly implied by the terms remains, and will always
remain, as fundamental, in the theory of education,
between the liberal and professional, between the general
and the special.

At the present time, preparatory or liberal studies
occupy the whole period of the younger student's residence
in the university, shortened, however, to three years; and
the graduates in arts—*i.e.* in the preparatory studies—are
in possession of all but a fraction of the endowments. In
the present scheme it has been proposed to deprive arts,
or liberal studies, of a large part of these endowments, in
order to provide for the protracted studies which are
requisite for the sciences. The sciences, arranged into
faculties—theological, legal, medical, mathematical, and
physical—are to be incorporated into colleges for the purpose of maintaining men into mature age, to study, profess,
and represent these sciences. When this provision has
been made by the appropriation of the whole revenues of
certain colleges, it remains that a similar position be
created, and provision made, for all those branches of
knowledge recognised among us, and generally considered
as belonging to the faculty of arts. A name is of little consequence, and it may be convenient to retain the term
" Arts" as the general designation of a number of very
distinct branches of pursuit. But the faculty of arts, if it
is to continue to be so called, must in every respect be
placed on a par with the other faculties. It must be

advanced from being introductory and disciplinal, to be final and scientific. Its degree must rank by the side of the degrees of the other faculties, and no longer be the road to them. Other universities, to avoid ambiguity, have disused the term " Arts," and instead of " Master of Arts," give the degree of " Doctor of Philosophy."

There must be at least three colleges, or incorporated, endowed, bodies of professors, in this faculty, call it what we will :—

1. A College of Classical Studies.
2. A College of Comparative Philology and the Science of Language.
3. A College of the Theory and History of Art.

The moral and political sciences, usually classified under this faculty, I have placed in that of Law. The classical college would require subdivision again into probably more than two sections. But the greatest flexibility would be desirable in the statutes of these colleges to enable them to adapt· themselves to the fluctuations of discovery and the progress of knowledge.

In the proposal to introduce the study of Art to a substantive share in the endowments for learning, many will see as great an innovation as in the introduction of the sciences, without as good grounds for the novelty. The sciences can plead ancient precedent, for though exiled for 300 years, there was a time when they formed an integral part of our occupations. But the study of Art would have to go as far back as the Greek μουσική to find a justification in example. The claims, however, of Art to a place in university education cannot be set aside as fanciful, now

that they have received public recognition from Mr. Mill.
In order to shelter myself under his authority, I must
introduce his words here, though all of us who occupy
ourselves with the question of university reform have been
reading them so lately.   He says :—

" The education of the feelings and the cultivation of the
beautiful are things which deserve to be regarded in a far more
serious light than is the custom of these countries (*i. e.* England
and Scotland).   It is only of late, and chiefly by a superficial
imitation of foreigners, that we have begun to use the word art
by itself, and to speak of art as we speak of science, or government, or religion.   We used to talk of the arts, and more
specifically of the fine arts.   By them were vulgarly meant
only two forms of art—painting and sculpture—the two which
as a people we cared least about, which were regarded even
by the more cultivated among us as little more than branches
of domestic ornamentation, a kind of elegant upholstery.   The
very words " Fine Arts " called up a notion of frivolity, of
great pains expended on a rather trifling object, of something
which differed from the cheaper and commoner arts of producing pretty things, mainly by being more difficult, and by
giving fops an opportunity of pluming themselves on caring
for it and being able to talk about it.   .   .   .   On these
subjects the mode of thinking and feeling of other countries
was not only not intelligible, but not credible, to an average
Englishman.   To find art ranking on an equality—in theory
at least—with philosophy, learning, and science, as holding an
equally important place among the agents of civilisation, and
among the elements of the worth of humanity ; to find even
painting and sculpture treated as great social powers, and the
art of a country as a feature in its character and condition,
little inferior in importance to either its religion or its government—all this only did not amaze and puzzle Englishmen
because it was too strange for them to be able to realise it, or

to believe it possible ; and the radical difference of feeling on this matter between the British people and those of France, Germany, and the continent generally, is one among the causes of that extraordinary inability to understand one another which exists between England and the rest of Europe, while it does not exist to anything like the same degree between one nation of continental Europe and another" (*Inaugural Address at St. Andrews*, p. 42).

Perhaps we shall have less difficulty in obtaining a recognition of art as an indispensable branch of a university foundation, than in coming to an understanding what is the proper function of a university in respect of art-teaching. Yet the line of demarcation is as clear here as in other of the professions. The practice of the art, or the teaching of drawing, belongs to the school, not to the university. This technical instruction is properly carried on in a special academy, supplemented by the *ateliers* of individual artists. This instruction, so far as it is obtainable in this country at all, has localised itself in the metropolis, where alone are any considerable collections. More elementary teaching in any branch of art may now be had in any of the numerous art-schools scattered over the country in affiliation to the establishment at South Kensington. Such a school now exists in Oxford and is doing excellent work. But it can no more form a portion of the university than a grammar-school can. The university has its own work to do in art, as in the other departments of mental training. It should no more undertake to teach drawing than it should teach French, or German, or arithmetic, or the practice of conveyancing. We should only be doing over again what the art-school is now doing, and not doing it so well. And we should soon have the usual summons to give scholarships and prizes to enable us to compete for pupils and keep our school full.

But, without descending to the work of an art-school, the university may do much in its own sphere, which would operate upon the profession of the artist, to elevate and liberalise it. The province of the university lies not in the technic, but in the science and archæology, of art. These are branches of knowledge which the English artist hitherto has either done without, or has had to pick up as best he may in other countries. The benefit conferred upon the profession of art by opening a sub-faculty in these subjects would react upon the university itself in its influence upon our classical and philological studies. In a university whose reputation is wholly classical, it may be doubted if there is at this moment a single scholar, who, if a monument of Greek art were placed before him, could give an opinion on its age.

An endowed art-college might provide for (say) four professors: Two, historical, dealing with—1. Classical archæology, Asiatic, Egyptian, etc., art; 2. The period from the revival of art to modern times. Two, of the science and æsthetic, dealing with—1. Painting and sculpture, theory of composition, chiaroscuro, style, etc.; 2. Architecture; mechanics, proportion, balance, etc.

The present chair of poetry, to which one of English literature might be added, might be incorporated in this foundation.

§ 3.—*Income of Professor-Fellow.*

The subject of amount of stipend is a very important

one, but it can only be properly considered by the authority, whatever it may be, which shall be commissioned to arrange details.

The principles to be held in view in such arrangement may be here stated.

1. Whatever be the scale of income intended to be created, it should not be expressed by fixed money-payments. The Commission of 1850 gave an opinion, that " the fixed salary of the greater professorships should, if possible, be not less than £800 per annum, and ought, where possible, to be more " (*Report*, p. 109). In the fifteen years which have elapsed since their report was issued, the fall in the ratio of the value of the precious metals to the value of commodities, which is always insensibly proceeding, has made itself sensibly felt. In the ordinances framed by the Parliamentary Commission of 1854, a similar error was committed in limiting the annual dividend of fellowships to a fixed sum— usually of £300. Mr. Fawcett has intimated that a further and rapid depreciation of gold is " a contingency which it would be prudent to make some preparations to meet. The practical importance of taking such precaution has not, as yet, been recognised in this country. For instance, fathers who wish to leave a provision for unmarried daughters, frequently settle upon them a fixed money-income, arising from an investment in the funds, and generally the investment is settled upon them in such a way that the investment cannot be changed (*Manual of Political Economy*, p. 506). As the professor-fellow is endowed out of landed estate, there will be no difficulty in securing him against any such risks.

2. On what principle must the amount of salary, which it is desirable a professor should receive, be determined? This is one of the most difficult parts of the problem of " endowments." One opinion on the subject, which meets with some favour among professional men, is, that the income of professors should be left, like the income of a practitioner in law or medicine, to be determined by the action of the ordinary laws of supply and competition in the market; in other words, that a professor should have what he can earn by fees and no more. Whether or no the law of supply and demand is directly applicable to superior education or not, I do not undertake to say. But even were it granted that it is so, it is only applicable to the teacher by profession, and cannot be directly applied to the class of men which it is the object of these Suggestions to call into being in the university. The professor-fellow is to teach, but his business is to learn, not to teach. If it be objected that you cannot override economical laws with impunity, without originating mischief, the answer is, that such endowment of learning is not really an exception to the law of supply and demand. It is only an indirect application of the law. It is only because, in a civilised community, there arises a demand for theoretical science, that the community becomes willing to pay for, and creates the conditions of its supply— viz. independence and leisure. Were endowments perpetuities, absolute freeholds and not beneficial trusts, there might be weight in the objection. But as long as they remain under the watchful control of the community which creates them, they are only the form in which it finds it necessary to pay for an article which it desires to

consume. The proposal that professors should be paid exclusively by fees is, in fact, a proposal for the abolition of endowments. It is therefore beyond the scope of these Suggestions, for the purposes of which we have assumed endowments, not in principle, but as existing in fact.

Dismissing as unpractical the doctrine that professors should be paid by fees only, it is however necessary to ask if the principle of partial dependence on exertion should not be applied to them, by allowing endowed professors to take fees ? This may be done in two ways :—(1.) The professor may be sufficiently endowed—sufficiently according to some standard to be settled—but may be permitted to add to his income, if he pleases, by forming paying classes. (2.) Or he may be insufficiently endowed, according to the same standard of what is sufficient, and left to make up the balance by his own exertions. The second arrangement seems to be indefensible. It is unfair to precisely the highest class of erudition, to science just in proportion as it becomes special. Even in the more popular subjects, and the more frequented class-rooms, the tendency of this system must be to lower the standard of lecturing. This has been shown by experience to be its effect in the Scotch universities. The professors of Greek, Latin, and Mathematics, in the University of Edinburgh, long resisted all attempts to raise the standard of instruction in their classes, on the ground of the loss of income it would occasion them (*Scotch Univ. Commission, Report,* p. 3). The former of the two modes of encouraging activity—viz. that of giving all professors an adequate endowment, but allowing them to make better incomes by devoting themselves to class-work, is the only scheme which can be enter-

tained. This is, I believe, the German system. Two circumstances recommend this plan—(1.) Without any un-
fairness to the professors of less popular subjects, it allows
any professor who can do so to improve his income ; (2.)
The student takes a keener interest, and attends with
more assiduity, a course for which he has paid money
than one which is gratuitous. It is true that any system
of fees carries with it one inseparable evil :—It leads to a
rivalry among professors of cognate subjects, a rivalry
determined in a wrong direction—that, viz., of adapting
their instruction to the demands of some examination. A
system of fees is a pecuniary interest acting directly
counter to a principle which it is one main purpose of these
Suggestions to enforce—viz. that the teaching-courses
govern the examinations, and not the examinations determine the teaching. If the taking of fees should be found,
upon trial, to have an important influence in lowering the
scientific level of the professor's lectures, it would become
necessary for the university, as the least of two evils, to
sacrifice the advantages derivable from the system.

3. Since the Commission of Inquiry in 1850, something
has been done by the university and the colleges towards
the endowment of various chairs; but in only one instance—
that of the Linacre professor of physiology—has the standard
of the commission, £800, been reached. Somewhere about
£600 a-year appears to have been tacitly agreed upon by
the university as the normal stipend of a professor. By
what calculation this particular sum was arrived at, I am
unable to say. It may have been by counting the professor
as two fellows, the fellowship being estimated at £300; or
it may have been only as a safe margin deducted from

the £800 of the commissioners. But then we do not know any more how the commissioners of 1850 came to fix on those figures.

4. The practice of foreign governments can afford us no help on this point. The whole scale of salaries for official persons in Germany is different from that which is found necessary in this country; and whatever the professors in a German university receive as salary comes out of the annual budget, and is not provided out of the rental of the land.

5. It has been said that the competition of the market is the only mode by which salaries can be determined. For what annual sum can you get good professors? So much, and no more should be given.

The reply is, that the fund out of which wages (or salaries) come, and the fund out of which our professors are to be paid, are totally different. The wage-fund is a portion of the profits of trade. The economical law which divides that portion among the labourers cannot reach that endowment-fund which we have to divide among our professors.

Nor is it enough to say that you must give in each case that which the individual whom you desire to place in the chair will accept as an equivalent for the performance of the duties; for a reference to our history will show that some of the most eminent names connected with Oxford have been glad to accept professorships of £100 a-year, while the most highly-endowed chairs are often filled by the least distinguished persons. This well-known fact is capable of an easy explanation — an explanation not creditable to the patrons of our chairs. But the explanation is irrelevant to the present purpose; the fact is only mentioned here to show that what the recipient will take can be no measure of the liberality of the university.

6. A measure of the requirements of a professor is thought to be furnished by the ordinary expenses of house-keeping in the locality. This seems at first sight to afford a practical standard; but on examination will be found quite inapplicable. Probably at this moment examples may be found of families of university officials living at all rates of expenditure, from £500 up to £3000 a-year. There is no ordinary level of necessary expenditure such as can fix the scale of income.

7. With respect to the men who would, under an improved system, be sought out to fill the fellowships, it must be remembered that for their commodity there exists no market, no competition, no demand. This very endowment fund, if applied as now proposed, would be itself the only fund seeking to employ scientific labour. There is therefore no general economical law directly determining the value of that labour. The representative name, the man who has become the leader of his science for the time, is an entirely unique man, and not one of a class. He has no appraisable value. Such men, whenever they can be found, the reformed university would endeavour to incorporate on any terms. The deputation sent by the States of Holland, at the instance of the curators of Leyden, to Scaliger, then living in France, stands in academical history as an ever-memorable precedent, applicable as long as universities shall be — a type of the spirit which will animate such a body whenever it is worthy of its high vocation. In this country, the universities will be the only

bidders for such eminent qualities. The division of Germany into small states, each having its own university, which has hitherto caused a kind of competition for the possession of celebrated men, will probably cease to operate in that country, and has no parallel in the circumstances of this. It is, however, highly probable that an improved standard of scientific attainment would bring about a more cosmopolitan feeling in our universities, and lead to an honourable rivalry among them. Already, and it is highly to their credit, more than one Scotch university has taken its professors from the south. Oxford has honourably followed in the same path, filling her chair of natural philosophy (1866) with a stranger, though not wanting abundance of her own of no common merit. The time may come when at Cambridge, in like manner, the claims of science may be recognised as superior to the college-tie. Even Trinity College, Dublin, may hereafter be drawn out of its national isolation, and be unwilling to see a scholar like Badham bury his learning in Australian exile, while it is filling its own Greek chair with a Dublin man whose name had never passed the precincts of his college.

8. Such leading celebrities must always be a small fraction of the whole number among whom the endowment is to be divided. The younger teachers, tutors, lecturers, professor-fellows, will constitute a class. And it is the object of the endowment to call such a class into being, and to provide for its regular supply. Some fixed scale of payment must therefore be adopted for this class. Without attempting to establish a theoretical principle, the practical rule will probably be accepted as sufficient, that, in order to make the profession of learning and science a

profession, it must be organised on the same footing as any other profession. If this new profession is to have only its proportionate share of the average talent of the·country, it must offer inducements to talent to embark in it not below the average. These inducements include income, but do not consist solely in amount of income. Position, distinction, the agreeable nature of the pursuit; above all, leisure—the indispensable condition of this profession, and the one by which it is distinguished from all others—go to make up the total of its attractions, and to make possible a rate of payment below what is necessary to fill the other professions. It is indeed a popular error to suppose that the life of the scholar or of the scientific man is an idle life. To overtake the ascertained facts, the extant knowledge, in any of the great departments of human thought, requires an assiduous tension of the faculties, prolonged through many years, which is more exhausting to the nervous powers than the exertions demanded by one of the active professions. Still, active minds not backed by the physical stamina requisite for public life, or the law, or medical practice, may compete in this new field. For these and other reasons a scale of salaries below what is necessary in the professions may be reasonably proposed for the universities. This scale must be such as will maintain the profession of learning, as a substantive profession, in efficiency. Hitherto, a university life has not been a life-profession. A fellowship and tutorship has been only held *in transitu* to a living. It is a principle of any reorganisation of the university, a principle had in view throughout these Suggestions, to erect teaching and learning, insepar-ably united, into a life-profession, for which a young man may regularly qualify himself, and look forward to it as a maintenance. The professions are so arranged, in connection with the university course, as not only " to assign a direction to scientific industry, but to provide the future means of bodily support. The university is designed quite as much to ensure the subsistence of the outer, as the glorified renewal of the inner man" (Kirkpatrick, *Of the University*, p. 80). Apart from any provision for learning, were teaching merely had in view in our arrangements, it would be quite necessary that the present anomalous position of the celibate tutor-fellow should be put an end to.

9. A new profession then, a profession which on its theoretical side has some specific branch of science for its matter, and on its practical side has teaching for its business, being erected, the candidate for its rewards and honours must see before him at least as good a prospect as if he were entering one of the old professions or any branch of the public service. Of the rate of salary thought necessary in public appointments a few quotations may be given :—

Deputy-Keeper of Rolls	£1000
Clerk of Assize—Midland, Northern, or Oxford Circuit	1000
Registrar of Court of Probate . .	1600
„ of County District Court—*e.g.* Exeter, Manchester, or York . .	1200
Police-Court Magistrate—1 at . .	1500
„ „ 22 at . .	1200
Land-Registry Office—Assistant Registrar	1500

These are all salaries charged upon the consolidated

fund, or voted annually by Parliament, and may therefore
be regarded as fixed as low as possible.   Where the salary
is payable out of fees, or suitors' fund, a more liberal scale
of estimate is taken, *e.g.*—

Commissioner of Bankruptcy — County District (Leeds)	£1800
Registrar, do.	1000

That this scale of salary is not unnecessarily extravagant is sufficiently proved by the fact that the same, or
even higher, is offered by commercial undertakings.   A
buyer, or head of a department, in a Manchester warehouse,
will often receive £1000 a-year, or even more.   The manag-
ing director of a bank has usually from £1500 to £2000,
and occasionally even more.

" It cannot be wise that county-court judges, police-magi-
strates, secretaries to railways and public boards, should receive
for the employment of their time £1000 to £1500 per annum,
while university professors are asked to perform duties
requiring great knowledge and abilities of a less common
description, without half the remuneration.   There should be
secured to a competent professor such an income as will enable
him to marry in his office, and look forward to continuance
in it as the work of his life.   The university, too, should be
in a position to command the services of the most distinguished
men in the several sciences, and to hold out to its members
the university professorships as rewards to a career of industry.   .   .   When once appointed, the professor should feel
his position (generally speaking) to be his home and his
destiny, so that he may continue to concentrate his interests
and exertions upon the subject" (H. H. Vaughan, *Evidence,
O. U. C.* p. 88).

An objection may perhaps be brought against any proposal to make science a profession, and to endow it with a scale of income not inferior to that which the other professions reach—an objection founded on a difference between the pursuit of knowledge and all other professions. It may be said that in all the other professions you pay for results, and only for results. The secretary of a railway board, say, has a definite quantity of work to do, a quantity the value of which can be estimated in salary. He has duties; and it has been found by experience that the energy he will display in their performance will bear a ratio to the remuneration. Even men of power, when shabbily paid, are apt to content themselves with a corresponding style of service. And, it is urged, here the analogy between the professions and science fails. No pecuniary inducements can create, nor can penury repress, literary genius or scientific ardour. Where services are required for which the average ability of mankind suffices, money can command those services. But in science, art, and literature, nothing has value but what springs from high incommunicable gifts or inspiration, which it is idle to speak of encouraging by rewards. Even in the professions the highest stamp of character requires higher motives. "Woe to the physician," says Hufeland, "who makes money or honour the end of his efforts! He will be in continual contradiction with himself and his duties. He will curse a vocation which does not reward, because he knows not true reward!" (Dr. Bird, *Address to the Harveian Society*, 1852).

This line of objection misplaces the profession of knowledge, for which these remarks are contending. It would be absurd to propose an endowment of genius. And we have carefully repudiated all notion of promoting discovery or providing for the progress of science. These are facts, taking place in a region of intellect over which economical laws do not extend. At least they do not directly apply. For indirectly it may be maintained, and is so by a recent writer, that "the love of wealth has not only produced all trade, all industry, and all the material luxuries of civilisation, but has proved the most powerful incentive to intellectual pursuits. Whoever will examine the history of inventions, of art, or of the learned professions, may convince himself of this" (Lecky, *History of Rationalism*, ii. 316). But all that middle region which lies between original productivity and the drudgery of teaching, that region in which are preserved and transmitted the extant types of the best culture, that region in which the professions have their roots, is governed by the same economical laws which regulate the ordinary conditions of life, and all the other known employments and occupations.

At the same time it cannot be denied that there *is* a difference in this respect between the cultivation of knowledge and other employments. Rich endowments have not been found in practice invariably provocative of mental activity. The corporate wealth of Oxford has not preserved it from a long period of torpor, a period of which we are now probably approaching the termination. That the wealth has produced the torpor is, I think, a mistaken inference from the facts; but it is a fact that they have co-existed. Mr. Gathorne Hardy, in the House of Commons on the 29th May (1867), jeered at certain "miserable philosophers who never gave anything out of their own

pockets for the furtherance of their views." Mr. Hardy is
a man of great wealth, and " the philosophers " whom he
was deriding are chiefly miserable in that they have to live
upon fewer hundreds a-year than Mr. Hardy has thousands.
For their littleness of mind in being satisfied with such an
inferior income, they no doubt justly deserve his contempt.
But, even if they were as rich and open-handed as Mr.
Hardy himself, instead of being poor and stingy, it would
be still true that they could not further their views by
putting their hands in their pockets. Opinions can be
directly propagated by endowments. But philosophic
education does not consist, as the member for the university appears to think, in the adoption of any peculiar
opinions. Its effect is rather to develop a power which
resists opinion, to call into being an individual intelligence,
a healthy organism of the soul, which enables it to outgrow
the tyranny of opinion, under which the uneducated, or
half-educated, live and act. Archbishop Whately used to
say, that the true way to counteract Catholicism was not
by trying to propagate counter-opinions, but by education.
Handsome appointments will not provide refinement of
mind, enlarged perceptions, devotion to the pursuits of
abstract thought or abstruse calculation. But if it be
desirable to create a school where these things may exist
and be practised, the humbler conditions of such a school
must not be neglected. The persons who are to labour in
it must have a maintenance, leisure, and tolerable freedom
from the anxieties of straitened means. So much is indispensable to the mere existence of a learned university.
More than this cannot be demanded. But there can be no
doubt that more will be cheerfully accorded by a country

P

not niggard in paying for what it values, as an appreciation of the importance of such a profession gains ground with the advance of civilisation. Let the profession once but barely exist as a profession, and leave it to conquer position and respectability by its own merits. A rich endowment of places for science, before there were men to fill them, or recognition in the country for them, even if it were possible, would be improper.

" We do not think," says a recent writer, " that any legislation will much alter the demand for a university education. In order to make Oxford and Cambridge thoroughly popular institutions, there is required rather a change in the nation than a change in the universities. Our whole conception of the value of learning, and of the dignity of a learned life, must undergo a change before our universities will be changed to any considerable degree ; and before we alter our opinion as to the value of learning we shall have to alter altogether our conceptions of the nature of learning, and these alterations will take a very long time, and will be but slowly affected by Acts of Parliament " (*Pall Mall Gazette*, 6th June 1867).

§ 4.—*Graduated Scale of Fellowships.*

While the endowment of the new profession of learning should be liberal, provision must be made for the encouragement of exertion, and guarantees taken, as far as may be, against the besetting danger of endowments—mental stagnation and apathy. This might possibly be attempted by a graduated system of promotion. Suppose that there were to be a fourfold scale of fellowships, rising in value :—

1. Tutors.
2. Lecturers.
3. Professors.
4. Senior Fellows (or Heads).

There would be fewer lecturers than tutors, fewer professors than lecturers. Lastly, Class IV. would be limited to a few places, some twenty or twenty-five, which would be the prizes of the profession. Any M.A. should be qualified to act as tutor. The tutor to be paid wholly out of fees, or, if necessary, to have a small stipend in aid of fees assigned him. Any tutor to be qualified as candidate for a lectureship in his faculty. The professor-fellow to be chosen out of the lecturers, but to be open also to other persons, even to those who are not M.A. of the university. The system of prizes recommends itself by the practice of all the professions, in which it has been found the most economical and efficacious method of dispensing reward. It is indeed in operation in the universities now. Better men are obtained, under the actual system, as college tutors, than would be secured by the mere income of their office, by the chance which they run of the headship, or of the one or two large livings which may be in the gift of the college.

§ 5.—*Patronage.*

Nothing is easier than to enact that promotion shall be by merit; nothing is more difficult to secure in practice. And, in fact, in this country, the army, the church, whole departments of the public service, are carried on without any recognition of such a principle. These services, to use the consecrated phrase, get on well enough without. It is true that an extraordinary strain on any department—as on the *Commissariat* in the Crimean war—places in a strong light the absurdity of conducting the public service on the hypothesis of the equality of capacities. But only for a moment. The danger past, the axiom enunciated by the truly English mind of George III., that " every man in this country is fit for any situation he can get," resumes its habitual sway.

In a university, however, the question of patronage is a question of life or death—" stantis aut cadentis academiæ." Promotion by merit, and by merit alone, is " a condition without which colleges are nuisances, and universities only organised against their end "—(Hamilton, *Discussions*, p. 364).

> ἐν τῷδε γὰρ κάμνουσιν αἱ πολλαὶ πόλεις
> ὅταν τις ἐσθλὸς καὶ πρόθυμος ὢν ἀνὴρ
> μηδὲν φέρηται τῶν κακιόνων πλέον.

It may be said that the English universities are, then, the purest public bodies in the kingdom, inasmuch as they distribute the mass of their places—viz. all the fellowships, by examination. But a little consideration will show that to give fellowships by examination goes but a very little way towards organising the service of the university on the principle of merit. In the first place, it applies to none of the more valuable appointments—headships, canonries, professorships; secondly, it does not apply to the honorary distinctions—the degrees, viz., which, from the M.A. to the D.D., the university bestows in consideration merely of an outlay of time and money; thirdly, as has been said above, the examination for a fellowship is only an unmeaning repetition of the class-schools by a less competent board of examiners. The fellowship examination does not profess to ascertain a definite stage of progress beyond the point reached by the first class. Lastly, even were these examinations conducted on an improved system—*i.e.*, were they in the hands of a general board, proposing to test a prolonged period of study subsequent to the B.A.—yet examination is a wholly inadequate test of scientific merit. Examination has its proper place in awarding honours and prizes to quite young men. As applicable to the public service, it can scarcely be held to have any other use than serving as an initial exclusion of incapacity, and a check upon nepotism. It cannot be the rule of promotion.

In the reformed university, examination will continue to be the test employed to award :—1. All scholarships and exhibitions to undergraduates; 2. The honour-degrees (M.A., etc.) at the termination of three years of study; 3. The few (two or three) prize-fellowships yearly proposed for competition among the M.A.'s, etc. The mass of the endowments arranged in the ascending order as proposed (1. tutors; 2. lecturers; 3. professor-fellows; 4. senior fellows, heads) cannot obviously be awarded by examination. At most, examinations would be applicable in the youngest stage, that of the tutor; but at this stage it will be unnecessary, as I propose that the honour-degrees (M.A., etc.) should of themselves form the habilitation for the office of tutor. Any one, on obtaining one of these degrees, may inscribe his name in the register of tutors and compete for pupils.

It remains to be considered where the appointments to the other three classes, of lecturers, professors, and senior-fellows, should be vested.

The modes of appointment at present in use in the University of Oxford are :—

1. Competitive Examination.   All Fellowships.
2. Computation of University Honours.   Eldon Scholarship.

3. The Crown. Dean and four Canons of Christ Church. Four other Professorships—Greek, Civil Law, Medicine, Modern History.

4. Election by vote of the Corporate Body. Heads of most Colleges.

5. Open poll of Large Constituency. Margaret Divinity.

6. Open poll of Convocation. Nine Chairs — viz. Camden Ancient History, Sibthorpian Rural Economy, Poetry, Vinerian Common Law, Clinical, Anglo-Saxon, Political Economy, Sanskrit, Logic.

7. Board of Academical Officials. Seven Chairs—viz. White's Moral Philosophy, Music, Laudian Arabic, Experimental Philosophy, Ireland Exegetical, Latin, Waynflete Moral and Metaphysical.

8. Board of Extra-academical High Official Persons. Seven Chairs — viz. Savilian Geometry, Savilian Astronomy, Sedleian Natural Philosophy, Chichele Modern History, Chichele International Law, Waynflete Chemistry, Linacre Physiology.

9. Board of Heads of Colleges. Exegetical Professor, Bampton Lecturer.

10. Vice-Chancellor. Two Chairs—viz. Mineralogy, Geology.

11. Single Patron. Lord Almoner's Arabic.

12. Boards of Curators. Two Chairs—viz. Taylorian, Hope Zoology.

13. Chancellor. Heads of three Halls.

If we except Nos. 2, 10, 11, 12, which are only applied in six cases, there is not one of these methods of appointment to offices which is not open to very serious objection; not one which has not in practice failed to secure promotion by merit.

Of No. 6, or election by open poll of the whole body of M. A., it may be said, without fear of contradiction, that it is, of all the modes of appointment in use in the university, the least defensible. The *pars sanior* of the electors themselves are, I believe, quite aware of the unfitness of Convocation for the exercise of this responsible trust, and would willingly surrender it into other hands, provided they were once satisfied it was properly lodged. There is only one class of places which might perhaps be left to be filled by this body of electors ; — non-resident professorships, of small value and limited tenure, by which some eminent person is retained to pay an occasional visit, and give his views to the public from the platform of a university chair, are by no means without their use. Such is the poetry professorship at present, to which might well be added a second professor of political economy, one of English literature, and one of the principles of art. These might still remain matters of popular election ; but in respect of all the permanent and more valuable appointments, it is urgently required, for the credit, well-being, and even peace of the university, that we should be relieved from the humiliating necessity of urging irrelevant considerations on a large body of electors, or even canvassing them under false pretences, in order to give a superior candidate a chance of success. While I write these lines, Convocation is preparing to elect two professors — one of poetry, and one of political economy. It is scarcely credible, but it is a fact, that the chances of the respective candidates are depending not on their fitness for the office, on their reputation, or past services, but on the support or opposition of the great theological party, which knows of no merit but adhesion to its ranks.

A board of official persons must either be composed of intra-academical or extra-academical officials. The petty intrigues, and the personal animosities for which, in the words of Schleiermacher, "universities, one and all, are infamous," make it impossible to entrust academical officers with the selection of their colleagues of equal rank. The worst form of patronage, according to Sir William Hamilton, is the appointment of professors by professors. Boards of extra-academical high officers of State are liable to the defect that the function of selection is an inferior appendage to a more important office. The appointment to a place in the university comes to rank in the eyes of a personage in such lofty station as but a portion of his patronage, which he distributes with the rest among the most hungry applicants. And for the steady maintenance of a scrupulous system of promotion, such boards would be wholly unfitted by the fluctuating nature of their composition. They are, besides, dependent for their knowledge of the character and services of individuals who are working in the place, upon information supplied from within the university itself. If this information be given unofficially, he who has no powerful or dexterous friend will never be brought under notice at all. He who has friends is likely to have enemies, and the just expectations of years of laborious service will be placed at the mercy of some personal ill-wisher or secret theological denunciator. If, on the other hand, the information be tendered in a responsible form, the elector loses his discretion, and is placed at the mercy of "Testimonials." Testimonials seem in theory an unexceptionable mode of obtaining information, and the extensive employment of the system in this country shows at least that it is found to answer some good purpose. Its defects, however, are many and well known. "Testimonials are strong in proportion to the partialities of the testifier, and the lowness of the standard by which he judges" (Hamilton, *ut supra*, p. 381). Without referring to these defects, it is sufficient to say that it is a system which can only be had recourse to, failing other direct and personal means of acquainting the patron with the character of the persons among whom his choice lies. And to work efficiently a graduated scale of endowed fellowships, such as is here proposed, there must be a patron on the spot capable of observing for himself the working and the diligence of the whole academical *personnel*.

The only other among the actual patrons who would be thought of as a trustee of academical appointments, on a large scale, is the Crown. The Crown acts as patron through the first minister. A comparison between the Crown appointments and those by intra-academical election, for a long series of years, would no doubt show greatly in favour of the former—*e.g.* the deans of Christ Church, who are nominated by the Crown, have been on the whole more distinguished men than the heads of any other one college where the corporate body elect. But it is only by comparison with a system more faulty than itself that the exercise of the Crown patronage by the minister can appear in a favourable light. The minister is wholly dependent upon a parliamentary majority. He is therefore the organ of one of the political parties in the State. The necessities of his position compel him to seek strength by using his patronage—clerical or academical— in the interest of his party. It has come to be thought that he *ought* to choose by this test, and not by that of capacity or fitness. Hence, among the competitors for

Crown professorships, the road to preferment has to be sought not by learning or diligence, but by political services, or loud-tongued advocacy of some powerful theological party. Much jealousy has been entertained in Oxford of Crown patronage as a danger to our corporate independence. Its real evil lies not in this imaginary danger, but in the degree to which it has tended to corrupt public opinion within the university, and to give the sanction of the country to nominations upon other considerations than the single one of fitness. A patron may err in any particular selection. That is an error of judgment which is to be regretted. But if it be known that he intended and desired, to the best of his discernment, to appoint the fittest man, his error will have no bad consequences beyond the single failure. But an appointment avowedly made on any other principle than that of " detur digniori," exercises a corrupting influence through the whole university. No intelligence and no liberality of the individual minister can rescue him from a necessity which is a necessity of his position. If any minister was ever in a position to be independent of party, it is the present prime minister, Lord Derby. To intelligence and liberality, to ancient lineage and great wealth, is here united no ordinary degree of classical culture, and its consequence, sympathy with education. Besides this, Lord Derby is Chancellor of the University—*i.e.*, official head, not of the Conservative party in the university, but of the whole body, and trustee of the Chancellor's appointments for the good of the whole body. Yet, in the exercise of the Crown patronage Lord Derby could not dare to overlook party considerations, or to appoint the best man, if he happened not to be a political Conservative. He may even have wished to do so, but he could not dare to do it. Public opinion would not merely allow him to regard his patronage as a political instrument rather than as a trusteeship for the benefit of learning, but it would not allow him to do otherwise. It will be obvious, I may hope, to every reader that I venture on this personal allusion, not as criticism on any particular appointment, but as an illustration, in a signal instance, of the fetters which political party have inextricably woven round the position of minister of the Crown—fetters which make it impossible for him to fulfil the conditions of an academical patron. Nor would it make any difference were the patronage lodged with a minister of instruction, if that minister, like the rest of the cabinet, was dependent on a parliamentary majority. Even in Germany, where there is no such dependence, a minister of instruction is too often the tool of a theological party. In Saxony (Jena), Hilgenfeld has been more than once passed over, and even inferior men promoted over his head, from the pressure of party considerations.

Convocation then, the Crown, boards of State officials, boards of academical officers, being alike ineligible as patrons, where are we to lodge this first and all-important trust?

I cannot profess to be able to offer a scheme which shall not be open to objections. Indeed it may well be that no such scheme is possible. Yet even if partiality cannot be, as no doubt it cannot be, wholly excluded, any system which shall *profess* the rule of scientific merit, to the exclusion of party connection, would be a great gain. Before, however, proposing a scheme of appointment, it is necessary to state the principles which must regulate the organisation of a system of academical patronage. This subject has been examined with great care, and wide acquaintance with its history, by Sir W. Hamilton. I may shortly re-state his conclusions. The grounds on which these are based may be seen by turning to his essay, which first appeared in the *Edinburgh Review*, 1834 (Hamilton, *Discussions*, pp. 348-385). This masterly and lucid statement of the question exhibits principles which must prevail in the long run, if universities are to continue to exist at all.

The conditions which should be practically fulfilled by any system of academical patronage are, according to Sir W. Hamilton, as follows :—

The patrons should be more than one, to obviate the errors of individual judgment, and to resist the influences that might prove too strong for a single will; to secure the animation of numbers, a division of labour, more extensive information, opposite views, and a many-sided discussion of their merits.

The patrons should be few, that the requisite intelligence may be possessed by each, that their responsibility may be concentrated, that they may understand each other and act in concert. A numerous body can elect only out of those whom a situation suits; a small body only out of those who suit the situation.

The patrons should be specially appointed *ad hoc;* the trust should not be an accidental appendage to a higher office.

They must be selected, not for social status or general respectability, but from peculiar qualification for the discharge of the office.

They should be conditionally permanent—*i.e.,* not holding the office for life, but re-appointed from time to time if their conduct merit approval. For the due discharge of the functions demands experience, and consistency and perseverance in a course of measures.

The patrons should have the recommendatory, but not the formal and definitive, appointment. This should belong to a higher authority.

The patrons should not select from those who solicit their suffrages, or even permit themselves to be solicited. They should themselves, on a vacancy, look round for the person of highest eminence in the given faculty.

To the conditions thus laid down by Sir W. Hamilton, the present scheme, which proposes graduated promotion through four steps, requires the addition of another condition.

The patrons must be, if not resident, at least in such constant communication with the university as to be themselves cognisant of the character and labours of all its working teachers. Their appointments must rest distinctly on their own knowledge; they must not be able to throw off any part of their responsibility upon the representations of others made by " Testimonials," or in any other way.

Two recommendations made by Sir W. Hamilton are here not adopted, intentionally :—1. That the patron should be also superintendent of the university. In the present scheme the superintendence is divided among the Vice-Chancellor, the Hebdomadal Council, and the Boards of the Faculties. Sir W. Hamilton's scheme seems only applicable to universities where the *curatorium,* or superintending body, is itself subordinated to a central minister of instruc-

tion.   2. That the patrons, with the report of their decision,
should be required to make an articulate statement of the
grounds on which their opinion has been formed, that the
object of their preference is the individual best qualified
for the vacant chair.   I reject this as likely to lead to
much rhetorical advocacy and counter-pleading, and as
reproducing the sophistic of "Testimonials" in another
form.

To fulfil the above conditions, let there be a Board of
five curators, to whom shall be made over the nominations
to the whole of the endowed places for which learning,
science, or literature, is the qualification, with any exceptions which may be desirable.

The curators shall have only the recommendatory
nomination.   They shall nominate to the Vice-Chancellor,
who shall have the power of declining their nominee,
stating the objection.   It shall be an admissible objection,
that there is another person, in the opinion of the Vice-
Chancellor, possessing superior claims.   The curators may
repeat the same nomination a second time, but if again
rejected by the Vice-Chancellor, such rejection to be final
for that vacancy.

The curators to be elected for seven years, to be
reckoned from date of appointment, and to be re-eligible.

Ineligible to the office of curator—Peers, or sons of
Peers; members of House of Commons; Bishops.   Not
more than two curators of one faculty at the same time.

Before entering on their function, an instruction,
passed by the university legislature, to be accepted and
signed by each curator.   This instruction should express,
in the most explicit terms, the obligation imposed by the

trust, of bestowing each place on the most eminent merit obtainable.

In excluding solicitation, it is not intended to prohibit applications. It is convenient that applications should be sent in, that the curators may know who are willing to accept the appointment. These applications are not to be specifications of the candidate's merits, but a short biography of himself, including a notice of the direction of his researches, and list of books, papers, articles, etc., written by him, and to be confined to matters of fact, to the exclusion of any promises for the future. The curators to be expressly charged in the instruction not to limit their choice to the applicants, but to make a tender of the office to the person, in their opinion, most qualified, even at the risk of being refused.

Lastly comes the question of election. Upon the integrity and judgment of these *Quinqueviri* will depend really the whole edifice of the university. If the right men, and none but the right men, could always be secured for the office of curator, the success of such a scheme as the present would be matter of certainty. But in no constitution, from Plato's Republic downwards, has the question, " Quis custodiet ipsos custodes ? " found a satisfactory answer. In every such construction, as in Aladdin's palace, there is one unfinished window. It is easy to lay down the maxims of good government, but no government can be good which is not administered by good men. The beginning of universities was not a place, or an institution, but a *man*. The men who, in the twelfth century, at Bologna or Salerno, came forward to teach what they knew, were not localised; they could at any moment go to another city, and open a school, which would become as frequented. "The personal influence of the teacher," says Dr. Newman, "is able in some sort to dispense with an academical system, but the system cannot in any sort dispense with personal influence. With influence there is life, without it there is none. . . . An academical system, without the personal influence of teachers upon pupils, is an arctic winter; it will create an ice-bound, petrified, cast-iron university, and nothing else" (Newman, *Office and Work of Universities*, p. 112). To expect of any system, whether on paper, or *de facto*, that it shall, by virtue of its own operation, secure a constant succession of the best men, is to expect what a system cannot do. No machinery that can be devised for the appointment of curators can, by its mere mechanism, turn out the right men. It may easily be that other methods of appointing the *curatorium* are as good, or better than the one about to be proposed.

In Sir W. Hamilton's scheme, the curators for the University of Edinburgh were to be elected by a board of six delegates. These delegates were themselves representatives, returned, one by each of six public bodies—viz. 1. The Faculty of Advocates; 2. The Society of Writers to the Signet; 3. The Royal College of Physicians; 4. The Royal College of Surgeons; 5. The Presbytery of Edinburgh (or the General Assembly); 6. The Town Council. Sir W. Hamilton himself, in later years, was inclined to think this scheme too complex, especially in that the principle of mediate election is not commonly practised in this country, and therefore not sufficiently understood. If indirect election could be employed, it might here be beneficial, and the difficulties arising from complexity would be less in a university than elsewhere. But to avoid the charge of proposing the impracticable, we may be content, for the present, with a direct election of the curators, and enact as follows :—

One shall be nominated by the Vice-Chancellor.

One by the professors of the faculty of mathematical and physical sciences.

One by the professors of the philological faculty.

One by the professors of law and history.

One shall be coopted by the board itself thus elected.

The nominee of the Vice-Chancellor to hold office only four years, in order that each Vice-Chancellor may have one nomination. He shall be nominated by the outgoing Vice-Chancellor just before laying down his office. The other four curators may hold office for seven years. The curators not to be salaried, but to have a paid secretary and a separate office.

This cannot be called a complicated arrangement. Even were it so, complex and artificial methods of appointment are not necessarily difficult to work when the machinery is seen to be conducive to a result. The wisdom of the Venetian government was proverbial; it was entirely due to a system of appointment to offices. " In Venice," says Antonio Serra in 1613, " the method of choosing magistrates is in such perfection that no one can come in by corruption or favour; nor can any one rise to high offices who has not been tried in the lower " (*ap.* Hallam, *Lit.* ii. 529).

It is not, however, so much from this or any system of appointment that the regeneration of the university is to be looked for. This can only come from a change in the spirit of the place—a change which legislation cannot enact, and which, if it comes at all, must be very gradual. The balance in which men have been hitherto weighed has to be altered. In the storms of the sixteenth century, the university acquired a party character which it has never since lost. It has always been assumed that university appointments should be made with a reference to the interests of the church, or those interests as interpreted by one of the parties in the church. This false standard, which has hitherto perverted our judgment of men and things, has to be got rid of. In our effort to shake off the yoke of party, we have encouragement and aid from a public opinion outside — a public opinion which is not hostile to the Established Church, but which is desirous to see it constituted on a more national basis. But it is not enough that a party standard of judging should die out here; it must be superseded by another and truer measure of academical fitness; and here we have the difficulty that there is no public opinion outside to aid. Beyond the circles of scientific men — circles so isolated as to be infected in no small degree with the spirit of clique — there is no public appreciation of abstract science or profound learning. The dependence of culture and civilisation on the maintenance somewhere in the body-politic of the theories of the various arts of life is not understood among us. We have in English no word by which to render the German *Wissenschaft*. We mean by *science* that which admits demonstrative or experimental proof, as opposed to art, practice, or literature. But the German term is much more comprehensive, and is applicable to the methodical and abstract treatment of any matter whatsoever. *Wissenschaft* expresses the purpose and aim for which a university exists. Not that in a university, any more than in the world at large, man is for knowledge. Much rather is knowledge for man. Not to enlarge the sciences, or to heap up libraries, is our object, but to maintain through successive generations an order of minds, in each of the great departments of human inquiry, cultivated to the utmost point which their powers admit of. Upon the prevalence and realisation of this idea depends the life of a university. But this is a conception which cannot be imported into Oxford from without, either by public opinion or the Legislature, because neither the public nor the Legislature can give an idea or a sentiment which they do not themselves possess. The idea, however, exists in germ in the university itself. It is sure to grow and develop itself under favourable influences. All that the Legislature can do is to create the conditions, or to remove the obstructions.

Sec. 6.—Of the Studies preliminary to the Degree.

§ 1.—" *Pass*" and " *Class*."

In treating the question, What studies shall compose the curriculum for young men passing through a university? one of two methods is usually adopted by speakers or writers.

One mode of treatment is the abstract. The writer lays down a psychological principle of education. He will say, *e.g.*, that the business of education is the communication of that knowledge which has most value for the conduct of life. And from this he will proceed to deduce the rule that a university should teach all those branches of knowledge, the practical applications of which are required to guide or adorn human life. To this a counter-theorist will reply, that education should be, not initiative into truth, but disciplinal; that its object is to develop faculty, and not to fill with knowledge; that if you pour in truths before you have created the powers of assimilation, mental growth is stunted. And from this he will deduce the rule that a university curriculum should be laid out upon such studies as form the best intellectual gymnastic, irrespective of their application.

The other method of deciding the question is the empirical one. This is to recommend promiscuously this, that, and the other study, which, for any reason whatever, has been found by experience to have value; to plant all these together in the university, and to let the student compose a curriculum, by taste or accident, out of any combination of these.

Essays of great value have been produced upon both these systems. To confine myself to English names, Dr. Whewell and Dr. Newman, Mr. Herbert Spencer and Mr. Mill, have contributed, from various points of view, most important elements to the discussion. A review of the controversy on the principles of complete education is not within the scope of the present " Suggestions." I am to confine myself to considering the existing arrangements of Oxford, and to proposing any modifications of those arrangements, which, without departing too far from our traditional practice, may tend to make that practice more consistent with itself, and less open to some serious objections, than it now is. The task to be here attempted lies midway between a philosophical investigation of educational principles, and framing the details of a statute of studies.

That not merely a revision, but an entire re-cast, of the statute " De Exercitiis," commonly called the " Examination Statute," is required, is, I believe, an opinion fast gaining ground among us. A labour so full of detail cannot be attempted by an individual. Nor is it one to which any of the existing machinery of our legislation is equal. It ought to be intrusted, not to a committee of Council or Congregation, but to a special delegacy constituted for the purpose, on the system of representing all the branches of study to be admitted here.

In saying that the business of such a delegacy would be to re-cast the examination statute, it is not meant that all that now exists would be swept away, and a new course of studies inaugurated. What is meant is that, for piece-meal amendment, which has gone on for some time, should be substituted an articulate organisation, founded on principles of education which we need not be ashamed to avow and defend against assailants. But the organisation would be an organisation of that which exists. Even the things studied would remain in great part what they now are. But they would be better arranged, classified, divided.

What are the general principles upon which such a revision must proceed ?

I must here assume that the reader has a general acquaintance with the courses of study at present prescribed for Oxford students. Those who desire more detailed information may find it in *The Oxford Calendar,* published annually, or in *Education in Oxford*, by Professor Rogers, or in *Pass and Class*, 3d edition, an Oxford guide-book, by Professor Burrows. An historical account of the successive changes in the course of studies from 1636, the date of the Laudian statute, will be found in the *Report of the O. U. Commission*, 1852, p. 60, *seq.*

In order to an understanding of what our arrangements actually are, a distinction must be attended to, the importance of which could not be gathered either from the examination statute or from any printed directions. This is the distinction between what is compulsory on all, and what is left to voluntary ambition — the distinction between "Pass" and "Class." The essential bearing of this distinction on the university question is not appreciated by the public outside. "The common impression is, that obtaining the ordinary degree is a very creditable and quite satisfactory achievement, while the class-list contains the names of some few wonderfully-clever and hard-working students, who are not uncommonly supposed to have ruined themselves for life by their exertions, and to be great fools for their pains" (Burrows, *Pass and Class*, p. 8). It is a great merit of Professor Burrows' guide-book that it insists on this distinction, and gives it its proper prominence. But because the "Pass" is a nullity, it is not enough to exhort the student not to rest satisfied with it. We must not close our eyes to the fact that the honour-students are the only students who are undergoing any educational process which it can be considered as a function of a university either to impart or to exact; the only students who are at all within the scope of the scientific apparatus and arrangements of an academical body.

This class of students cannot be estimated at more than 30 per cent of the whole number frequenting the university.

§ 2.—*The Pass Examinations.*

The remaining 70 per cent not only furnish from among them all the idleness and extravagance which is become a byeword throughout the country, but cannot be considered to be even nominally pursuing any course of university studies at all. For the pass-man, the university is but an unmeaning repetition of the school. Sent up here at nineteen, not having learned what he might have learned by sixteen, we have the option of teaching him nothing at all, or of teaching him over again what he has already been five or six years in not learning. The attempt even to do this is often vain, owing to a habit of dunce-hood which has been acquired by the passive resistance of the mind to the reiteration of the same matter.

It was at one time the fashion to say that the idleness of the pass-man was due to the narrowness of the university course. " Give them," said Sir Charles Lyell, " instruction congenial to their tastes, and let them see clearly that it has a distinct bearing on their future occupations and callings" (*O. U. C. Evidence,* p. 119). The university *has* admitted modern subjects. A small but valuable class of men has been withdrawn from inactivity by the new career thus opened to them. This is the class who, either from ill health, want of early opportunity, or other cause, had not a grammatical grounding early enough in life to allow of their entering as competitors in the regular classical competition. But their number is small. The total of those who take honours in the other three non-classical schools together, only amounts to some 50 per annum. The bulk of the pass-men still remains to be dealt with.

A favourite remedy for the evil with the first race of university reformers was a matriculation examination. "The very first step to university reform," says Archbishop Whately, "should be a university examination preliminary to matriculation." And the commissioners "fully concur with the general opinion to the same effect expressed in the evidence" (*O. U. C. Report*, pp. 68, 70). Since 1852, when this was the prevailing opinion, "Responsions" has been advanced to the first term of the student's residence, and has become, in fact, a matriculation examination. For though to pass "Responsions" in the first term is an option and not an obligation, yet the colleges endeavour to bring up the standard of their matriculation examinations to what is required by the university at "Responsions." With what success we learn from one of the masters of the schools, Mr. O. Ogle. Out of 168 candidates in March 1863, fifty-one were plucked, sixteen took their names off after paper work, and 101 passed. Out of the fifty-one plucked, forty-three were in a state of unfitness to undergo any examination.

"I am perfectly clear that the failure of all of that class whose work I have had the opportunity of examining was not owing to special ignorance of the particular subjects required, but to ignorance of such a nature as to render them unfit to undergo any examination whatever, on any subject whatever. An ignorance of the easiest principles and rudiments of language, an inextricable confusion of thought, a perfect inability to do more than guess at the meaning of a question asked, an absence of ordinary facility in spelling or constructing a sentence in English—these are the unhappy characteristices of the whole class. . . . Thus a large minority of the young men who matriculate are not only entirely unfit to satisfy the requirements of the place, but are in a state which renders it almost hopeless to expect that they ever will be fit to do so. Their hope and the hope of their friends is, not that they will rise in time to the standard, but that in time the standard will be low enough to meet their cases, and that, with luck assisting, they will so get through. And this is a perfectly legitimate hope as matters now stand. The standard has been sensibly lowered, and the proportion of plucks has sensibly increased. As a private tutor of considerable experience, I am bold to say that ever since the introduction of the new system . . . the standard of requirement in responsions has been falling lower " (O. Ogle, *Letter to the Vice-Chancellor,* 1863).

A matriculation examination, then, for such the " Little-go " now practically is, has been proved by experience to be no remedy for the evil. That it must have failed as a remedy is a result which can surprise no one who has had the opportunity of observing closely the working of examinations. While a competitive system stimulates ambition and effort, a minimum standard of requirement depresses all to the level of the lowest. It is the difference between voluntary work for a prize and compulsory task-work—the difference, so well understood in economics, between the value of free and slave labour. The paralysis of intellectual action produced by a compulsory examination is not more remarkable than its effect in depressing moral energy. For as examinations have been multiplied upon the unhappy pass-man, the help afforded him to pass them

has been increased in proportion. He has got to lean
more and more upon his tutor, and to do less and less for
himself. It is become a favourite view with us to pride
ourselves upon our superiority to the last academical
generation on the ground that the college tutors "work"
so much harder. They do indeed work; they drudge.
For they aim at taking upon themselves the whole strain
of effort. It is a point of honour with them to get their
pupils "through." The pupil has ceased to struggle, to
help himself; more and more is done for him. The pupil's
mind is wholly passive. The old metaphor, "clay in the
hands of the potter," is no longer applicable to the process.
For no form is imposed upon the ductile material. *Molle
lutum* it remains to the last. The examinations have
destroyed teaching, which may be said to be a lost art
among us. The student is not taught the things in which
he is examined. He is prepared to pass an examination in
them—a very different process. The first generation of
Oxford reformers, represented by Archbishop Whately, may
be pardoned for having overlooked the distinction between
competitive and compulsory examinations. This important
difference naturally escaped notice in our first enthusiasm
for examinations. Seeing the marvellous effects of the
examination system inaugurated in 1800, in awakening life
in this place, a belief grew up that examinations could
accomplish everything. We now know better the limits of
their power. The inertia of the pass-man is not to be
overcome by multiplying examinations upon him, and
taking upon yourself to find the additional power required
to force him through them.

A different remedy for the evil complained of has been

recently proposed, and received among us with some favour—to reduce, viz., the three years' residence to two. The fact alleged—viz. that all which we now profess to teach in three years might be taught in two—cannot be disputed. But, on the same ground, the two years might be reduced to one. For the final examination at the end of the third year does not exact a more advanced knowledge of Latin and Greek than the preliminary examination of responsions, passed in the first term. The books are changed, that is all. The undergraduate is worried by a succession of three examinations, but in point of acquirement is left at the end of them where they found him. Accordingly, some more logical and hardy reformers have already asked, " Why should he reside in Oxford at all ? Why one year any more than two ? As preparation for an examination is all, let him prepare himself how and where he will; provided he passes our test, that is all we need know of him."

It will be impossible in the end to resist this inference, whatever compromise with time may be accepted for the moment. The university has placed itself in a position, with respect to the pass-men — *i.e.* 70 per cent of her whole scholars—in which no reason can be shown why their presence in her lecture-rooms should be required at all. For as the pass-standard requires no special knowledge, such as can be possessed only by professors, but is equally shared by hundreds of teachers, masters in schools, clergy, and others up and down the country, the preparation can be more conveniently and cheaply made at home. The university can still do all she does at present—examine and give the degree.

While time is slowly preparing this result—that, viz., of resolving the university of Oxford, like that of London, into an examining body—let us fairly face the question, Is this operation of examining against a pass-standard one worthy of a university, and is the minimum attainment required for a pass worthy of being denoted by a degree in arts? Nothing but tradition and habit could ever have reconciled us to such a degradation of our laurels. The progress of things, should it take the direction of the present " Suggestions," will answer this question. Let Oxford once resume its higher functions, let it become the home of science and the representative of the best learning of the time, and what is now called a pass-degree will be seen at once to be an incongruity. It is an incongruity which the examination system has served to place in a clear light. While the B.A. was conferred for residence alone, as was the case from the Restoration to 1800, it denoted an unknown quantity of culture derived or derivable from four years of pupillary existence. When a pass-examination was instituted, was clearly severed from the honour-examination, and the quantum of attainment actually designated by the B.A. ascertained, those two letters lost their mysterious significance. It is now well understood that they denote no grade of intellectual cultivation, but have a merely social value. They are an evidence that a youth has been able to afford not only the money, but, what is impossible to so many, the time, to live three years among gentlemen, doing nothing, as a gentleman should.

It is thought by many university reformers that any proposal to revive the real meaning of degrees, higher or lower, is a piece of antiquarian pedantry. The degrees have become social badges; men are willing they should remain so, and that the revival of the university should be sought by means which should leave its mere forms undisturbed, to die out, or to continue as empty forms unworthy of attention. I quite agree as to the impolicy of seeking .reform by the method of resuscitating a bygone age. The folly of feudal revivals is a lesson not likely to be forgotten by those who remember events in Prussia twenty years ago. This is no question of a recurrence to a defunct past, of restoring meaning to decayed symbols, a mere ritualistic phase of academical reform. I would as soon .think of proposing to prohibit by statute the use of the title " Esquire " by those not legally entitled to it, as of proposing that the letters B.A. should once more signify that the bearer had acquired the seven arts. But I cannot think that any academical reform will ever be a radical cure, which does not deal with, and remodel, the degrees both higher and lower. These " Suggestions " are revolutionary, not in any dangerous sense, but inasmuch as their aim is to transfer the whole fabric of the university from the ground of social prestige—wealth, rank, and aristocratical connection—on which it now stands, to that of science, learning, and culture. The university should say to the candidate for matriculation, in the words of Theophrastus, " ἤτοι τὸν λόγον ἄφετε, πολὺς γὰρ ὁ πόνος, ἢ καλῶς αὐτῷ πρόστητε " (*Diog. Laert.* v. 41).

Let us once realise our lofty calling, and we shall find that we have quite enough to do in maintaining and adorning the vast structure of human knowledge to have time to occupy ourselves in the inculcation of the rudiments. There is a time and a place for everything; and school is surely the place where the attainments now required in the three examinations for the B.A. degree (pass) should be found.

The arrangement, then, at which we should aim is, that the university should cease the pass-business altogether. College-tutors should no longer have imposed upon them the drudgery of working men up for these examinations. The examinations themselves should be discontinued by the university as a body, and its degrees no longer conferred for passing them. Instead of the three pass-examinations, now compulsory on matriculated students, an extension might be given to the present middle-class examinations, by which the grammar-schools might be included under those examinations. Such an examination would be like the *Abiturienten-examen* in Germany. It would come at the end of the school course, instead of at the end of the university course. The candidates would not be matriculated students, either in act or in prospect. The examination would not be conducted by the university as a body, though the examiners would be mostly, no doubt, university graduates. The examiners would not be academical officers, but would form a delegacy (or delegacies) *ad hoc*, like the *Wissenschaftliche Prüfungs-Commission* in Prussia. Those who pass this examination might have any titulation which it might be thought expedient to give them. But as the standard must necessarily be a not very high one, they should not obtain a university degree, even the lowest.

If such a proposal is calculated to excite alarm, as tending to empty the colleges, and to send away at once 70 per cent of our students, let the following considerations be weighed :—

1. It is not possible, nor is it proposed, that such a measure as the abolition of the pass-degree should be taken at once, before the other parts of the university organism are ready for the change. Before the college endowments shall have been remodelled, and the college buildings gradually appropriated to the use of the professor-fellows of the several faculties, a generation of college tutors must have moved off to church preferment.

2. Even supposing that the proposal were such as to imply the removal from Oxford of all the non-reading men, and that the colleges thereby incurred the loss of the room-rents, and the profit on their board, with what face could we complain? If any gain is illicit, the gain made by pretending to teach those who do not learn is surely such.

3. But no such proposal is now made. Let the pass-examination, with its attendant pluckings, and the whole occupation of drilling men to "get through," cease. This is not to send away students, but to remove an obstacle out of their way. Let the gates of the university be freely open, and let all the world enter. Let all who choose be admissible to our lectures, our libraries, museums, and our voluntary examinations. But they shall not be compelled to seek a degree, under peril of disgrace if they do not obtain it. Under this arrangement the class of "Pass-men" would still be largely represented here. They would not seek a degree which they do not want, but they would seek such education as they could pick up, or as their friends would wish them to obtain. Some, whom the disgust of the compulsory examination now alienates from books, would become voluntary competitors for the classes. And as the area covered by the collective class-lists of all

the schools would be wider than at present—wide enough
to include anything that can be considered substantial
knowledge in any of the departments of study—the percentage of "Honour-men"—*i.e.* of candidates for a degree—
would be greatly increased. Thus, the only denomination
of students who would be banished the university by the
new arrangement, would be those who at present come
purely to obtain the degree apart from the education, who
want for social purposes the social prestige of the M.A.,
without any intellectual qualification. Is it possible that
any of us can seriously wish to see this species of student
retained in the university?

It may be objected to this scheme for doing away with
the compulsory examination, that a powerful instrument of
discipline is thus thrown away. Granted, it may be said,
that the training for the pass-degree gives no intellectual
training, yet its moral restraint over idleness and dissipation is valuable, nay indispensable. How helpless would
not the dean or tutor become when he could no longer
hold *in terrorem* over the head of the insubordinate the
annually-recurring examination which he must pass!

To this I reply that experience has sufficiently refuted
the hypothesis that compulsory examinations produce
habits of industry. The preparation for them takes up
time. But the total of idleness is not thereby lessened. A
distaste is engendered for books and reading them, and the
youth compensates himself for the hateful hours spent upon
his " grind " by taking all the rest of his time to " himself."
This temper is not generated in the university, but is already
formed in the boy before he appears as a man. It is chiefly
characteristic of one or two great schools, but seems to

have been propagated to others, which are not known as
"public schools." Spoiled by the luxury of home and
early habits of self-indulgence, the young aristocrat has
lost the power of commanding the attention, and is not
only indisposed for, but incapable of, work. Profound
idleness and luxuriousness have corrupted his nature. He
is no longer capable of being attuned to anything. He is
either the foppish exquisite of the drawing-room, or the
barbarised athlete of the arena, and beyond these spheres
all life is to him a blank. Congregated mostly in one
college, they maintain in it a tone of contempt for study,
and a taste for boyish extravagance and dissipation, which
infects the moral atmosphere far beyond their own circle.
As they lead the fashion, and are conscious of their right
to do so, in dress and manners, this social superiority gives
weight and currency to their notions and opinions on moral
conduct. From this source are propagated through the
whole place ideas of style and expenditure incompatible
with the means and future position of the general body of
the young men. The fear, but too much justified by facts,
of infection by the tastes of wealth and idleness operates to
deter parents from sending promising sons to college.
After the experience of more than fifty years, it is plain
that compulsory examinations are no remedy for a moral
tone which has its causes in social relations beyond the
university precincts. Our examinations harass these
students, but do not affect their ideas. They are punish-
ments which do not correct. It is a violation of a first
principle of education to use learning as an instrument of
chastisement; much rather should we hope for the mitiga-
tion of a sentiment which sets itself against work, by

R

aiding the growth in numbers and influence of the "reading men." Only public opinion among the undergraduates themselves can make ignorance and idleness disreputable among them. It is far from hopeless to win over a percentage of the aristocratical idle to an interest in intellectual pursuits. There is much generosity of temper among them, and no lack of quickness of apprehension. In the "minor morals," they often contrast favourably with youths of inferior breeding. This is not a case for laws and statutes, but for individual enterprise. A reform of Christ Church, it has been said, would be half a reform of the university. If only the sympathies of a minority of the young aristocracy could be enlisted on the side of self-improvement, a vast step would have been gained.

§ 3.—*The Examinations for Honours.*

It is with a sense of relief that we turn from the case of the pass-men to that of the honour-students. It is to turn from our most conspicuous failure to what is at least a comparative success. The honour-students—*i. e.*, about thirty per cent of our whole number—receive here an education which benefits them in intellect and character. As this result represents the total product of the university as it is at present constituted, it is natural and desirable that it should be closely scanned and criticised. A just estimate of the qualitative value of an Oxford training is very difficult to arrive at. It has been as severely censured by its enemies as it has been extravagantly lauded by its advocates. The value of the Oxford mintage is more than ever just now a topic of debate in speeches and pamphlets. It is no longer now, as in the days of

Coplestone and the *Edinburgh Review,* an attack and defence of existing institutions; it is a genuine desire on both sides to ascertain the true principles of a liberal education.

As has been already said, these "Suggestions" do not embark on this wider philosophical discussion; but as there are some points in our system of examination for honours which seem to require emendation, it is necessary, for the explanation of such proposed emendations, to refer them to the principles on which they proceed.

The compulsory examination and the pass-degree being supposed abolished, and a voluntary examination outside the university for youths under eighteen substituted for it, the next step follows as of course. The present standard of honours must become the qualification for the degree. The B. A. is superfluous, and may be dropped. The M. A. degree may be taken at the end of three years' *residence* by all whose names appear in any of the four classes in any of the schools.

Residence must be at all costs preserved as a qualification. It is easy to foresee that the proposal for diminishing or abolishing residence will be received with growing favour as an easy solution of the university difficulty. It is one of those solutions which cuts the knot it ought to untie. It saves expense and time, it preserves from dangers and social contamination, but it does so by abolishing education. Mr. Goldwin Smith's scheme for allowing persons brought up in affiliated colleges to get the *Oxford* degree by examination, is an exaggerated development of the examination system. So far from giving a further extension to that system, it seems to me that the time has arrived when

it is imperatively necessary to curtail it of the undue proportions it has acquired among us. The system inaugurated,
or rather restored, in 1800 has been to us a means of
renewed life. But its work is now done. It has made us
aware of the value of education, and given us energy to
pursue it. But we now find that, after first encroaching on
education, it has ended by destroying it. Teaching is extinct among us. Oxford is now, with respect to its
candidates for honours, little more than an examining body.
The professors, we are told, lecture to empty walls. The
enemies of learning exult over this failure, which they pre-
dicted, of the professoriate. What has caused this failure?
The tyranny of the examination system. This tyranny has
destroyed all desire to learn. All the aspirations of a
liberal curiosity, all disinterested desire for self-improvement, is crushed before the one sentiment which now
animates the honour-student, to stand high in the class-list.
Dr. Pusey has painted, for our avoidance, a picture of a
German sophist preaching some wild and novel theory in
order to attract a crowd of unfledged enthusiasts round his
chair. That theories have power to attract, implies at least
enthusiasm for knowledge, an enthusiasm with which we
cannot but sympathise, however much we regret its mal-
appropriation. No professor here in Oxford need fear to
become dangerously popular by a similar course. If he
wishes for any auditors at all, he must make himself subservient to the examination schools. That "enthusiastic
veneration which young men of loyal and well-conditioned
minds are apt to contract for men of intellectual eminence
within their own circle" (Masson, *Mod. Culture,* p. 303),
is not unknown among us, but it is bestowed, not on science

or attainment, but on the trainer who has turned out the largest number of winning horses.

Let it not be supposed that I am desirous of directing a diatribe against examination. Examination has its place in education, a place perfectly understood by us all in theory, however widely our practice may have deviated into extravagance. It is the sequel and supplement of a definite course of study. It is necessary to the student as "the only means of making distinct to him his knowledge and his ignorance" (Dr. Arnold, *Letters*). It is necessary to the teacher to find out at what point to take up his instruction. Coming at the close of the university curriculum, it ascertains and proclaims to the community with what industry the course of study has been followed. It is only when the relative position of the two momenta of the student's existence is inverted—when, instead of being questioned on the matters learned, he learns only how to stand being questioned, that examination becomes an evil. A sophistic art is found to have taken the place of a scientific training. A vague and windy rhetoric has supplanted solid acquisition. As early as 1838 the tendencies of an overdriven system of examination had become apparent in Cambridge. Dr. Whewell clearly perceived the danger, and laid down the just relation between teaching and examining :—

"By indirect teaching, I mean a course of education in which the student's exertions are directed mainly towards examinations, disputations, or some other public trial of his acquirements ; and in which he is led to acquire knowledge principally by the prospect of the distinctions, honours, or advantages, which attend upon success in such trials. I distinguish such teaching from that direct teaching in which instructions are given as claiming the student's attention on the ground of their own value ; and in which they are recommended to him by his own love of knowledge, by the advice and authority of his instructor, and the general sympathy of the body in which he lives.

" In the English Universities there has always been a combination of these two kinds of teaching ; and such a combination is, I conceive, the best scheme of education. In the selection and management of each of these elements there are some considerations of grave importance which I will briefly state.

" The college lectures and other college instruction appear to have been, till recently, of the nature of direct teaching. The studies thus presented to the pupil were considered as sufficiently recommended by the injunctions of the college and the parental authority of the tutors, without reference to ulterior objects. The public disputations, and those which must be performed in order to obtain a degree, formed a scheme of indirect teaching ; and the college teaching was consistent with this, but was far from being considered as merely ministerial to it. Several subjects were introduced into the courses of college instruction which have no reference to those public trials, and which were selected by the authorities of the college because they were considered as valuable for their own sake, and proper parts of a liberal education. But a strong disposition has manifested itself of late years, in the University of Cambridge at least, to give a great preponderance to the indirect system ; to conduct our education almost entirely by the means of examinations, and to consider the lectures given in the colleges as useful only in proportion as they prepare the student for success in the examinations.

" The university must have tests of proficiency, to be applied before her degrees and honours are granted. There must therefore be university examinations. On the other hand, it must always be recollected that examinations are a means, not an end ; that a good education, a sound and liberal cultivation of the faculties, is the object at which we ought to aim ; and that examinations cease to be a benefit when they interfere with this object.

" The knowledge which is acquired for the purpose of an examination merely is often of little value or effect as mental culture, compared with that knowledge which is pursued for its own sake. When a man gives his mind to any subject of study on account of a genuine wish to understand it, he follows its reasonings with care and thought, ponders over its difficulties, and is not satisfied till all is clear to his mental vision. When he studies for an examination, he does not wish to understand, but to appear to understand ; he cares not for unsolved difficulties in his mind, if the examiner detect them not ; he wishes to see clearly only, in order that he may express himself clearly. What is acquired for an examination is likely to be soon forgotten ; the mind is bent upon it with an effort, which, though strong at the time, is felt to be temporary, and is followed by a relapse into apathy and obliviousness. The habit of preparing for examinations makes other studies appear flat and insipid. The mind craves for the excitement to which it has been accustomed ; it becomes restless and volatile, and loses the appetite for quiet thought and patient study. If examinations become too frequent, all good courses of study are interfered with. It is impossible to arrange public examinations so as to point out a succession of subjects which forms a good system for all " (*On the Principles of English University Education*, 2d ed., 1838).

Towards the meritorious working institutions for higher education which are rising up in our centres of population, at Manchester, Liverpool, Birmingham, fear, jealousy, or contempt are not the sentiments we can feel. Let us wish them all success in their efforts in the common cause, and give them sympathy, and, if in our power so to do, aid. But let the Oxford degree remain the stamp of an Oxford education. " Education is a high word; it is nothing less than a formation of mind." It is impossible for those who enter into the significance of this dictum of Dr. Newman not to join with him in his indignant protest :—

" I protest to you, gentlemen, that if I had to choose between a so-called university which dispensed with residence and tutorial superintendence, and gave its degrees to any person who passed an examination in a wide range of subjects, and a university which had no professors or examinations at all, but merely brought a number of young men together for three or four years, and then sent them away, as the university of Oxford is said to have done some sixty years since, if I were asked which of these two methods was the better discipline of the intellect—mind I do not say which is morally the better, for compulsory study must be a good, and idleness an intolerable mischief—but if I must determine which of the two courses was the most successful in training, moulding, enlarging the mind ; which sent out men the more fitted for their secular duties ; which produced better public men—men of the world, men whose names would descend to posterity— I have no hesitation in giving the preference to that university which did nothing, over that which exacted of its members an acquaintance with every science under the sun. And, paradox as this may seem, still, if results be the test of systems, the influence of the public schools and colleges of England, in the course of the last century at least, will bear out one side of the contrast as I have drawn it " (J. H. Newman, *Discourses on the Scope and Nature of University Education*, 1852, p. 232).

This, then, is a principle to be kept in view in recasting our statute " De Exercitiis"—viz., that the examination must be restored to its proper place, and that is one of subordination to the curriculum of study, whatever that curriculum may be. Instead of, as now, the examination regulating the student's preparation, and the examiner being supreme over the teacher, the position should be reversed. The examination should follow the course of study, arranged from time to time among the professors of each faculty, organised into a college of studies for that faculty.

Here emerges the question as to compulsory attendance at courses of lecture. Are the students, as part of the qualification for the degree, to be required to attend given courses of lectures, and to produce a testamur of attendance from the instructor, along with a testamur of proficiency from the examiner?

There is much to be said against this requirement. It seems to introduce in another form that compulsion to learn which we have said defeats its own end, and to avoid which we have abolished compulsory examination. Our own experience seems against it. The attempt, some years ago, to compel certificate of attendance on two (at least) courses of professors was abandoned after a short trial as a confessed failure. The experience of German universities is, I believe, not favourable. The Belgian reporter on the University of Berlin says:—

" Among us in Belgium, the student, on entering the university, finds his programme of study ready for him, and he has but to undergo it passively. In Germany each student forms his own programme, and displays in following it the ardour which might be expected in the pursuit of subjects of his own choosing. In the selection of his professors he enjoys the same entire freedom as in the selection of his subjects.

According to his tastes and his abilities he attaches himself to this or that teacher. He is not even bound by the partition into faculties which serves as the basis of the teaching. Till the day of his examination he does not belong rigorously to any one faculty, but takes up with any professor or any course which happens to suit him. Thus, from the first days of his academical life, the German student is habituated to act and judge for himself, and thus is developed in him that spontaneity which is the germ of true science. This is the secret of the high value which Germany has always attached to free study" (Banning, *Rapport sur l'Université de Berlin;* Bruxelles, 1863, p. 24).

Hörfreiheit, however, does not imply a liberty to attend *no* lectures, but only a freedom of choice as to what, and in what order, he will select. In some universities (*e.g.,* Jena, see rescript of 12th July 1852) students who have not, at the end of the first week of the semester, given in their names to any lectures, are to be summoned before the authorities and compelled to inscribe themselves. Faculty students, too, who are about to enter a profession, are obliged, before passing their public examination, to present a certificate (*abgangszeugniss*), on the face of which appears the courses they have attended. *Zwangscollegien,* by which term is denoted given courses which must be attended, though an experiment often tried, have always been given up as failures. The utmost that is usually attempted is advice as to the order in which lectures should be taken. The experience of Erlangen, as recorded by Von Raumer, may be taken as the general experience:—

" Here the rule used to be that every student must attend in his first year courses on universal history, physics, logic, philology, mathematics, and natural history. At the end o the time the poor wretches were examined, all at once, on all these subjects, and till they had passed this examination they could not begin their faculty studies. These six courses were called derisively the Freshmen's courses (*Füchsen collegien*). They were attended reluctantly and negligently, and were as oppressive and discouraging to the professors who had to give as to the students who had to attend them" (Von Raumer, *Geschichte der Pädagogik*, iv. 224).

Fleisstabelle and *fleisscontrole*, or attempts to enforce diligent attendance, have also, though often tried, had to be abandoned. Where they are still maintained, they are easily evaded. Cases are said to be not rare where a student has obtained a certificate of attendance at a given course of lectures, while he was known to be not even residing in the place, or even to be engaged in some other occupation, such as private tuition in some nobleman's house. It can hardly be, as one hears sometimes alleged, that there are material difficulties in the way of registering attendance. There is, I think, a secret dislike, shared both by teachers and learners, of the restraint — a dislike which makes the most stringent official rescripts and injunctions on this head inoperative. This is not from any ignorant impatience of control; — no people are more docile to police regulations than the German — but from a keen perception of the inutility, as learning, of what is compulsorily learned. Taubmann long ago defined the student as "animal quod non vult cogi sed persuaderi." MM. Beer and Hochegger, in their criticism of the new system of studies, introduced into the University of Vienna in 1856, say —

" The rule prescribing a fixed and graduated course of progressive study for each year of the student's residence, has not, in our opinion, justified itself by its results. The unlimited choice of studies (*studienfreiheit*), which is allowed in some other German universities, has in no instance been productive of any bad consequences. Nowhere has this liberty undermined (as it was urged it would) the order of sequence arranged for the public lectures. Yet, in other universities, youth is not less thoughtless nor less lazy than in the Austrian, if these were faults which ought to decide in favour of the principle of compulsory courses (*lehrzwang*). But, we may ask in return, has the system of compulsory courses anywhere been found to fill the lecture-rooms, or to call out scientific exertion in the student? Looking to the vast differences of individual capacity, can one common course of lectures for all be said to be the treatment indicated? We are convinced, for our part, that freedom in the choice of his courses can be allowed the student without material danger to the benefits of a university life. Let admission to the public examination for the civil and other services be made dependent upon a certificate of attendance at a given number of lectures in the faculty of law and the political sciences, by all means. Require also that *some* courses of lectures in the philosophical faculty shall have been attended, but do not go on to exact attendance at any given course of lectures in any faculty. . . . Beyond fixing the number of compulsory attendances, all may be left to the student himself. Should any individual pupil make a preposterous selection of courses, he will be admonished by the deans and professors, whose duty it is. But there is little reason to fear this, since in all German universities there is a traditional order of succession in which the courses are taken, and a similar system had naturalised itself in Vienna even before 1855. We have had no rescript fixing the courses for the faculty of medicine, yet the common sense of the students has directed them to the proper order. It would never occur to a medical pupil to attend a clinical course before he had laid a foundation by courses on anatomy, physiology, and pathology. A system of guardianship and tutorial nursing is as prejudicial in science as in economics" (*Die Fortschritte des Unterrichtswesens*, 1867, vol. i. p. 641).

Experience and reason seem to be both united in favour of the " voluntary principle " as an indispensable condition of the higher education. But all liberty must be realised through law. We offer the degree, but on conditions. We exact residence ; we test proficiency by examination. May we not go further, and prescribe a curriculum of lectures ? I think we may, if such a condition is not arbitrary, but is founded in the nature of the case. The failure of our former enactment, requiring certificated attendance on two courses of professors' lectures, was owing to this being an arbitrary enactment. It was seen to be intended to keep up the professors, and provide them with an audience. The professor was an excrescence on the examination system. To compel the student to attend him did but demonstrate his uselessness. For the professor is there as a teacher of science, and the examination was to be passed, not by acquiring science, but by being crammed for passing it. Under the scheme now proposed this will be no longer so. A degree will be offered as a prize to the student on two conditions— 1. That he has gone through a defined curriculum of study ; 2. That he has done so with attention and profit. The courses of lectures delivered by the public teachers will henceforward be the centre of the system. When the teacherships are filled by men of real knowledge, and who are imbued with the idea of science, the teacher will no longer condescend to be guided in what he shall say by an examination in prospect. The trade of the sophist will be gone when examination in fixed text-books is abolished.

It may be objected that this predominance of the chair over the examination schools, of the teacher over the examiner, may be attainable in the sciences properly so called, certainly in the experimental and progressive sciences, and possibly even in the deductive; but that it can never be attained in arts—*i.e.* in literature, where the book, the literary *chef d'œuvre*, is the object of study, and the expositor must necessarily be subordinate to the author. In the study of the classics, *e.g.*, chamber-study must always be not only indispensable, but superior to any courses of classical lectures. I shall be reminded of cases like that of Friedrich August Wolf, who found Heyne useless to him, and made himself what he became by shutting himself up in his lodgings and exhausting in solitude the contents of the Göttingen library.

It might be replied that Wolf did not forsake the lecture-room till he had learned much from Heyne; that he took care, after he had quarrelled with his teacher, to keep himself informed through his fellow-students, of all that was done in Heyne's classes; and that there was in his seclusion more bad temper than conviction of the inutility of oral teaching. But, apart from the merits of a single case, it must be admitted that the contemplation of literary beauty must always be chiefly a devotion of solitude. So far as literature enters into the curriculum— literature as distinct from philology—the class-room can do little; the man will mostly be less than the book. But this will be the case, I apprehend, in no other department. If, then, it shall appear that the cultivation of a literary taste ought no longer to be the central occupation of the academical student, and that the study of classical models should henceforth form only a subordinate part, instead of nearly the whole, of the business of a student in arts, the objection to a compulsory curriculum of public lecturing will lose its force.

Besides, the really objectionable part of compulsory attendance is to compel attendance on a given course, or a given teacher. It was this against which Adam Smith's censure was directed. When he stigmatised the privileges of graduation only to be obtained by attending certain lectures, as a "statute of apprenticeship," he was thinking of his Balliol experience, where, under the college system (1740), each student entered as the pupil of one tutor, from whom alone he was to derive all the instruction he got. This monstrous abuse, by which a university ceases in fact to be a university, still maintains, it must be remembered, a modified existence among us, inasmuch as the student is still a compelled attendant on the three or four tutors of the college of which he happens to be a member, and is not free to attend lectures in another college. Let this monopoly be destroyed; let the scholar be free to select his teachers, and we need not anticipate any difficulty in getting the candidates for honours to submit to a prescribed order of the subjects taught. If occasionally humour, or self-conceit, should lead to a contempt of methods and teachers, we may be confident that such cases will be exceptional ones. The fact that at present the student for honours neglects the professor's lecture-room for the private lessons of a tutor, only a few years his own senior, is an artificial necessity created by the present system of examination. Let the pressure of that system be removed, and the instincts of ingenuous love of knowledge and liberal curiosity will resume their sway; the student will seek to learn from those who know. Adam Smith says —

" Where the masters really perform their duty, there are no examples, I believe, that the greater part of the students ever neglect theirs. No discipline is ever requisite to force attendance upon lectures which are really worth the attending, as is well known whenever any such lectures are given. Force and restraint may, no doubt, be in some degree requisite, in order to oblige children or very young boys to attend to those parts of education which it is thought necessary for them to acquire during that early period of life; but after twelve or thirteen years of age, provided the master does his duty, force or restraint can scarce ever be necessary to carry on any part of education. Such is the generosity of the greater part of young men, that, so far from being disposed to neglect or despise the instructions of their master, provided he shows some serious intention of being of use to them, they are generally inclined to pardon a great deal of incorrectness in .the performance of his duty, and sometimes even to conceal from the public a good deal of gross negligence " (*Wealth of Nations*, v. 1).

These assertions may seem at first sight not borne out by our own experience of the university student; but we must remember that Adam Smith wrote from an experience of Oxford before the establishment of an examination compulsory on all. The divergence between his words and the facts with which we have to contend may perhaps afford a measure of the alienation from knowledge brought about by our compulsory system. The spectacle presented to Adam Smith was that of indolent, easy-going tutors, and neglected undergraduates willing to learn, but with no man to guide them. It is highly probable that it is an expression of his personal feelings. A fact recorded of him by M'Culloch, though not mentioned by his biographer Dugald Stewart, represents the authorities of Balliol as not merely neglectful of their pupil, but as seeking to check his aspirations after philosophy : — "Something had occurred, while Dr. Smith was at Oxford, to excite the suspicions of his superiors with regard to the nature of his private pursuits ; and the heads of his college having entered his apartment without his being aware, unluckily found him engaged reading Hume's *Treatise of Human Nature*. The objectionable work was, of course, seized ; the young philosopher being at the same time severely reprimanded " ("Life of Adam Smith," in M'Culloch's edition of *Wealth of Nations*, p. 2). Our experience presents us with the reverse picture : tutors zealous, diligent, inculcating industry, and spending their strength upon their pupils ; the pupils, on the other hand — seventy per cent of them — languid, uninterested, with their intellectual instincts and tastes not only undeveloped, but blunted by school grind, and overborne by a gladiatorial appetite for feats of the cricket-field. A compulsory attendance at lectures, when enforced for the sake of the purse, or the convenience, of the tutor, or for the purposes of discipline over the student, this compulsion was justly condemned by Adam Smith. But education is the being passed through a prescribed course, and subjected to a discipline. We not only may lay down such a course, but, if we offer education at all, we *must* do so. It is a

S

chief business of the university to lay down correct lines of study, to indicate the high road of education among the innumerable cross-roads and by-paths of learning; from the vast mass of all that may be learned and may be taught, to select what should be taught and learned. As, on its scientific side, the university is to be the cultivator of real learning and productive science, as distinguished from the pedantries of erudition, or the vain subtleties of a metaphysical philosophy, so, on its elementary side, it is to offer a systematic course of initiatory study, which shall be the result of all the experience of the past, of the long educational experiment which has been going on ever since reason and intelligence began to be objects of cultivation.

The existing system of Oxford education, regarded in its principle, is an attempt at an adjustment between two conflicting claims. I speak here of the honour-courses, which alone come within the range of the higher education, or deserve consideration in a discussion on university training. The conflict of claim is that between the special and the general. Every man has either to earn his bread, or at least to fulfil his functiom in life, through and in a profession or calling, and for this purpose he requires the special knowledge and accomplishment proper to that calling. Every man is also a member of civil society, a participant in a common humanity, is a soul or mind capable of a development or perfection of its own, and for this purpose he may be the subject of a general or humane training and accomplishment. Every one of us is, consciously or unconsciously, working out this double problem, to combine specialty of function with generality of culture. Different times and countries have formed different estimates of the value of these two elements of life respectively. These different estimates immediately influence the conduct of the higher education. At one time it will tend towards becoming wholly liberal and propædeutic, at another it will be absorbed in the acquisition of the details of knowledge for practical application.

In the last generation—*i.e.* thirty years ago, to go no further back—the Oxford curriculum was wholly liberal. Professional knowledge, whether for the three learned professions or for any other, could not be had at the university. We continued, nevertheless, to bestow the insignia of accomplishment in divinity, law, and physic, but we made no attempt to teach a knowledge of them. The titles of D.D., D.C.L., and M.D., were, in fact, sold at a fixed price by the university, for the benefit of its exchequer, to any one who thought them worth purchasing. But no instruction was given here except in the faculty of arts. Arts were not treated as a faculty co-ordinate with the other three, immersed in a special investigation, and issuing in a separate pursuit; they had come to be considered as entirely disciplinal. A good deal of energy, though blind and ill directed, was expended upon the three (or four) years over which this course was spread. Looking back upon that course at a distance of thirty years, those who passed through it know that it was not inoperative. It was, on the contrary, a powerful agent in stimulating the mind to grapple with difficulties. It was not truly, what it claimed to be, liberalising. It was too often productive of a narrow self complacency, a supercilious disdain of all that lay outside its own sphere—*i.e.* of the whole circle of real knowledge. But the old double-first, with its merits and defects, is now a thing of the past. It is only cited here as exhibiting an education which attempted to liberalise without instructing, to form without informing. The Oxford first-classman of that day was received by the outside public and by the scientific world with mixed feelings. They submitted to the prestige of his honours, were irritated by his presumption, and astonished at his ignorance. This latter soon became the point of attack upon the system. After a long struggle with opinion we had to give way. In 1850 two new schools—that of law and history and that of physical science—succeeded in establishing themselves, but in a subordinate position to the school of classics. Fifteen years more (1865), and the new schools had thrust aside the once supreme classics, and become alone a qualification for the degree. Classics may now be dropped entirely at moderations.

This is the adjustment between the general and the special which was spoken of above. Up to 1865, for more than three centuries, Oxford education had been wholly general, preparatory, formative. In 1865 half the university career was surrendered to special studies. General education may, if the student so chooses, terminate in his second year of residence. The remainder of his time he may devote to the acquisition of real knowledge. We have compromised with public opinion, which charged, not untruly, the Oxford model man with being an ignoramus, by offering to confer the Oxford stamp in half the time, and to give up the remaining half to special studies.

Whether public opinion in this country will be satisfied with the concessions it has extorted from us I cannot pretend to say. But I am sure that we ourselves shall not long rest content with the clumsy adjustment of the problem which we patched up two years ago. We have made a breach in the system of education through the " classics " which was introduced by the Rénaissance. We must prepare ourselves to abandon that system altogether. The steps which we have already taken are, I venture to think, steps in a right direction, but to make them safe we must go on. Our present arrangement can only be regarded as transitional—can only be satisfactory to those who consider them as a halt or stage to break the shock of revolution.

What is meant by saying that the steps have been in a right direction is, that the recognition of special studies as qualification for *a* degree is in conformity with the true principle of university education. I believe that a different view is current among English university men, and has the sanction of great names. To mention only three— Schleiermacher, Dr. Whewell, and Dr. Newman, representative men of their respective universities, seem to inculcate that the function of the university is disciplinal and formative only, and that special study belongs to a later time, and not to the period of education. They may not agree as to the fittest medium of such liberal education— Schleiermacher holding it to be modern philosophy, Dr. Whewell language and mathematics, and Dr. Newman (if I understand him rightly) classical literature; but they seem agreed upon the principle of general training (Schlei-ermacher, *Gedanken über Universitäten, Werke*, i. 561, etc.; Whewell, *Principles*, etc., 2d ed. p. 37, etc.; Newman, *Discourses on University Education:* Dublin, 1852). On the other hand, the German university exhibits a system in

which the university course is almost wholly special; the
liberal and própædeutic studies are relegated to the grammar-school.   I think the arrangement to which circumstances have driven us in Oxford to be in principle much
nearer the truth.   That is, we have opened the way for the
division of the university curriculum into two stages.   We
assign, *v.g.*, the first year and a half, or three semesters, to
complete and carry further the general training begun at
school, and then allow the student to transfer himself to the
professional study of some one of several distinct branches
proposed to him.

The vindication of the principle that the end and aim
of the highest education must be the exclusive devotion of
the mind to some one branch of science, cannot be
attempted here.   Such a vindication involves both a discussion of our mental constitution, and a survey of the
history of universities, either of which are much beyond
my present limits.   No one will dispute that, in the
development of the mind, there comes an epoch where a
discursive ranging from province to province of information must give way to the inverse process of concentrating
the energies of the intellect in undivided intensity upon
some one object.   The necessity for so doing is forced
upon most men by the external pressure of a profession.
Even to the favoured few whom fortune may have raised
above such compulsion from without, the conviction is soon
brought home by experience, that if they would know anything as it can be known, they must restrain their investigations to narrow limits.   The division of labour is the
law of mental, no less than of manufacturing, production.
" In every instance of genuine originality, a powerful

mental bias in the direction of some one particular subject never fails to manifest itself along with that activity of the reasoning faculties which constitutes the essential characteristic of intellectual maturity. The most marked peculiarity in the practical education of manhood, when compared with that of an earlier period, is perceived in the fact of its being accomplished by means of specific and definite studies, instead of mere generalities " (Kirkpatrick, *Conception of the University,* p. 72). That this change in the direction of the mental powers takes place in life must be admitted as a fact. The only point that can be questioned is, Ought this change to be postponed till after education is finished ? Can the higher education be completed by general processes ? Can intellect be fully formed by formal discipline without special knowledge ?

The old university system, from the twelfth to the sixteenth century, answered this question in the negative. The practice of Oxford, for the last three centuries, since the introduction of the classics as the instrument of education, has been founded on the opposite theory. It is essential to the revival of the university that it should recur to the older system. The principle of the old university system was a combination of the general and the special. The Faculty of Arts was not a faculty coordinate with those of divinity, law, and medicine, but was a course of study introductory to them. It was disciplinal, not scientific ; a means, not an end ; incomplete until carried out into one of the faculties. No one could commence student in any of the three faculties till he had taken the degree of M. A. The university is " founded in arts," was the old dictum ; and, historically, the other

faculties came into being subsequently to that of arts, out
of which they were developed. As the faculties grew out
of arts, so the colleges grew out of the faculties; for a
main object of founders of colleges was to provide the
means for poor regent masters to " continue " (continuare)
or go on residing as students of one of the higher faculties.
Hence the usual condition of a fellowship in the older
foundations was the proceeding within a time fixed to the
degree of Doctor. The prolonged term required for the
faculty studies necessitated a provision for the student
during the process.

The proposal made in the first part of these " Suggestions," for the application of the college endowments, was
in fact a proposal for the revival of faculty, or special,
studies. The proposal provides for a permanent, or at
least a continued, residence in the university of the recipient
of the benefaction. It was therefore only a provision for
after-studies, and not for education properly so called.
Besides, the number of persons who could be employed as
professor-fellows must be small — insignificant in comparison with the whole number of those who would be
candidates for a degree. The principle I am now
contending for goes further still in the direction of
specialising study. I am contending for the introduction
of definite, or faculty, studies at an earlier period of the
curriculum, and for all students — not for those only who
become recipients of endowed funds. Here it may be
objected that this is by no means the old university system,
for that system gave seven years to the preliminary course
in arts, before the faculty studies could be commenced;
while what is now proposed is to begin, and, for the mass

of students, to complete, the special studies within the three years.

It might be sufficient to answer, that, of the septennium required for the arts degree in the old system the greater portion is now spent at school. The modern student does, in fact, give a greater, and not a less, time to general studies. For the B.A., which now terminates general education, is seldom taken before twenty-two, while it is probable that twenty-one, or earlier still, was formerly the usual age for the attainment of the M.A. But it will be understood that, in appealing to ancient precedent, nothing is further from my purpose than a mere restoration of the old for restoration's sake. That a practice was in force in the thirteenth century, forms no reason at all for recommending its adoption now. The necessity for founding the higher education on faculty studies lies in the reason of the thing, and not in the weight of authority or force of precedent. The higher education must be thorough; it must take hold of the highest mental faculty, and form and develop it. This faculty is the scientific reason in its perfect form. The higher education must not quit its hold of the individual; nay, cannot be said to have taken hold of him, till it has developed in him the scientific habit. The imagination and the taste; the employment and discernment of language; the perception of beauty by the eye; to speak, to write, to argue, to reason;—all these are capacities or accomplishments to be improved, or formed by education at some period. But all these, beautiful as adjuncts, form only a superficial mental character, if the great work of education, the establishment of an exact habit of judgment, of the philosophical intellect, has not been achieved. The acquisition of this habit cannot be made through generalities, or through literature, or by promiscuous reading. Still less is the scientific habit generated by the pantological schemes now so much in favour, which those who are their dupes describe as " an adequate acquaintance with the fundamental principles of all the principal departments of science." It can only be educed by setting the understanding to investigate for itself the laws of some one chief department of knowledge, or division of objects. It is not the matters known that make science, but the mode of knowing. Popular language, which identifies science with physical science, creates much confusion in discussions on education. Anything whatever may be studied in a scientific spirit—*i.e.* with a determination to know it exhaustively in its causes and mutations. " Science is nothing but trained and organised common sense; and its vast results are won by no other mental process than those which are practised by every individual in the humblest and commonest affairs of life. The man of science simply uses with scrupulous exactness the methods which we all habitually, and at every moment, use carelessly " (*Westminster Review*, April 1861, article by Mr. Herbert Spencer). Hence no reception of truths as dicta on authority is science to the recipient; and a man may be " acquainted " with the principles of all the sciences without having had a scientific education.

Any object-matter constituting a distinct division of existences may become the object of scientific investigation. But it is obvious that, not every such division of things that can be known is equally fitted for selection as an educational instrument. We cannot wholly neglect the results of knowledge in our selection. The special destiny of the subject of the education in his after-life must usually determine the character of the theoretical study to which he will attach himself. The higher education, as the portal through which the boy is to enter upon the duties of the man, must conform in its arrangements to those of the social system to which he belongs. Even the higher education, great as is the prerogative claimed for it, is not sovereign over life; it must adapt itself to the requirements of daily existence.

" An institution," says Mr. Kirkpatrick, " which stakes its whole credit and power in society upon refinement and intelligence, not evinced in any one particular form of efficiency, will inevitably disappear more and more from connection with a world of flesh and blood into a kindred cloud-land of unrealities and abstractions." Hence, in drawing up a curriculum for a university, or fixing the subjects to be studied, we must not be guided by the philosophical chart of human knowledge, absolutely viewed, but by the bearings of knowledge upon life. The old division into the three faculties of divinity, law, and physic, was a rude classification adapted to a simple state of society. It was true in principle. Our more complicated social system demands many more subdivisions of the university course, corresponding to the main lines of practical life as now open to the ambition of every Englishman. The church, the bar, and medicine ought no longer to be treated as peculiarly " the learned professions." There is no reason why every class of vocation in which intelligence and refinement are applicable, and in which a career of prosperity is opened to the practitioner, should not have a corresponding " Faculty" arranged for it in the university, where an appropriate training—not practical and professional, but theoretical and scientific—might be had. Why should commerce and industry choose to remain under the stigma which the feudal system branded upon them, as base employments, which necessarily excluded from the education which was reserved for the territorial seigneur and the cleric?

The London University now gives degrees in science (since 1858), in addition to those in arts, laws, and medicine. The title is an absurdity. A degree in " science," which is no science in particular, is not an intelligible mark or designation. But the thing intended to be done is good, and the example ought to be followed by us. What the re-arrangement of the faculties should be, and of the schools and courses leading up to their respective degrees, is matter which will require profound deliberation by special committees. Nor can it well be arranged by ourselves without the advice and co-operation of the Inns of Court, the Medical Council, the Heads of the Government Offices, and other chief interests and occupations, which will in future come in for their share of liberal training.

It will easily be understood that the degree in each of these schools, seeing it is to be obtainable at the end of three or three and a half years, cannot imply any profound and exhaustive knowledge. Such a knowledge is not to be looked for till a later stage, and from those graduates who will continue in the university as teachers, public or private, with the view of becoming candidates for a lecturer's place (fellow-lecturer) in their faculty. For the

degree, we may adopt the words of the earliest examination statute (1800) : " Nihil triste aut asperum molimur.
Lenitati ubique consultum volumus, modo ne ea sit, quæ
juniorum socordiæ patrocinari videatur " (*Add. Statutt.*
tit. ix. sec. ii. § 2, 1800). The class-list will not be more
exclusive than it is at present. Indeed, with the enlarged
choice of schools which will be offered, the various lists
may be well expected to comprehend together a much
larger total of names. The stimulus to be given by academical reform is to be looked to, to add to the numbers
of honour-students, not to screw up their exertions to an
unnatural pitch. The efforts made at present by the best
average students are probably as severe a strain as can
safely be put upon the nervous energies at their time of
life. The arrangement now proposed has in view to give
a better direction to their studies, not to intensify the
severity of the test. The examinations to be held in the
new final schools, and the character of the preparatory
study, will hold a place midway between the vague rhetorical philosophising at present in vogue in the school of
Literæ Humaniores on the one hand, and merely technical
and professional acquirement on the other. The faculty-
student is not to be expected at twenty-two to have
exhausted his subject; but he may have been initiated into
an exhaustive method of learning it. He will not have
become an accomplished philologer or a thorough phy-
siologist; but he will have learned, by and through
philology or physiology, what it is to know anything. He
will have seen that " the highest excellence—and no lower
object can be proposed by him who is destined to accomplish what is even creditable—is alone to be attained by

one who does not disperse, but gathers his powers of perceptions into a piercing intensity and singleness of view, enabling him to reach beyond the facile and commonplace into the dim and distant region of the undiscovered. The law of genial precognition in the subject is in the highest degree analogous with that of life and beauty in the object. Intensest unity is the soul of contemplation and ideal action, no less than of creative organisation " (*Kirkpatrick*, p. 75).

4.—*Faculty of Arts—Honour Examinations.*

It remains to determine in what relation these faculty-studies, and the degrees which terminate them, are to stand to the Faculty of Arts. Is the whole university course of three or three and a half years to be confined to the special faculty selected by each student to graduate in ? Or is the first portion of residence to be assigned to a course of general and preliminary studies common to all alike ? Do the conditions of the modern university require the recognition of a faculty of arts ? and, if so, what are the " arts " that should be studied in the faculty ?

Turning to our existing practice, we find the arts degree in a quite anomalous state. Three schools stand side by side with the old school of Literæ Humaniores—viz. the mathematical, the physical, the law and modern history. In these three schools the studies are special—so special as, in the physical and law schools (at least), to be of the nature of faculty - studies. In the school of Literæ Humaniores, on the other hand, the studies are general, liberal, introductory to knowledge. Yet, by the present statute, the degree of M.A. is given indifferently to the successful candidates for honours in all these schools. It is not that it designates equal proficiencies in distant subject - matters, which might be tolerable; but it is awarded indiscriminately as the title earned by a course of special, or by one of general, study. It would be more intelligible, as well as more conformable to usage, that the faculty degrees should bear each their proper name, and that the term " arts " should remain restricted to that course common to all the students before they have diverged into their several faculties. This common course of study is at present represented by the moderation and final school of Literæ Humaniores. For pure mathematics are so little followed in Oxford, that the mathematical honour course may be thrown out of the account in describing our existing practice.

The arts course then is at present entirely governed by the two schools—Moderation Classics, and the final school of Literæ Humaniores. Rather the student's whole time is taken up in preparing himself for these two examinations, under the guidance of his college-tutor; for the university knows nothing of any course or " curriculum " of study. Under this guidance the honour-student usually confines himself, for the first year and a half of residence, to what is known in Oxford as " scholarship." In this process he perfects and brings to a head all that he has been six or eight years preparing at school. He extends his classical reading, but in the same direction; the only addition to the school circle of study being the elements of logic. So far his training is wholly " formal," and almost wholly verbal. No real knowledge is acquired. But the formal education of the memory, imagination, reasoning, and analytical powers, is well sustained and carried out. After moderations—*i.e.* at the end of one and a half or two years of residence—the student in classics enters for the first time upon forms of thought which are new to him. He prepares philosophy and history for the final examination. A perusal of the statute, or of the directions printed in the Oxford Calendar for the use of students, will convey a very imperfect idea of what is required in this school. For the classical authors there specified form in fact but a portion of the matters examined upon. The questions set have of late years ranged over a limitless field of logical, metaphysical, moral, and political speculation. Language is here subordinated, but not dropped. For though the Greek language no longer, after moderations, forms itself one of the direct objects of study, yet passages of Greek and Latin, set for translation into English, constitute an important item in success, and a large part of the learner's time is occupied in preparing what he calls " the text " of the books out of which these passages are taken.

It is, as has been already said, difficult or impossible for one who is himself of Oxford to offer any general valuation of the results of this " curriculum." Any such estimate would require to be based on a wide acquaintance with men of every variety of class and training in more countries than our own. Without invidious comparison with other systems, one cannot fail to recognise in the type of character and understanding resulting from our training many valuable qualities, and an emancipation from some of the more common intellectual defects. Our system is not inoperative or feeble. It takes a powerful hold, and moulds the man towards a fine ideal.

It may be said, How can one who so thinks desire change? Is not, to grant so much as I have granted, to preclude all proposals for reform of the studies preliminary to a degree? If we are doing such good work, is it not better to leave well alone, to persevere in a course which is already so satisfactory?

The answer to this is that I do not desire to overthrow, but to improve. He is an "unprofitable servant" who is content to do well where he sees his way to do better: τὸ ἐμὸν σὺν τόκῳ. We have greatly improved the character of the work done here in the last thirty years; but that is all the more reason for desiring to carry those improvements further. "The old English universities," Mr. Mill admits, "in the present generation, are doing better work than they have done within human memory in teaching the ordinary studies of their curriculum" (*Inaugural Address at St. Andrews,* p. 40). This is high approbation from a quarter certainly not prejudiced in our favour, but we cannot sit down and fold our arms, satisfied with having earned it.

The principle of the improvement which appears to me possible in our system of studies is that of specialisation. The latter and larger half of the whole time of residence should be set apart for "scientific" study. This term is employed, as already explained, for want of another, in the wide sense of the German "*wissenschaftlich.*" Any of the great departments of human knowledge may be scientifically studied, when studied thoroughly in its laws and their developments. Professor A. de Morgan has given an excellent exposition of this idea. He says—

"In looking over the various branches of human inquiry, I do not find that what is learned in a second period is merely

T

a certain portion added to that which was acquired in the first. If I were to teach geometry for two months, I conceive that the geometry of the second month would not merely double the amount which the student gained in the first, but would be, as it were, a new study, showing other features, and giving additional powers, with the advantage of its being evident that the second step is the development and consequence of the first. Suppose that, instead of employing the second month in geometry, I had turned the attention of the student to algebra, would he have been a gainer by the change? I answer confidently in the negative.

" To carry this further, let us take the whole career of the learner, and apply the same argument. There is in every branch of knowledge a beginning, a middle, and an end. A beginning, in which the student is striving with new and difficult principles, and in which he is relying in a great measure on the authority of his instructor; a middle, in which he has gained some confidence in his own knowledge, and some power of applying his first principles. He is now in a state of danger, so far as the estimate which he is likely to form of himself is concerned. He has as yet no reason to suppose. that his career can be checked—nothing to humble the high notion which he will entertain of himself, his teachers, and his subject. Let him only proceed, and he will come to what I have called the end of the subject, and will begin to see that there is, if not a boundary, yet the commencement of a region which has not been tracked and surveyed, and in which not all the skill which he has acquired in voyaging by the chart will save him from losing his way. It is at this period of his career that he will begin to form a true opinion of his own mind, which is not done by many persons, simply because they have never been allowed to pursue any branch of inquiry to the extent which is necessary to show them where their power ends.

" For this reason I think that, whatever else may be done, some one subject at least should be well and thoroughly investigated, for the sake of giving the proper tone to the mind upon the use, province, and extent of knowledge in general. . . . There should be in every liberal education at least one subject thoroughly studied. What the subject should be is comparatively of minor importance " (*Lecture at University College, London, in App. to Modern Culture*, p. 388).

The dispute between science *versus* classics in education will not be settled on paper or by discussion. It will be settled, in fact, by the establishment, somewhere or other, and in some form or other, of a system of scientific education, the results of which will vindicate themselves. We may argue, and vested interests may resist, but the tendency of things is unmistakable—the sciences will end by conquering their place. It is, however, probable that the struggle will be a long one. I would gladly see, but can hardly hope to see, our own university, instead of being dragged ignominiously in the wake of practical opinion on this question, come forward, and, on grounds of theory, at once restore to science that place in our curriculum which of right belongs to it. For the instincts of the practical men are sufficient to make them right in their aim, though, when they come to argue their case, they lay themselves open to easy refutation by the defenders of the existing system. The form in which the claims of science to a place in the higher education are presented is too often that of " an acquaintance" (I believe that is the word) " with the fundamental principles of all the principal departments of science,"—science being in the mouths of most of the " scientific men," identified with inductive science, or with that portion of the sciences which are at present in the inductive stage. If this were only the ideal of the popular lecturer on the question of " science," we might afford to pass it without notice. But it would almost seem that no other idea of scientific education is entertained even by our greatest men. It is with the utmost dismay, and consternation that I read the following, endorsed by a name which I cannot write without an expression of the homage of profound veneration. Sir John Herschel, consulted about a scheme of instruction for a South African college, wrote as follows:—

" A good practical system of public education ought, in my opinion, to be more real than formal—I mean should convey as much of positive knowledge, with as little attention to mere systems and conventional forms, as is consistent with avoiding solecisms. This principle carried into detail would allow much less weight to the study of the languages than is usually considered its due in our great public schools, where the acquisition of the latter seems to be regarded as the one and only object of education ; while, on the other hand, it would attach great importance to all those branches of practical and theoretical knowledge whose possession goes to constitute an idea of a well-informed gentleman—as, for example, a knowledge of the nature and constitution of the world we inhabit ; its animal, vegetable, and mineral productions, and their uses and properties as subservient to human wants ; its relation to the system of the universe, and its natural and political subdivisions ; the constructions of human society, including our responsibilities to individuals, and to the social body of which we are members. In a word, as extensive a knowledge as can be grasped and conveyed in an elementary course, of the actual system and the laws of nature, both physical and moral" (Sir John Herschel, ap. *Modern Culture*, p. 365).

The London University has actually established an examination which covers " as extensive a knowledge as can be conveyed in an elementary course of the laws of nature "—viz. its examination for the degree of B.Sc. The error, however, committed at this stage, is redeemed at the next, and to some extent cured; the examination given, or proposed to be given, for the degree of Doctor in Science, implying a thorough and scientific study of one branch—a course of mental effort capable of conferring not merely knowledge but training. Thus the examinations for B.Sc. may be regarded as a "preliminary examination," determining who shall be admitted to the final trial, and, like all other "preliminaries," doing no other harm than wasting a certain amount of time in cramming for it, while it has no influence on the vital part of the process of culture (Appendix E).

If, indeed, our choice lay between an education which aimed at a little encyclopædia of elementary "knowledge" of as many branches of natural law as possible, on the one hand, or, on the other, the fearful waste of time and labour which is involved in the system of Latin and Greek grammar, it might be not unreasonable to choose the first, as the least of two evils. Real knowledge is always respectable, and may be useful; it is, at any rate, truth. But out of the barrack grammar-school are turned—in the proportion, it would seem, of 70 per cent of the whole—youths who have neither acquired the languages they have spent six or eight years in learning, nor any other knowledge; but who *have* acquired the mental habits which render them for ever incapable of learning anything, their senses of observation dulled, their curiosity extinguished, and a secret antipathy generated for all mental exertion. But though, in our recoil from the evil of the school-barrack, artificially maintained by examinations, scholarships, and prizes, we might fall back upon the pantological schemes of "extensive information" which are so popular on the platform and in the press, when we sit down calmly to consider academical organisation, we must reject any such "impotent attempt at polymathia" as not being within the scope of a university which is to exhibit the most perfect scheme of intellectual training known to its age.

Whatever may be the ultimate direction given to school training in this country, it may be assumed that, for the present, it will remain classical. I believe no prudent advocate of scientific instruction urges a revolutionary transfer of the school system from the Greek and Latin basis. We must accept it as a fact that liberal or preparatory training is to continue classical. The question, then, is, Is entrance at the university to be the point where the transition is made from the general to the special? Is liberal education to end at school, and scientific study to commence at the university? This is the system which has come to prevail in Germany. There, general education is conducted wholly at the gymnasium, and is terminated by the *Abiturienten examen.* On his arrival at the university, the student, from the first moment, considers himself as dedicated to a *Fach* —*i.e.* some special province of research, often, indeed, in a very limited field, and always much narrower than that of the faculty in which he matriculates. We in England think we see in the German practice evils directly traceable to a premature discontinuance of liberal training. At any rate, in retreating from our own usage hitherto, that of making the whole university course, throughout its entire length, "general," we ought not to rush into the opposite extreme.

Moderations afford a boundary ready to our hand. Let school exercises—*i.e.* general education—terminate at Moderations. Let this examination be placed at the end of the first year from matriculation. That passed, let the student declare his faculty, and commence his special, or scientific, studies. These are to be according to a prescribed curriculum, for each faculty separately, to be spread over two years and terminated by the degree.

I have more than once already explained the sense in which the word "scientific" is here used. In this sense the studies in all the faculties, and not in that of science only, may be scientific. Distinctly so in the Faculty of Arts. This will lose its general and preliminary character, and, in its two branches of "Philology" and "Classics," will become scientific. The remains of classical antiquity have by no means yet ceased to offer the material of fruitful inquiry to the nations of modern Europe. It is possible that, in individual instances, these inquiries may have degenerated into frivolous pedantry and unprofitable antiquarianism. But, in spite of occasional abuse, to penetrate into the mind and character of the Romans and the Greeks, to understand their institutions and interpret their modes of thought, will long remain one of the most fruitful fields of real knowledge. Only on this condition—viz. that it has itself intrinsic value as a material to be explored by men— can classical literature continue to be employed as a medium of the higher education of youth.

At Moderations, then—that is, at the end of his first year—the "Arts" student will discontinue his school training. Moderations would become purely a test of "scholarship," and not a mixed test of reading and scholarship in

an indefinite combination. The final examination in the
two alternative schools of the Arts Faculty—the philological and the classical—would be purely a test of scientific
study, and not a mixed test of reading, plus an uncertain
quantity of scholarship, as at present. An entire separation
between an earlier and a later stage seems more reasonable
than the attempt to carry on two distinct kinds of training
together, through the whole curriculum. And the last two
years of residence are too short, and too valuable, to admit
of the vast expenditure of time and labour required to keep
up the school facility in "composition." The dispute between scholarship and learning, between skill (*Können*) and
science (*Wissen*), between faculty and knowledge, would
thus be arranged, and the vexed question of the value of
" Latin composition " simplified.

I would gladly have avoided this question, as it is one
on which recent discussion has exhausted all that can be
said, as well as the patience of all scholastic men. But a
review of the studies preliminary to the degree would be
incomplete without facing the inquiry, What place in the
university course is to be given to Latin and Greek composition? To exclude it from the final examination, and
to confine it to Moderations and the first year, will hardly
be considered a sufficient concession by the advocates of
realist education. Their main argument—viz. the waste of
time occasioned by the practice in schools—is not broken
by this concession. That the time and labour of a majority
of schoolboys *is* wasted by the practice, it seems to me impossible to deny. Surely it can only be a profitable exercise to that minority who carry it far enough to become an

instrument of intellectual mastery over the language, and appropriation of finished forms of thought. On the other hand, schoolmasters and tutors cannot be controverted when they affirm that, without the exercise of at least writing it (if not speaking), a language and its literature cannot be thoroughly understood and enjoyed, and consequently cannot serve as an instrument of culture. If these two positions of the contending parties are both true, it follows that the dispute about the maintenance of the practice of composition in schools and the junior classes in our lecture-rooms, is really a dispute as to the maintenance of classical studies as the common instrument of a liberal education. If classical literature is to continue to be this instrument, it involves the necessary maintenance of classical composition. If other and better subjects of study claim the time now given to Latin composition, it follows, not only that composition should be disused, but also that Latin and Greek must be given up. To abolish, in a school, Latin writing, and divert the time to the acquisition, *e.g.*, of some useful knowledge, is merely to add an imperfect training by science to an imperfect training by literature, in the expectation that two faulty halves will make together a perfect whole.

The true and ultimate solution of the difficulty appears to be the extension to our schools of the system of bifurcation. In other words, schools will have to be separated, as to their higher classes, into two divisions—the Grammar side and the Real side. The changes which are going on in the university, and which will have to be carried much further in the same direction—viz. that of specialising study—will force some system of bifurcation upon the school course. But this is beyond the scope of these " Suggestions." As long as classics form in fact the staple of general education in the schools throughout the country, the university, which is itself to take up and to continue general education for the first year of residence, must employ *all* the tests of scholarship. And among these tests, " composition," by common consent, occupies a foremost place.

We must even, I venture to think, go further. It is not enough that we retain composition as a test of knowledge of the language. The set that has been made for some time past against Latin composition, by the realists, has had an insensible influence upon us. We maintain the practice in our schools, it is true, but that is all. The pressure upon us has been so great that we have pared down our standard of attainment. Latin writing is kept up, but it is by no means the efficient instrument of training that it once was. Pains are taken, perhaps greater skill and knowledge than ever are brought to bear, upon our writing Latin which shall be free from grammatical faults. The exercise thus answers its purpose fully as a test of grammatical proficiency. It is a grammar exercise. But the higher arts implied in the word composition are comparatively neglected. Not only beauty of style and expression, but the art of presenting our meaning, and putting together the parts of a discourse, are hardly at all cared for. We have retained the " Latin writing" which was introduced into the schools in the sixteenth century, but we no longer use the exercise for the purposes for which they employed it. The " Rhetoric" class was the next step above the grammar-school, and occupied the first year of the quadriennium, or as we should say, of residence. In it the exercises were not merely grammatical, but involved the practice of composition in all its parts. Thus the time expended on Latin composition by our forefathers was given not merely to an accurate acquisition of the language, but reached far beyond this into the region of æsthetic construction. It was the mode in which they aspired after and appropriated beauty of form, and cultivated that literary taste which never died out in the universities, even at the time when philological knowledge was at its lowest. It was the sudden revival of a sense for this perfection of form in classical literature which constituted the *Rénaissance.* It was not the discovery of the MSS. which created the sense. The converse was the case : the sense and the aspiration led to the disinterment and multiplication by copies of the MSS. The cultivation of literary beauty was soon, by the efforts of the enlightened minority, introduced into education as an integral part of the university course. The Jesuits followed the same system in their schools. From the sixteenth-century curriculum, accordingly, we have inherited "Latin writing." But our Latin writing, with all its scrupulous correctness, seems to be losing its attractions and its efficacy as an exercise in artistic production, and sinking to the level of a grammatical test.

There are other causes for this insensible change. But one cause, probably, is to be found in examinations. The grammar-test may be applied to a written exercise immediately and unhesitatingly. Every candidate can be required in three hours to translate a short passage of English adequately and correctly. But it is absurd to expect a literary composition, which shall have merit as a work of polish, to be produced in the same time. Such merits too, where they exist, require an expert eye in the judge, while a grammatical solecism speaks for itself.

I would not speak with discourtesy even of the plat-form-orator, who declaims against " Latin verses" from a one-sided point of view. With the realist movement in education I heartily sympathise; and its victory is certain. Our courses of instruction are becoming constantly more and more scientific. But there is a time for all things. School is one thing, the university is another. This distinction we seem to have almost forgotten. If the university has got too much into the way of doing over again the work of the school, the school has invaded the province of the university. Exercises are giving way to philological lessons. Colleges encourage this by setting papers on " Philology" to candidates for scholarships, and a considerable amount of such knowledge is often displayed on these occasions by schoolboys. In this error we are imitating that Germany, from which we are so reluctant to learn when we might learn with advantage. The rector of a gymnasium, who is often a deeply-read and scientific scholar, sometimes yields to the temptation to prælect to his boys, as if they were students, upon some abstruse point of philology which is interesting himself. And, generally speaking, the instruction given in the higher classes of the gymnasia is carried on in too academical a manner. This mistake, however, has attracted attention, and is in course of being checked in Germany, just as we are beginning to fall into it. We are underrating and letting slip that one feature in our grammar-school system, which the German theoretical *Pädagogik* has stamped with its approval, and which practical schoolmen in Germany would wish to naturalise at home. We are slowly imbibing from the example of German universities a habit of scientific examination of the material contents of classical literature. Are we not, in the process, in danger of throwing away a discipline of which the German schools envy us the possessiòn ?

We are re-reading the classics in the university, as we have never read them before, in the light of German philology. That is *our* business in the *university*. But the business of the *school* is something quite different. The appropriation and mastery of verbal expression, from the earliest efforts of the infant to the crowning achievement of the consummate orator, is to be attained not by the study of rules but by practice. Exercise, practice, *Uebung*—the constant effort to express with neatness, precision, and elegance what we have to express—is the only road to the language faculty. The constructive and imitative stage of education in language-training must precede the analytic stage of linguistic science. In cutting down, as we have done, in submission to the press and platform demagogues, our " composition" in our grammar-schools to the minimum which tests grammatical correctness, and filling its place with knowledge about language, we have been going counter to the natural law on which education in language is founded. Grimm long ago (Pref. to *Deutsche Grammatik*, 1st ed., 1819) denounced the teaching of German grammar in schools as a preposterous mode of learning the mother-tongue. But it is no new discovery of modern psychology. I cannot deny myself the pleasure of placing before the reader, in the original, some fine sentences of a scholar of the last century. Facciolati says :—

" Quod si ardentessimæ illi proficiendi voluntati aliquando respondisset ingenium—ut certe nunquam respondit ; nec vos hoc tempore plebeio dicendi genere molestissime detinerem, nec ullus esset hac ætate latinus orator cui de orationis nitore, numero, perspicuitate, ullo pacto concederem. Nunc vero in magna virium infirmitate si quid valeo, qui valeo sane minimum, totum Ciceroni, Terentio, Livio, Cæsari, Virgilio, Horatio, cæterisque ejus ætatis scriptoribus elegantissimis debeo. Nihil a me repetundarum jure postulet Priscianus, nihil Donatus vindicet, nihil Valla, nihil Sanctius, nihil ille ipse, deliciæ quondam nostræ, Alvarus — quos omnes una cum crepundiis vel abjeci, vel deposui. Excidere jamdiu animo eorum monita, excidere leges, nihilque mihi potest ad stilum retardandum contingere infestius, quam tristis quædam eorum recordatio ac metus, unde solent arida omnia, sicca, exsanguia proficisci. Quid est enim aliud grammatice loqui, quam omnino latine non loqui, si credimus præceptori maximo Quintiliano ? (*Instit.* i. i. 6). Nam ut omnia grammatici vere dicant, utrum aliud efficiunt, nisi ut sine barbarismis, sine solæcismis sit oratio ? In quo si tota laus consistit latinitatis, jam ne ipse quidem Cicero latinus est, cujus libri, si ad grammaticorum cavillationes exigantur, solæcismis non carent."

On the conditions, then, that Latin exercising be confined to that select class of boys who show a decided aptitude for language, that it be cultivated far enough to become a rhetorical, and not merely a grammatical, exercise, and that Greek composition be not attempted at all, or be confined to a still more select circle, it seems to me that such exercise must constitute an integral and valuable part of school training. The same exercises will be continued in the university up to Moderations. But the demands of " scholarship" must be satisfied with Moderation honours— the Ireland, the Hertford, and the composition prizes. All the foundation scholarships which shall be appropriated to the Faculty of Arts will also be decided by the scholarship test. But the qualification for the degree in the classical (and of course in the philological) school, and the two years' curriculum after Moderations, must be science, not skill, if "Arts" is to rank on a par with the other degrees, and if classical study is to be a pursuit for a man, and the aditus to a special profession.

As I would remove logic and philology from Moderations, and make that examination an examination purely in scholarship, I would make the final examination for a degree in the Arts Faculty wholly scientific.

The final examination in the school of Literæ Humaniores, as it at present exists, is the heart and life of our system. It is that upon which we have bestowed most pains, and which we have wrought out to a perfection which makes it confessedly a powerful intellectual stimulus. It may be that it is rash to tamper with what works so well. It is impossible, however, not to be aware that that examination, and the curriculum which leads up to it, are open to serious objection on grounds of educational theory.

It is impossible to convey to a stranger—to a German university man, *e.g.*—an idea of what it is that is exacted, ascertained, or tested by our classical examiners. Such an idea cannot be collected from the words of the statute which prescribe the "matter of the examination" (De materie examinationis secundæ). The statute (vi. 2, § 8) enacts as follows :—

" The *Literæ Humaniores*, for the purposes of this school, we define as, in addition to the Greek and Latin languages, the histories of Greece and Rome, with those handmaids of history—chronology, geography, antiquities, rhetoric, and poetics, and the moral and political sciences, so far as they are derivable from ancient writers. These last, however, we allow

from time to time, as shall appear expedient, to be illustrated
from modern authors. Dialectic (logic), which we add to the
Literæ Humaniores, as above defined, must always be offered
by candidates for a first or second class; and proficiency in
logic shall have great weight in the distribution of honours."

This is all that the statutes of the university lay down
as to the "matter" of the examination. The translation I
have given is of the statute as it now (1867) stands; but
the definition of the "materies" is substantially the same
as in the original enactment of 1830. Yet, since 1830, a
totally new character has been gradually given to the
examination, and consequently to the preparatory study.
This is not mentioned as a defect in the statute, but only
to show how entirely inadequate the words of the law are
to convey an idea of the practice under the law. The
present practice is for the candidate to offer a list of six
to eight books—viz. Aristotle—Ethics; Plato—Republic;
Thucydides (the whole); Herodotus (the whole); Livy,
1-10; Tacitus (a portion). To these are sometimes added,
Bacon—Novum Organum, i.; and Butler—Sermons. It
is not usual to name any logical author; logic is examined
in as a subject, which the candidate learns from books or
from lectures, as suits him best.

A list of books, however, does not explain itself. More
than one system of examination, implying totally distinct
lines of study, may be raised upon the same books. The
Oxford examination in "classics" takes a very peculiar
form,—a form which could never reveal itself to the
unassisted eye of a student. It is in drilling him in the
preparation of "his books" in this form, that the great
arcanum of tuition resides. First, a distinction is drawn

between "text" and "matter" of each author. Close and correct translation of the text is inexorably exacted. This requires careful preparation of the six Greek and Latin books above named. This preparation is usually made by aid of a translation, or some of the innumerable explanatory commentaries, which are, in fact, abridged translations of the difficult passages.

When the text is thus gone through, the candidate commences the preparation of the "matter." Some thirty years back the getting up of the matter of the books was a simple affair. It was set about in the same servile and memorial way in which the getting up of the text is proceeded with now. It was then enough to recollect the contents of the books as they stood on the page. We have outgrown that stage. The abject method of cramming then encouraged could not be long continued in face of the criticism which it provoked. There was a call for "philosophical development of the faculties." Accordingly, without altering the "materies examinationis," philosophy was gradually infused into the examinations, till it has become their most material component. The questions set range over the widest field of speculative philosophy— ethical, social, political, religious. The educational test of the University of Oxford, in this its most elaborate and intense instance, may be said to be made up of two parts— exact translation and speculative power; for though Latin and Greek "composition" is nominally retained, it exercises little or no influence on the result. It is indeed almost reduced to the mere rendering of a passage of English into Latin. To take the alternative "Greek prose," instead of the "history of philosophy" paper, is regarded suspiciously

as a symptom of "weakness." The preposterous attempt
of the friends of "scholarship" to thrust in their subject
without regard to fitness of time or place, has been defeated
by the nature of things. Like ignorant but well-meaning
nurses in the sick-room, because quinine is good for con-
valescents, they insist upon pouring in the bark into the
patient's food.

Of the two elements of the test, exact translation and
philosophical power, the first succeeds pretty fairly in
inducing a close and careful, though somewhat mechanical,
reading of the text of six very valuable classical authors.
Beyond this, I think, it does not reach. A classical philo-
logian trained in a freer system would be astonished to find
that, the special preparation of six Greek and Latin books,
for which two years are allowed, was compatible with a
total neglect of all the philological inquiries to which those
books necessarily give rise. All such inquiries are looked
upon by the student with contempt, as extra-parochial. A
Wolf or a Ruhnken, a Heyne or an Ernesti, would lecture
here to empty benches, or would have an audience only of
Tutors. We have in the final school of classics "an educational test," which, in the words of Dr. Donaldson,
"closes the access to a progressive development of the
studies on which it rests." It chills the genial fire which
a free study of classical literature is capable of communicating, and which is one of the best mental results of
that study. However, this part of the test does produce
some real knowledge. If its negative effect is cramping,
its positive effect is good in compelling thorough and
repeated perusal of the six given classical texts, instead of
dipping, hasty running through, or casual inspection. It

does not pretend to secure thorough knowledge of the books offered; but it lays a sound basis for the after-acquisition of such knowledge.

The reason why the six books offered are so incompletely studied is to be found in the fact that, the greater part of the candidate's effort is given to meet the other half of the test, in the examination in philosophy. Of this part of the examination, the classical books offered by the candidate afford rather the excuse, than the material. If the strictly classical part of the preparation was calculated to invite criticism by its confined limits, the philosophical department of the examination must excite our wonder for the opposite reason—the boundless space over which it ranges. There seems to be scarcely any of the debateable questions of politics, morals, and metaphysics, on which the candidate may not be asked to give his views. The horizon of the examination is as wide as that of philosophical literature. Will it be insinuated that the questions are there for show, and that, like many other examination papers, so ours serve to parade the knowledge of the examiner, rather than to test the powers of the candidate? Far from it. The suspicion is very wide of the mark. The best of our *eléves* are found fully equal to the emergency. They are not overwhelmed by the magnitude or the variety of the moval problems proposed to them. A clever youth, trained by a skilful private tutor, can discuss, with a masterly air, as many of the questions mooted by the paper, as three hours of rapid penmanship permit. The quantity of original writing produced in the time is of itself surprising. But the quality is still more so. The best papers are no mere schoolboys' themes spun out with hackneyed commonplaces, but full of life and thought, abounding with all the ideas with which modern society, and its best current literature, are charged. So totally false are those platform denunciations of the Oxford classical system, which assume that it lands its alumni in old-world notions, and occupies him with matters remote from modern interests! I do not believe that there exists at this moment in Europe any public institution for education, where what are called "the results of modern thought," on all political and speculative subjects (the philosophy of religion, perhaps, alone excepted), are so entirely at home, as they are in our honour examinations in the school of "Literæ Humaniores"—the examination, be it observed, not as prescribed by statute, but as actually worked.

Indeed so palpable a fact is the free modern life of speculation which now pervades our classical school, that it must be distinguished as the characteristic stamp of the young men whom we have turned out for the last ten years, and who are now rising into distinction in their several professions. Recognising, as I must do, in that race of athletic and accomplished intellects, the very flower and hope of England for the next generation, it is impossible to deny that the school in which they were trained must possess a high educative power. Yet there appear to be reasons for thinking that the philosophical part of the curriculum in the School of Literæ Humaniores cannot be continued on its present footing—that it has done its work. The philosophical has been a transition stage, by which we have risen above the mere belletristic treatment of classical literature. It has now outgrown the classical books upon which it has been raised, and it is time that it should be transferred to the basis of real science.

It appears to me to be a fatal objection to our " philosophical" course, that it encourages speculation not based upon knowledge. The fluent deductions and wealth of " thought," which the best candidates have at command, overpower and dazzle us, till we ask ourselves the question, By what mental process were these brilliant speculations arrived at and appropriated ?   A philosophical " idea" is a general proposition, colligating, or being the short expression for, a number of observed facts.   Such a proposition does not possess an intuitive validity.   It is only probable in a greater or less degree.   The degree of its probability is an essential element of the conception.   In other words, the evidence for a moral conclusion must be collected, examined, sifted by the mind itself, before it can justly appropriate the conclusion, affirm it, and proceed to reason upon it.   " To give the net product of inquiry, without the inquiry that leads to it," says Mr. Herbert Spencer, " is found to be both enervating and inefficient.   General truths, to be of due and permanent use, must be earned. Easy come easy go, is a saying as applicable to knowledge as to wealth" (*On Education*, p. 61).   We teach this principle of investigation in our inductive logic, but we violate it in our educational practice.   We comment upon Bacon's reiterated criticism of the schoolmen for their inane subtleties, and we insist, in his words, that the road to truth is " interpretando," and not " abstrahendo ad placitum." Yet the " thoughtful paper," which is rewarded in our examinations, is but a mass of generalisation arrived at by that very method of the schoolmen which we condemn. That brilliant " philosophy-paper," thrown off in three hours, and teeming with the " results of modern thought," from what source was it supplied? From a diffusive reading of the best modern books. The student himself will tell you that he answered such a paper " out of Grote," and such another " out of Maine" or " Austen." And are not, it will be said, Grote's *History of Greece,* Maine's *Ancient Law,* Austen *On Jurisprudence,* valuable books, the best of their kind in the language? No doubt of it. Each of them is the result of a consummate learning, of years of experience and study of one subject, and models in their respective lines of enlightened investigation. But we do not employ them as models. We encourage the student to grasp the results without the investigation, to appropriate the conclusions without testing them, and then to parade them as his own. There is such a thing as " cramming" philosophy. To glean rapidly the current ideas floating about the schools, to acquire the knack of dexterous manipulation of the terms that express them, to put himself into the hands of a practised tutor, to be set in the way of writing in the newest style of thought upon every possible subject, and inserting the quotations from Aristotle in their proper places—this is all that the student has time to do between moderations and the final school, if he is to stand up to such an examination as we then propose to him. Ideation is stimulated by the process, the philosophical imagination awakened, a desire for knowledge created, and an acquaintance with much of the results of knowledge acquired. But as mental training, it is surely most unsound. It cannot be called " philosophical." It is rhetoric expended upon philosophical subjects. It is the reappearance in education of the σοφιστική of the schools of Greece, condemned by all the wise. Its highest outcome is the " able editor," who, under protection of the anonymous press, instructs the public upon all that concerns their highest interests, with a dogmatism and assurance proportioned to his utter ignorance of the subject he is assuming to teach. In the schools of Oxford is now taught in perfection the art of writing " leading articles."

I may illustrate my meaning by a specimen of the examinations.

I have said that the examination in the final school consists substantially of two parts—one in the text of the books, and one in general philosophy. I have purposely omitted to name " history," as the historical part of the examination has entirely a philosophical character. A paper of questions on " Roman history," set in 1866 is before me. Among the questions are the following :—

" 1. Italian history begins at a far later stage of civilisation than Greek or Germanic.
          " Examine this statement.
" 3. In what way did a career of conquest affect the internal development of Sparta and Rome respectively?
" 4. The southward movement of races in Italy, in its effect on the fortunes of the various states.
" 8. Estimate the force and character of religious feeling at Rome during the early empire.
" 9. The extinction of the Cæsarean family as an epoch in the development of the empire.
" 10. The various forms of alliance, union, or dependence, existing between early Rome and other cities. Are similar relations between cities found in Greece?
" 13. How far is the unsatisfactoriness of Livy's First Decade traceable to defects personal to the writer himself, how far to defects incident to the age in which he wrote?"

These are very striking questions, evidently resulting,

in the mind of the examiner who set them, from a fresh
and original study of the ancient authors. But what kind
of knowledge can they be the test of, in the examinee?
The whole paper contains thirteen questions, and, though
no candidate would be expected in three hours to answer
all the thirteen, he would probably write upon half the
number, say six, at least. For the preparation of the
whole of the subjects of this examination he has, at most,
two years. There is, in this space of time, the text of six
books to be read and re-read, and carefully prepared.
There are the contents of the " Ethics " and " Republic "
to be conned and understood. There is philosophy and
the history of philosophy to be surveyed. There is Greek
history, on which a paper, similar in character to this on
Roman history, is set. Logic cannot be put aside, for,
though the elements of it may have been learned before
Moderations, the logic paper in the final examination goes
much more deeply into the subject. What portion of his
two years can the student properly allot to Roman history?
Not one-fourth, possibly one-eighth, of his time and attention. But, if he had the whole of two years for this one
subject, he could hardly be in a position to make any of
the above inductions for himself, or, when made by others,
to test them by the facts on which they rest—*i.e.* by comparison of the original sources. What he writes on them
so effectively is, therefore, by the unauthorised adoption of
the unverified conclusions of others. Such an exercise has
no claim to be considered " philosophical." It is purely
rhetorical. It is to play with philosophical terms as with
counters. What he has acquired in this way is not merely
not knowledge, it is imposture — an imposture of which

himself is the dupe. For he goes his way, thinking that he possesses, in his improvised theories, the master-key to history.

I am aware that the school of Literæ Humaniores, or the philosophical element which is now so largely infused into the training for it, is menaced at this moment by a formidable enemy. This aspect of the question is so important, that I may be permitted to turn aside for a moment to contemplate it.

The wave of Catholic revival, which is passing over all the countries of the west of Europe, has reached our shores in two distinct currents—one, communicating an impulse without the National Church; the other, within it. Of this influence I wish to speak here only so far as it touches our educational theory and practice. With its doctrinal or ecclesiastical aspect I am not now concerned. The effect upon the Roman Catholic body in this country has been to arouse, in the minds of their spiritual guides, a jealous alarm at the encroachments made by the higher education upon the wealthier classes. This alarm, first conceived on occasion of the erection of the Queen's Colleges in Ireland, has become more intense since the partial opening of the English universities has made it possible for Catholic students to enter here, if they can find a head of a college willing to admit them. A few Catholic students, braving the difficulties which the colleges continue to throw in their way, have found their way to Oxford. The expediency of interfering to prohibit their resort to us, few as their numbers were, was anxiously debated. In spite of the resistance of a small minority of English and Irish

Catholics, it has been decided by the authorities of the Church of Rome, that Catholics are to be discouraged by their priests from sending their sons to the Queen's colleges, to the English universities, to any place of mixed education. Especially is Oxford denounced as "dangerous to the faith." Separate education, and a Catholic university, are now the aim of the authorities of the Church, for these islands.

A similar alarm animates the Anglican party within the National Church. The growing strength of this party, which has been hitherto used chiefly to fill university appointments with its partisans, or to influence elections, is about to be turned against the school of Literæ Humaniores, as now administered. The challenge has been thrown down, and the leaders of the party have denounced the system of training in that school as " dangerous to the faith." One of them is quoted as having said, " Education at Oxford is infidel to the core" (*Dublin Review*, Oct. 1867).

For my own part, I think the fears of the Catholic party, whether within or without the National Establishment, are substantially well founded. With one qualification, however. Dr. Pusey, living on the spot, can discriminate between the " Pass" and the " Class" curriculum. There is, he is well aware, no danger incurred by a candidate for a pass degree. The Roman Catholic authorities may be relieved from any apprehension as to "the faith" of the students of their church, provided they confine their studies to what is required for the degree. There is no danger to principles or faith in a "pass" course, because such a course is not "education." It does not reach the intellect or the soul. I appeal to any of the Catholic students, who have taken the ordinary degree in Oxford since 1854, to say if anything has been taught them officially, which has been calculated to interfere with their religious belief. Nor even in the honour curriculum for the other schools is danger supposed to lurk. It is the school of classics (Literæ Humaniores) only, and, specifically, the philosophical subjects which have developed themselves within that school, which alarm the church party. This the party must either conquer, or be content to see all the minds that come under the influence of that training—that is, all the minds of any promise that pass through Oxford—hopelessly lost to them. They are beginning to turn their efforts to overhaul and remodel the method and subjects of this school. Such is the ascendency of the party at this moment in the councils of the university, that it is probable they will be successful.

I trust it will not be supposed that I wish to see any part of our training either maintained, or changed, for any such reason as that it is hostile or favourable to the aims of any party in Church or State. There are scientific principles of education, and it is endeavoured in these "Suggestions" to refer our arrangements to these principles. It is only where a party puts forward, or takes its stand upon, educational principles which do not seem to me to be true, that these pages have any business with party names.

In the collision which is impending between the Catholic, or catholicising party, and the liberal party in Oxford, on the subject of the philosophical teaching in the final school, there is such a principle at stake.

And this principle is no other than the existence of the

higher education—a training of the intellect, as underlying accomplishments and useful knowledge, " arts," in old academical language. An education, which proposes to itself to induct the pupil into the highest course of knowledge, must offer to train the intellect to the investigation of the laws of nature, man, and society—an investigation which shall be based upon an exhaustive knowledge of the phenomena in each case, and shall employ all the powers of the reason in ascertaining the relations between the phenomena. Nothing short of this, I conceive, can be the aim of any establishment for superior education, such as is a university. " The mind that is in harmony with the laws of nature, in an intimate sympathy with the course of events, is strong with the strength of nature, and is developed by its force " (Maudsley, *Physiology of Mind*, p. 30). This is the mental result at which a university education must aim. Not that this goal, or perfect development, is attained by the student on taking his degree; but he is launched on this career, initiated into this method.

An education, of which this is the aim and method, must come into conflict with any system which proposes to provide *à priori* conclusions in any branch of knowledge relating to nature, man, and society. Any system or corporation, which supposes itself to be in possession of such propositions, may propose them to its pupils as true, and require their acceptance upon the authority of the teacher. The Roman Catholic Church does suppose and profess this. Even lately the supreme catholic authority has put forth a syllabus of eighty propositions which are condemned as " false." Perhaps they are so. I do not know.

It is not material to my present purpose whether they are so or not. But, under such a system, education must be something very different from what we understand by the word —education, I mean in its last stage, as academic. For in its earlier stages, in the nursery, the home, and the school, education is founded on tradition and faith. By the child, knowledge is received on authority.

In the Catholic system, then, as understood by the modern authorities of the church, there can really be no higher education. Catholic schools there may be, but a Catholic university there cannot be. Catholic education may be excellent in respect of all the accomplishments, and may embrace many important branches of useful knowledge. It may comprise mathematics, mechanics, the rules and graces of composition and style, taste in literature and art. It cannot really embrace science and philosophy. The "philosophy" course in a Catholic seminary is, in fact, only logic and rhetoric—the deduction of consequences from premisses furnished by authority, or the collection of probable arguments for the defence of those premisses. They appear before the public as teaching science and philosophy, but it is sham science, and a mockery of philosophy. Propositions in science and philosophy may be inculcated in their classes—possibly true propositions. But the learning of true propositions, dogmatically delivered, is not science. Science is the method of scientific investigation, which is one and the same in respect of all phenomena. The Catholic authorities, therefore, cannot allow their youth to share our universities. They demand a separate university, not that they may conduct education in it, but that they may stop education at a certain stage.

This position of the Roman Catholic body towards the universities of Great Britain and Ireland must be also the position of any other party, which conceives itself to be in possession of any important moral, social, metaphysical, or physical truth which has been arrived at in any other way than by an exhaustive investigation of the pertinent facts. Such a party must necessarily be made uneasy by the present state of the Oxford schools. It cannot, consistently with its principles, rest till it has either introduced into our system the teaching of propositions in moral and social science on authority as true, or has eliminated science altogether.

If the character of the training given by the classical honour school be a source of uneasiness to the church party, is it because that training is a thoroughly sound training in the method of scientific investigation, a method which knows nothing of truth delivered upon authority? I am sorry to be unable to think so. The character of the "philosophical" element in that training has begun to be questioned by other than those who have surrendered their judgment to a theological party, and on other grounds. Mr. T. Acland, M.P. (to cite one who cannot be charged with speaking from party bias), writes, "I venture very earnestly to urge the conviction that the intellectual freedom for which Mr. Mill gives Oxford credit, and which, within the bounds defined by Christian humility, I do not desire to abridge, would be more safely exercised, and would be stronger and more healthy, if there were less ignorance of common principles and laws of nature, more security for sound training in exact studies, admitting of definite certainty, requiring care in the statement of the datum and the quæsitum, imposing due regard to the statement of evidence, before young men are plunged into an ocean of doubt about the reality of the faculties, intellectual and moral, with which we are endowed by our Creator. . . . Some subjects are postponed so that they are hurried over, others are excluded; abstract questions and doubts are prematurely forced on minds ill prepared to master them. For example, Aristotle's rhetoric, a favourite with statesmen and orators from Lord Grenville downwards, has been squeezed out; the Ethics and Butler are unread by many who seek honours in law and modern history. The orators are excluded from the course of history; logic, as now taught, with its unsettled and unsettling theories, is forced on all; a wide range of physical science is approached by men who have had no training in geometry or mechanics treated mathematically; and while men are encouraged in almost any branch of special and separate study, there is one to which no distinctive honour is allowed in the final examination, and that is the higher philology" (*Letter to the Vice-Chancellor :* Parker and Co., 1867).

The particular criticisms offered by Mr. Acland in this passage I cannot adopt. And, in general, I must venture to differ from his wish to " squeeze in " more matters into the honour curriculum. That curriculum is already bursting from being overcharged with matters, and our reforms must take the direction of further specialising study. But in the general drift of his remarks, as bearing upon the final classical school, many besides myself will be ready to join with him. But I would prefer to state the objection in another form. That logic " unsettles " minds cannot be an objection to it. For that would imply that they were

" settled " before; before, that is, education commenced. Mr. Acland seems to say that the student should enter upon his education with a mass of " settled " propositions in those moral and social sciences which he comes to learn. Mr. Acland cannot mean this; for such a system would be, like the Catholic system, a negation of science, and, consequently, of academical education. The objection justly chargeable upon the " philosophical " training, as now administered in Oxford, seems to me to be that it mainly consists in a " settling " of opinions. It deals with opinions, and administers ready-made results to the mind, instead of training it in the methods of investigation. I have already touched on this head in speaking of the historical part of the examination. It shall only be added here that our philosophical teaching at this moment is, viewed in its logical principle, identical with that adopted in Catholic schools. The propositions enforced, recommended, encouraged, or current in the two schools, differ widely. But the same objection lies against both systems —viz., that, as the result of the training, the student carries away a mass of unverified conclusions. To the Catholic youth these conclusions come recommended by the " authority" of the teachers and the Church. To our students they are recommended for adoption by the " authority" of fashion, or the current turn of thinking of living philosophic minds, and of the prevailing philosophical literature.

The causes of this educational error are not far to seek. They lie in the present constitution of the teaching body. " Philosophy " is taught, not by professors who have given a life to the mastery of some one of the branches of moral or political science, but by young tutors. He is often too young to have had the time to study profoundly. He never will obtain the time, for his business as tutor is conceived to be, to push his men through the portals of some examination which is awaiting them. Accordingly he reads, in his vacation, or in such moments of leisure as he can snatch, the last new book upon the subject. He becomes, of course, an immediate convert to the theory of the latest speculator; he retails the same in his lectures, recommending it, perhaps, by eloquence and learning all his own ; and when he becomes examiner he examines in it.

Let it not be thought that I would imply that the outgrowth of philosophical speculation which has shown itself in the classical school among us has not been productive of very great advantages. It has undoubtedly done signal service. Mr. Mill has lately said, " A university ought to be a place of free speculation. The more diligently it does its duties in all other respects, the more certain it is to be that. The old English universities, in the present generation, are doing better work than they have done within human memory, in teaching the ordinary studies of their curriculum ; and one of the consequences has been, that whereas they formerly seemed to exist mainly for the repression of independent thought, and the chaining up of the individual intellect and conscience, they are now the great foyers of manly inquiry to the higher and professional classes south of the Tweed " (*Inaugural Address at St. Andrews*, p. 40). The praise thus bestowed upon us has been earned exclusively by the spirit which has reigned, for some years past, in the school of classics. In stimulative efficacy the training has been all that could be desired.

x

But it has done nothing more. Surely an education should aim at more than rousing curiosity. It should satisfy and guide—guide, not by dogmatic delivery of truths, but by scientific training in the method of inquiry. " A university exists for the purpose of laying open to each succeeding generation, as far as the conditions of the case admit, the accumulated treasure of the thoughts of mankind " (Mill, *Inaugural Address*, p. 38).

Our system of class-lists has fairly run away with us. In our anxiety to perfect the conditions of a race, we have substituted examinations for teaching ;—competitive tests for an educational course. Yet each phase through which the Oxford examinations have gone since 1802 has been a step in advance. The first generation of examiners looked for " scholarship." Then came a generation of examiners (from about 1834-1854) who required of a candidate " knowledge of his books." The present fashion is to look for speculative " power." We must not forget that this latest phase is a step in advance upon that which preceded it. But it is time that the test of " power " should give way to that test for which it has been a valuable preparation— scientific knowledge of things. We are ripe for the change. There are plenty of signs around that mere brain-spun speculation is losing its attractions and its hold. Slashing style, and daring assertion not based on knowledge, are falling into discredit, even in newspaper writing. It is time that the university should assume its function—of teaching. The young tutor of " speculative ability " must be superseded by the middle-aged professor of scientific knowledge. On this point, at least, I cannot but think that Positivism has brought forward an opportune truth. " En procedant du simple au composé suivant les lois qui régissent l'univers, les sciences non seulement apprendraient aux hommes à mieux connaître et à mieux exploiter le globe qu'ils habitent, mais encore disposeraient le cœur à la generosité, et l'esprit à la modestie. Les verités capables d'être démontrées, et que tout le monde peut vérifier, substituent leur sûre et bienfaisante discipline à l'ancienne et invérifiable discipline, écartant les discussions oiseuses ou irritantes, sans valeur moralisitrice et constructive " (*Rev. de. la Philos. Pos.*, July 1867).

To avoid misunderstanding, I must repeat, at the risk of wearying the reader by the reiteration, that, by science and scientific, I mean the proper method of knowing and apprehending the facts in any department whatsoever. What has been said in deprecation of " philosophy," as now employed in our Oxford schools, is by no means intended as an exclusion of the " philosophical sciences," to use a term employed by Dugald Stewart. " The first proper and adequate object of philosophical inquiry is, as he repeatedly tells us, human nature considered as one great whole—*i.e.* in the sum of its phenomena. This is the foundation of what, according to Stewart, is the ultimate aim of speculation—viz. the determination of the various special ends and methods of the sciences, and the analysis of the ground of our certainty regarding real existence as well as formal truth, or the constitution of a rational logic. . . . This general study of human nature affords the exclusive condition and the means of true liberal culture" (Veitch, *Memoir of Dugald Stewart. Works*, x. p. xxxiv.) The moral sciences are not to be expelled from the Oxford curriculum. On the contrary, in a recast of the " schools" these sciences will hold a more independent and substantive position than they now do. Instead of lurking under the guise of a spurious commentary upon the "Ethics" or the "Republic," I propose to provide them with a school of their own. We have long ceased to teach "Physics," with Aristotle for a text-book. Surely it is not less absurd to be teaching moral science out of Aristotle. Not that I would displace the "Ethics" to substitute any other text-book. The philosophical sciences can only be indoctrinated by a master, carrying the pupil along with him on a graduated method, which shall begin at the beginning. This line of study I would place either as a sub-faculty, or at least as a separate school, under the Faculty of Law.

The present classical school would then become a school of philology; but a school of scientific philology—not a mere repetition of the Moderations examination. With Moderations the training and the tests of "scholarship" should end. In the thoroughness of its scientific method, the classical school should march *pari passu* with all the other final schools. Not only the principles of literary criticism, as applied to the interpretation and authentication of ancient documents, but all those principles of investigation which must be applied in order to reproduce a complete idea of the life and thoughts of the ancient world—these would be its subject-matter. Thus, after expelling the rhetorical "philosophy" which now reigns in the school, the school of classics would still be in a true sense "philosophical." Aristotle and Plato would continue to be read in this school; but as what they really are, precious remains of the Greek mind, not forced into a false position as manuals of social science for to-day's use.

The close study of such a work as Plato's Republic and Laws, the grandest product of the philosophical imagination extant in literature, is indispensable to the understanding of the ancient world. The book called "Aristotle's Ethics," in its double form—the Nicomachean and Eudemian—is a philological problem of the highest complexity, capable of calling out all the critical powers of the classical student. Even as we read them, these books are found to exert a powerful influence on the minds of youth. How much more will this be the case when they are restored to their proper place in the classical school! when the absurd attempt to compose a theory of morals out of a combination of "the Ethics and Butler" is relinquished, and when the candidate for a degree can read Plato in a free spirit, relieved from the constant pressure of the terror of an examination in the contents of the pages.

Within the sub-faculty of classics, as part of the curriculum, might be established something of the nature of what is called in Germany a "Philological Seminary." "Two of the greatest scholars of the university assemble all the best and most advanced pupils, and encourage them to give in criticisms on classical works, and to write exercises, and practise themselves in translation; they preside over and control those exercises, and even give prizes for excellence" (Dr. Perry, *Evidence on Mr. Ewart's Bill*, 1867). The object of such a seminary is not only to encourage learning, but to train teachers. The necessity of a normal school for training the teacher is recognised in the elementary department, and our national schoolmasters receive an elaborate professional preparation. But for the vastly more complex art of intellectual education it is not imagined that any preparation is requisite. A practical teacher of much experience says :—" Whilst the mere possession of knowledge is enough to teach advanced classes . . . the teaching little boys and stupid boys well is a thing of wonderful skill " (Thring, *Education and School*, p. 110). This statement appears to me to be the reverse of the truth. I shelter myself under the authority of Professor Veitch, who, speaking of Dugald Stewart's course of academical teaching, calls it " an art of which there have been but few masters " (*Memoir of Stewart*, p. xxxiii.) It is not perhaps wonderful that we should deny the existence of an art which is almost extinct in this country. Between the sparkling oratory of the public lecture on the one hand, and the " exercising " in preparation for an examination on the other, lies the place of " teaching." We have the platform lecture and the exercises in abundance, and they are quite indispensable parts of any system of education. But a teacher of the higher branches of science must himself be a master in that branch, and how many such can we reckon among us ? And yet it is not enough that his science should be familiar to his thoughts and to his tongue ; the art of conducting another along the road he has travelled himself is not an art which is acquired without practice. At present what skill any academical teacher may acquire in this respect must be acquired at the cost of his classes, and to his own great mortification and discouragement. Dr. Peacock long ago (1841) complained that " the great majority of the persons to whom the duty of private tuition is entrusted are young men of very limited attainments, without experience, and perfectly incompetent to convey to their pupils any correct or enlarged views of the subjects which they teach. . . . The veriest tyro in classical or mathematical knowledge will consider himself qualified to teach as far as he has himself been taught, though in the most superficial and imperfect manner, and thus becomes the instrument of propagating crude and inaccurate knowledge through successive generations of pupils" (*Observations on the Statutes of Cambridge*, p. 154). And Dr. Donaldson complains of "the belief, that teaching is a business which requires no apprenticeship, and that the attainment of even the highest academical distinctions qualifies a young man to pass from the status of a mere learner to that of an instructor of others" (*Classical Scholarship and Classical Learning*, p. 258).

I should therefore establish, in the faculty of philology at least, a systematic course for the training of schoolmasters and tutors. What the exercises should be in such a course is matter of detail. Attendance on this course would not be required for the degree of M.A. But there can be little doubt that the course would be attended by all who wished to qualify as professed teachers, whether within or without the university. Certificates of attendance and proficiency in the Philological Seminary, issued by the Board of Studies of the faculty, would be far more reliable than "Testimonials," which breathe the warmth of private friendship, and which would probably in time be supplanted by such official certificate.

There remains much more to be said under the head of the present section. But it is time to draw these observations to a close. I am impatient to abdicate a censorship —an office to which I become in each page more sensible that I am quite unequal, and which was only forced upon me by circumstances. I will only touch on one point more—viz. the duration of a course of lectures.

Mr. Gladstone has intimated his opinion that the Long vacation is too long. This is probably only a form in which our former—must I not still say our real?—representative in Parliament brings home to us the feeling among the public that Oxford is idle. Oxford *is* idle. But the Long vacation is not too long. For the fact is, that Oxford is at once idle and overworked. In respect of seventy per cent of its students it is idle—hopelessly and incorrigibly idle. In respect of the honour curriculum, I am inclined to think that there is too much, rather than too little, done for the pupils by the tutors, and too severe a strain placed upon the anxious mind of a nervously-sensitive examinee. More freedom of spirit is required, for a real appropriation of ideas, than most men can now feel under the pressure of constant examination. Too much is at stake upon the accidental condition of his physical and nervous system during the examination-week. Mr. Mill said, in the same *Address at St. Andrews*, " The majority of those who come to the English universities come ignorant, and ignorant they go away" (p. 4) ; and a few minutes afterwards, " The English universities, in the present generation, are doing better work than they have done within human memory" (p. 40). Mr. Acland suggests that these statements are inconsistent (*Letter to Vice-Chancellor*, p. 25). They are both true. To shorten the Long vacation would be to cripple the " better work" which we can do, in order to set us to do worse work which we ought not to attempt to do. To shorten the Long vacation would be to legislate for the idle majority. I contend that our principle of legislation ought to be to legislate for the studious minority. The suggestions contained in these pages have for one object that of slowly turning this minority into a majority. It is absurd enough that a place of study should be divided into " reading" and " non-reading" men; into " students" who study, and " students" who don't study. It would be more absurd still, if our arrangements for " studies" should be framed with a view to the supposed interests of the students who do not study. Let us by all means encourage all to become reading men. But do not let us imagine that we can force any one to become so by compulsory examinations.

For the working student and the working tutor, in the honour curriculum, the vacation is not a time of idleness. It is only a change of labour. The student requires to exchange the strain upon his receptive powers for the repose of digestion. After the infinite variety of matters forced upon his attention during the term—a variety which, by its rapid succession, stuns and bewilders rather than illuminates—four months of repose are not too much. He requires to recover his balance and his self-possession. I may here recall words written many years ago in a now forgotten paper :—" The stagnant lethargy of the old days enjoyed one supreme privilege, which the system that woke us to life has robbed us of. In the then undisturbed repose of academic leisure, the student had at least the full fruition of thought and books. He had time to read. ' Deep self-possession, an intense repose,' could do for the higher faculties what no ' getting-up' of books ever can do. ' There is a source of power,' says De Quincey, ' almost peculiar to

youth and youthful circumstances, that not always are we
called upon to seek; sometimes, and in childhood above
all, are we sought:

> ' There are powers
> Which of themselves our minds impress ;
> And we can feed this mind of ours
> In a wise passiveness.'

Such a condition was a sacrifice of the many for the benefit
of the few. We should be on our guard that we do not
now reverse the case, and sacrifice the best minds to the
necessity of stimulating the many. . . . We ought to
remember that intellectual character is the true preparation for life. It may be questioned if the bustle and stir
which accompanies our training here be favourable to
character. There is in it more of restlessness than of
energy. ' No great intellectual thing,' it has been said,
(Ruskin, *Pre-Raphaelism*, p. 11), ' was ever done by great
effort.' There is an overwork caused by the ambitious
desire of doing great or clever things, and the hope of
accomplishing them by immense efforts—' hope as vain as
it is pernicious, not only making men overwork themselves,
but rendering all the work they do unwholesome to them.'
This excitement with us in Oxford is a consequence of the
degradation of our studies, of our being occupied with the
trivial, and not with one object which can permanently
engage and sustain the intellect. The best and most
zealous teachers endeavour to make up for the want of
leisure to do one thing well, by a spurious activity which
endeavours to do many things."

In the present state of things, the Long vacation affords
the only opportunity which an actively-engaged teacher has

of refreshing his teaching by a recurrence to its sources. But he would be relieved, instead of burdened, by another change, which would probably effect all that Mr. Gladstone had in view—viz. lengthening the terms. "The short period of an eight weeks' term, an arrangement which has probably no parallel in any other university, makes it impossible to lecture on a great subject with that steady and thorough procedure which is requisite to let it make its due impression on the mind." This evil, felt to be so twelve years ago, is aggravated now, as even more is done now than then. Instead of three terms of residence in the year, I would have only two. The first should begin 10th October and end 23d December. The second should begin 14th January and end 1st June. The examinations should be held only once in each year, in the month of May.

The reasons for the selection of these days will be obvious at once. The advantages of the change would be : —(1.) A substantial addition to the length of the academical year. The "residence" of an undergraduate student is now considered to be 168 days out of the 365 ; under the new arrangement it would be increased to 210. Even if ten days were allowed at Easter, a whole month would still have been added to his attendance on lectures. (2.) What would be gained, by this addition to the quantity of teaching, is of less moment than the improvement which might be expected in its quality by the freer space and elbow-room which the teacher would obtain. In the hurry and rush of an eight weeks' term, he is straining to do as much as he can crowd into the time, and nothing is done as well as it might be. We are ever beginning, and leaving off before we have well begun. Though the

teacher's course would be lengthened by the new arrangement, I believe he would lecture through 200 days, when
divided into two semesters, with more ease to himself than
he now does through 168 divided into three terms.   (3.)
By ending residence in May, and thus cutting out the
month of June, we should strike a heavier blow at the
cricket and boating than by any other means known to me.
If any proof could convince the advocates of intramural
residence of the futility of " college-discipline," such a
proof might be found in the mastery which the athletic
furor has established over all minds in this place.   So
entirely are the tutors beaten by it, that, to cover the disgrace of defeat, they are obliged to affect to patronise and
encourage the evil.   I know, therefore, that on this head I
must look for no sympathy from college-tutors.   I appeal
from the tutors to parents and schoolmasters.   Can parents
and schoolmasters possibly go on any longer pretending to
think that cricket, boating, and athletics, as now conducted, are only recreations—are only the proper and
necessary relaxation, which fills up the intervals of lecture
and private study ?   It is quite time that this delusion
should be dispelled.   They have ceased to be amusements;
they are organised into a system of serious occupation.
What we call incapacity in young men is often no more
than an incapacity of attention to learning, because the
mind is preoccupied with a more urgent and all-absorbing
call upon its energies.   As soon as the summer weather
sets in, the colleges are disorganised; study, even the
pretence of it, is at an end.   Play is thenceforward the
only thought.   They are playing all day, or preparing for
it, or refreshing themselves after their fatigues.   There is a

hot breakfast and lounge from 9 to 10 A.M.; this is called training. At 12 the drag which is to carry them out to the cricket-ground begins its rounds, and the work of the day is over. I have called the academical year, under the existing arrangement, a year of 168 days. It is actually not so long. Some five or six weeks must be deducted from the summer term, and charged to the vacation side of the account.

Commemoration, which serves no really good purpose, and seems to give an official sanction to much frivolous dissipation, would at the same time be discontinued. The serious work of the examinations, and the publication of the various honour-lists, would be the concluding " act " of the academical year.

§ 5.—*Summary of Arrangement of Studies.*

The arrangements which have been suggested of the " Studies preliminary to the Degree " would then stand as follows :—

A student would come up at once, without previous notice, and matriculate. All matriculations are in October. He would inscribe his name on the register of the university, and not on the books of any college. All that would be necessary for this purpose would be that he should be presented at the Registry Office by an M.A. whose own name was on the roll of " tutors "—*i.e.* the lowest or junior grade of university teachers. There is no matriculation examination, no responsions, and no " pass " examinations or lectures. The tutor would give what instruction he thought fit, and require his pupil's attendance at any courses of professors' lectures he judged expedient.

The student would lodge where he liked. If he chose

to rent a set of rooms in any college, or if he obtained a scholarship attached to any college, he would have, of course, to comply with such regulations as to hours, etc., as the college thought good to make. Outside college-walls he would be amenable to the disciplinal regulations of the university and the directions of his tutor.

If he be a candidate for a degree, and for honours—which are the same thing—he must attend public lectures in such sequence as shall be from time to time directed by each of the Faculty Boards. But the first university test he will encounter will be Moderations. There will be no limit of age or standing imposed on candidates for Moderations. But it would be usual to pass the Moderation-school at the end of the first year of residence—*i. e.* in the May following the October in which he matriculated. But there would be nothing to prevent any young man from offering himself for this examination before matriculation. If he passed it, he would not thereby reduce the three years of his attendance on lectures to two. But he would gain the advantage of having got a mere "preliminary" examination out of the way, and of getting three years' scientific instruction instead of only two. In Moderations there would be (at least) two schools :—1. Classical; 2. Mathematical and Physical. The names of those who passed this examination would be arranged in four classes in each school. The appearance in one of the classes to be indispensable to obtain the final degree. Candidates to make their option between the classical and the mathematical school.

Moderations would thus take somewhat the place which the " Previous Examination with additional subjects " holds at Cambridge. This part of the arrangement is a concession, to what seems a present necessity, for the present. It draws the line between the general and preliminary education, and the scientific, or properly academical, course. It gives the student an academical year (October—May) to complete and improve his school-discipline. From this moment he takes leave of disciplinal studies, and commences as student in some one of the faculties.

Having, after Moderations, chosen his faculty, he must attend the courses of lectures in that faculty in the order prescribed by its Board of Studies. Any other lectures besides these he is free to attend, if he likes. If he intends to become a professional teacher, in or out of the university, his tutor will recommend him to inscribe his name in the " Philological Seminary." These courses last two years. At the end of two years from Moderations he presents himself in the school of his faculty for examination for the first degree. The faculties are :—

Theology.
Law, with two sub-faculties.
    1. History.
    2. Moral and Social Science—*Staatswissenschaft*, etc.
Medicine.
Mathematics and Physics in two subdivisions.
    1. Chemical and Biological Sciences.
    2. Natural Philosophy.
Language and Literature in three subdivisions.
    1. Comparative Philology and Science of Language.
    2. Classics.
    3. Theory and Archæology of Art.
Civil Engineering, Architecture, etc.

The faculty of theology must be considered in abeyance for purposes of education at present. There is indeed a scientific theology, and, in the Christian records of the early and later ages, the amplest material for various learning and critical investigation. But theology has not begun to exist as a science among us. In the present state of the public mind in this country, it is hopeless to propose to assign to it the place and rank which is its due. I must be content with having marked this place, as being side by side with the other schools which entitle, each of them, to a degree, and which have a defined course of studies leading up to that degree. But I cannot venture to propose what is obviously impossible. Theology will, I fear, in practice, continue to occupy its present degraded position of an extraneous appendage tacked on to the fag-end of every examination in every other subject. In this respect the academical traditions of the sixteenth century, when all education was theological, have been continued into our day, partly from mere habit, partly with the idea that, by thrusting in theology into every examination, we were making education religious, as the Puritans of a former age imagined, that by the employment of Scripture phraseology they sanctified common conversation.

The scientific faculties, then, in which the university offers definite courses of instruction, and crowns those courses with a degree, are nine. Those students who have attended these courses, and pass the examination which is instituted upon the courses, will be arranged in four classes in each school, and will be entitled to the first degree. This degree confers the title of "Master," and all the privileges and franchises attaching at present to a "Member of Convocation."

The second degree confers the title of Doctor of the

faculty to which the graduate belongs. But, while the first degree is general and public, open to all who have passed through the prescribed courses, the doctorate is only for those who design the practice of one of the professions. It is conferred by the university, but requires, besides the previous attainment of the degree of "Master" in the faculty, the performance of such exercises or conditions as the authorities of the profession may impose. For the profession of teacher (whether in or out of the university), the university is itself the sole authority, and may impose its own conditions, therefore, on the doctors in arts, etc. The master's degree is, alone, to qualify for the rank of Tutor. But before the "Tutor" can be promoted to be "Lecturer" in his faculty, a further test might perhaps be applied. At all events, attendance in the philological seminary would be required.

I should anticipate that no inconsiderable number of students would at all times be found here, who were not candidates for a degree, and who resided irregularly for the benefit of the lectures. We have naturally grown into thinking that every one who entered our walls was to be taken in hand for drill, and was to be forced through a given course, and that if he were not so engaged he had no business in the place. This mode of thinking seems to have been founded upon a secret consciousness that the instruction imparted had no intrinsic value, but derived its value from being the medium of getting through an examination. As soon as the university teachers shall be in a condition to give instruction which is in itself valuable, we shall not grudge to admit all who will, freely to it, without exacting from them that they shall be candidates for a degree. When this is the case we shall hear no more of the call for a " matriculation examination " now so loudly made—a call which proceeds upon the theory of " compulsory " learning. That theory is itself but a part of the popular conception of the university as a school. The *Studirfreiheit* of the German universities is the correlative of the superiority in learning of their teaching body. As our teachers rise to a higher level of instruction, we shall hear proportionably less of schemes for compelling unwilling students to learn.

It will be obvious that the feasibility of these sugges- tions on the studies preliminary to the degree, depends on the adoption of a previous part of the scheme as to the employment of the endowments. Scientific teaching can- not be substituted for "scholarship" and " philosophy" unless there are scientific men to give it. A change in the destina- tion of the endowments is therefore the first step required to be taken. It is impossible to take in hand the recon- sideration of the examination statute, till the endowments have been first transferred from their present employment as educational prizes to be a provision for learning and science. To revise the examination statute is to reconsider what the university ought to teach. If we were to proceed to recon- sider this question now at once, we should probably decide that we ought to continue to teach classical scholarship, philosophy, and the elements of mathematics and physics. An immediate revision of the examination system is, there- fore, by all means to be deprecated by all who wish to see Oxford rise to a level of instruction above the school elements with which she occupies herself at present.

SEC. 7.—CONCLUSION.

I am by no means insensible to the evils of change. But the alternative of change is not a conservative persistency. To be perpetually changing your system, without plan or methodical purpose, cannot be a good thing in any department of public administration. In a university even the desire for change, and the political agitation which attends it, are directly destructive of the purposes of the place. In a seat of learning, says Bacon, there should be " institutions and ordinances for government, all tending to quietness and privateness of life, and discharge of cares and troubles; much like the stations which Virgil prescribeth for the bees :—

> " ' Principio sedes apibus statioque petenda,
> Quo neque sit ventis aditus.'"
>
> (*Advancement of Learning,* p. 108.)

We cease to wonder that the " hautes études " cannot exist in France, when we find that the whole system of education has been changed from top to bottom eight times since 1802. Only last year M. Duruy issued a circular to the rectors of the academies, ordering them not to teach grammar by rules, and giving reasons for the order. The discontinuance of " grammar " happens to be in accordance with the best experience, and in this, France is but following in the wake of Germany. But M. Duruy's successor may, perhaps, next year issue a rescript that grammar shall be taught by rules, and give reasons for doing so. This kind of change—the degradation of waiting upon the whims of any " petit maître " who may climb the stool of office, we may well be thankful that we are not exposed to. We have in Oxford a vitality of our own, which is quite equal to detecting and correcting faults of detail. All machinery is brought to perfection by watching its working, and constantly striving to strengthen or to substitute. This is progress, not change; indefinite advance of an institution towards a perfection which it will never reach.

Such progressive development of the powers and uses of our university can only be worked out by ourselves. But such action implies, that we are once for all set in the right road; that we have placed before us a distinct aim, which prescribes our duty. The proposal which runs through these "Suggestions" is not of the character of improvements of detail, it is nothing less than a change in the aims and objects of Oxford. The greater part of our institutions have gone through such a revolution, have been put on a new footing, and adapted to the requirements of our civilisation. Other parts of our social system the revolution is only now beginning to reach. The English universities have come down to the year 1867 substantially what they were in the reign of Elizabeth—what they were left by the storm of the Reformation (Appendix F). The other nations of the continent, who are in a parallel stage of civilisation with ourselves, have dealt with their universities long ago. France, in the paroxysm of the Revolution, found her universities in the sixteenth-century shape, and, too impatient to reconstruct, destroyed them. She has still no university except in name, though some of the functions of a university are fulfilled by the *Institut,* the *Collége de France,* and some other public bodies in the metropolis, which keep alive, though faintly, the tradition of learning.

Catholic and conservative Austria, though the latest in the field, has preceded us. In 1850 Count Thun inaugurated a new era in the Austrian universities, and set on foot a series of reforms which are still proceeding. The University of Vienna, which in the hands of the Jesuits had been made a mere instrument for promoting the interests of Rome, and had consequently been reduced to the most abject intellectual decrepitude, is now rapidly reviving, and bids fair to become one of the principal *foyers* of science in Germany, as it is already the largest in point of numbers (2200 students). In Vienna, where, up to the end of the last century, every graduate had, on taking his degree, to take an oath to the immaculate conception of the Holy Virgin, and where, till recently, the whole university went in procession to receive the sacrament of the altar on Holy Thursday, now, non-Catholics are admissible to the doctorate, the professorate, and the academical senate, and endeavours are made to obtain from foreign states men of eminence to fill the chairs.

We, at last, made a beginning in 1854. It was but a beginning. And very fortunate it was that no more was done then—that the Act of Parliament was so moderate, and the executive commission so timid. Much good was done by the reforms set on foot then, and no irreparable harm. The college endowments are substantially intact, and the ideas of most of us who took part in the discussions then, as to the capacities and obligations of a public endowment, have become greatly enlarged. But it is still only a small minority, and chiefly of academical and scientific men, who yet see their way through the difficult problem of university education. The conception of an organised profession for the preservation and transmission of the tradition of knowledge has not yet become familiar to the English mind. The state of elementary and of middle-class education interests the public. Of the very existence of the higher education, as a distinct gradation in mental culture, the public is not aware. It does not believe in it; for the very sufficient reason, that it has no extant example before its eyes. Middle education, and university education, are supposed to differ in respect of cost, and in nothing else. They are known to be intended for classes socially distinct; but the education is supposed to be the same.

Class-education would seem to be as rooted an idea in the English mind, as denominational religion. But if the universities are only schools for the wealthy classes, why should they enjoy a large national endowment? Endowments mean, then, gratuitous education. Why should the nation, out of its national endowment-fund, provide gratuitous education, to the extent of £200,000 a-year, for the sons of precisely that class, which is best able to pay for whatever education it may think proper to have?

If the university be a school, of which heads, canons, professors, and tutors are the teachers, and which is frequented exclusively, or chiefly, by the rich, it is impossible that it should claim any longer to preserve its endowments. All our experience is against gratuitous instruction being provided for any class in the community, even the poorest. But if gratuitous class-education is to exist at all, it certainly cannot continue to exist precisely for the wealthiest class.

The object of these "Suggestions" has been to insist that

the university shall be no longer a class-school, nor mainly a school for youth at all. It is a national institute for the preservation and tradition of useful knowledge. It is the common interest of the whole community that such knowledge should exist, should be guarded, treasured, cultivated, disseminated, expounded.

At the same time, a school of the highest form of education can only exist on condition of being attached to such an institute. Such an organised institute of science and scientific training may be properly endowed. Nay, if we want to have it at all, we must endow it. The profession of learning will not exist at all, as a profession, with regular succession, unless it is created by endowment. There is no other fund but this reserved portion of the national domain, seeking to employ the practitioners of such a profession.

The issue in the debate now on foot in university reform involves, among many other things, our title to the endowments. Our mere *possession* of an endowment, which is the *property* of the nation, can surely not constitute a title. The British nation is at this moment deliberating if it shall not resume the endowments at present in possession of the Irish Church, with the view of reappropriating them to some other purpose which it may prefer to the present purpose. We cannot foresee what will be the issue of that deliberation; but the deliberation will be likely to be impartial, and the decision to be wise, in proportion as the deliberating body realises its full and complete right to re-enter on its own domain, to resume possession, and to confirm, annul, or alter the present destination of that domain. With the same freedom let us deliberate on the application of the endowments now enjoyed by the universities. If we shall conclude that we want an organised institute for the cultivation and transmission of the best knowledge extant, we cannot do better than locate it in the universities. There are the endowments ready to our hand; and it is certain that, without those endowments, such an organisation of science will not be. If, on the other hand, the nation shall decide that it does not want such an institution, it has the endowments in hand to appropriate to education. Endowments of education mean gratuitous education. Will the nation choose to employ its public fund in bestowing gratuitous liberal education on the children of the rich, or, rather, in providing gratuitous elementary education for the children of the poor ?

Should the deliberation reach this later stage—should the destination of the endowment-fund hang in doubt between paying for educating the rich and paying for educating the poor—it is obvious which way the decision would be. Is there any hope that it will not reach that stage; that we shall elect, in the first instance, to have a university which shall be an organisation of science ?

Is there any hope that this idea can be created in the mind of the public ? The signs of the times are not encouraging. English instinct, or what we call so, seems against its reception. The literary cynic sneers at the " sophists ; " the religious demagogue denounces the heresies of " German professors ; " the hurry of business and pressure of practical life make " culture for culture's sake " sound like cloistral and pedantic talk.

But there is a side from which the necessity of organised science is likely to force itself upon the convictions of Englishmen, and that at no very distant time. All that we have hitherto accomplished, all of which we have been proud—our colonies, our commerce, our machinery—has been the achievement of individual enterprise. These splendid results have been due to the energy of will—to character. But civilisation in the West has now reached a point where no further triumphs await mere vigour, undirected by knowledge. Energy will be beaten in the practical field by combined skill. The days when the knight, cased in his armour, lorded it on the field by the prowess of his arm, are gone for ever, and battles are now decided by the evolutions of masses directed by a central intellect. We have had lately some rude reminders—in the *fiasco* of our railway system, in the catastrophe which in a few weeks ruined the edifice of our credit, in the incapacity of our boasted self-government to secure us the most indispensable sanitary regulations—that there is something wrong, somewhere, which is not want of energy of purpose. The conviction must ere long reach us that our knowledge is defective, and that such is the length of art and the shortness of life, that knowledge can only be made available for public purposes by concert and organisation.

I decline, for myself, to be bound by the theory of those who maintain that education is for life, and life as it is. A Christian looks for a life beyond this life, and thinks that no theory of education can be perfect, as theory, which does not take account of that hope. The development of mind as mind, or culture for culture's sake, is to him the true ideal. But, for the present, it will be a great step upwards if the higher education can be organised on the basis of positive knowledge. We, in Oxford, have entirely lost sight of the connection between training and knowledge.

We have forgotten that we ourselves—the teachers—are here as learners; that we have any obligations on the side of knowledge. We are absorbed in our anxiety to perfect the conditions of an examination—to see that the race between the competitors is fairly run. Provided we stimulate the candidates for the prizes to exert themselves to the utmost, and provided we secure that the award is impartially made, we are satisfied. We care not in what subjects the race is run. We care not what we teach, provided it is some material which allows of decisive comparison of merit (Appendix H).

As we own no obligations to knowledge, so there is no public opinion to enforce any upon us. I am aware that the purport and aim of these "Suggestions" is one which can appeal to the sympathies of a very small minority. I must console myself by the hope that they are a growing minority. New circumstances are bringing with them the new conviction that abstract science and adjusted theory are, after all, conditions of successful practice. When we have reached this conviction, England will have arrived at that truth upon the belief of which was founded the earliest university known to history—the University of Athens,—οὐ τοὺς λόγους τοῖς ἔργοις βλάβην ἡγούμενοι, ἀλλὰ μὴ προδιδαχθῆναι μᾶλλον λόγῳ πρότερον ἤ ἐπὶ ἅ δεῖ ἔργῳ ἐλθεῖν.—(*Pericles ap. Thucyd.* ii. 40.)

APPENDIX.

(A, p. 45.)

A Memorial from the HEBDOMADAL COUNCIL of the UNI-
VERSITY OF OXFORD to the Right Hon. Sir G. GREY, Her
Majesty's Principal Secretary of State for the Home
Department, respecting the POLICE of OXFORD.

1. Under the present system the responsibility and expense
of maintaining a Police Establishment in Oxford is shared be
tween the University and the City ; the University maintaining
a force for duty by night, and the City maintaining a force for
duty by day.

2. The share taken by the University in the Police arises
out of the right of " Watch and Ward " possessed and exercised
by the University from a very early period ; this right consisting of an *exclusive* right of keeping " the Night Watch," and
" a joint right with the Mayor and Bailiffs of ' Ward ' during
the day-time."

3. The objects for which these powers of " Watch and
Ward " were given to the University Authorities were the
protection of the Scholars and Servants of the University, and
the maintenence of order amongst them.

4. By Statute 6 Geo. IV. c. 97, after a recital " that it is
expedient to add to the means anciently provided for maintaining peace and good order in the Universities of Oxford

and Cambridge," the Chancellor or Vice-Chancellor is empowered to appoint so many Constables as he may think fit, who are to have the ordinary power of Constables within the precincts of the University and four miles of the same.

5. Since the passing of this Act, and under the powers conferred by it, the University, up to the present time, has maintained a force for general Police purposes by night over the whole town, besides the staff in attendance upon the Proctors for purposes of University discipline.

But the University holds that it is not under any legal obligation to maintain an efficient Night Police for the whole City and suburbs, however large they may become ; and that it may at any time relieve itself of the charge of the Night Police (so far as that is required for the purposes of the City apart from the University), by withdrawing, after due notice, such portion of the Force as may not be necessary for the purposes of University discipline and morality.

6. The Force maintained by the City for Police purposes by day is raised and managed under the provisions of the Municipal Corporation Act.

But this arrangement does not exclude the authority of the University in Police cases affecting its own Members, whether by day or night. Such cases are always dealt with by the Vice-Chancellor.

7. The division of the Police into two separate bodies under distinct management, one taking the duty by day and the other by night, is productive of great inconveniences, and very injurious to its efficiency.

These inconveniences are common to the University and City, and cause general dissatisfaction on both sides.

8. On the part of the University it is also felt that the

City of Oxford and its Suburbs have grown, and are rapidly growing, in extent and population, whilst there has been no corresponding increase of the University and the persons and property belonging to it.

At the Census of 1821, next before the passing of the Act before mentioned, the number of inhabited houses in Oxford was 2431, and at the Census of 1861 the number of inhabited houses was 5234.

The population (including members of the University and other persons living in the Colleges and Halls) had increased during the same period from 16,364 to 27,560.

The University portion of this population cannot be estimated at more than 2000.

With respect to property, the rateable value of the University, Colleges, and Halls, as assessed to the General District Rate under the Local Government Act, is in round numbers £32,000.

The rateable value of the City and other property included within the Oxford District, as assessed to the same rate, is in round numbers £100,000.

9. The Night Police Force at present maintained by the University consists of—

> 1 Inspector.
> 1 Sub-Inspector.
> 1 Assistant Sub-Inspector.
> 17 Constables.
> 3 Supernumeraries.

Besides this Force, the Proctors' staff, for purposes of discipline, consists of a Marshal and three Proctors' men.

The cost of maintaining this establishment may be stated in round numbers as about £2000 a-year.

10. The inefficiency of the Police Force under the present system, by day as well as by night, is admitted on all hands.

To make the Night Police adequate to the wants and requirements of the place would entail still greater cost upon the University; and it is felt that the burden of such responsibility and expense for so large and growing a town ought no longer to be borne entirely by the University: while, with the increase of the area, and the population, and property to be protected, the evils of a divided, and therefore inefficient, police are becoming daily greater and more manifest.

11. A strong opinion accordingly prevails on the part of the University, and (as there is reason to believe) on the part of the City also, that for the remedy of these evils there ought to be one common Police Force, available for day and night duty, under common management; and, with the view of coming to an arrangement for the establishment of such a Force, negotiations were commenced some time ago between the Vice-Chancellor and Hebdomadal Council of the University on the one side, and the Mayor and Council of the City on the other side. But the proposals hitherto made on either side have not proved acceptable, or led to any satisfactory results.

12. And the last proposal made on behalf of the University, to refer the whole matter to arbitration, having been rejected by the committee acting on behalf of the Town Council, it has been thought advisable to bring the case under the notice of Her Majesty's Secretary of State for the Home Department, in the hope that his intervention may lead to a speedy solution of the existing difficulties, and to the establishment of a Police Force in Oxford upon fair terms, and under an efficient system, which may be satisfactory to all parties.

Oxford, June 4, 1866.

(B, p. 59.)

Matriculations in the University of Oxford from 1854.

1854 . . . 393	1861 . . . 433
1855 . . . 344	1862 . . . 433
1856 . . . 385	1863 . . . 452
1857 . . . 380	1864 . . . 476
1858 . . . 399	1865 . . . 524
1859 . . . 419	1866 . . . 517
1860 . . . 410	1867 . . . 501

Matriculations in the University of Cambridge from 1861.

1861 . . . 425	1865 . . . 530
1862 . . . 407	1866 . . . 540
1863 . . . 448	1867 . . . 572
1864 . . . 519	

Frequenz of the universities of Prussia, (corrected) from returns collected by Lord Russell in 1859.

Berlin . . . 2000	Breslau . . 770
Bonn . . . 800	Königsberg . 380
Greifswald . 300	Halle . . . 640
	Total . . 5890

Total *Frequenz* (*i.e.* the number of students resident at one time) in the two older English universities . under 3,500.

Population of Prussia in 1859 . . 18,000,000.

Population of England and Wales . . 21,000,000.

Frequenz of the universities of the Austrian Empire, (corrected) from returns obtained by Lord Russell in 1859.

Vienna . . 2200	Grätz . . 310
Cracow . . 280	Olmütz . . 80
Prague . . 1120	Inspruck . 290
Pesth . . 1190	Lemberg . 530
	Total 5850 drawn

from a population of (say) 24,000,000.

The universities in the other German States had (before the Prussian annexation) a total *Frequenz* of more than 6800. This gives a total of more than 16,000 young men receiving a university training. This total is drawn from a population which may be roughly estimated at 50 millions.

The total *Frequenz* of Oxford and Cambridge together may be stated as 3500, drawn from a population of (say) twenty millions. But the disparity is really much greater than these figures represent it. We must take into account—(1), the much greater wealth which exists in this country; and (2), the fact that, while the larger part of our clergy frequent Oxford and Cambridge, a very small fraction of the Catholic clergy approach their universities.

(C, p. 150.)

The course of studies in Yale University, which is stated to be a poor and hard-working seminary, is as follows :—

Freshman's Year.—Homer (*Il.* and *Odyss.*), Herodotus, Lucian, Greek Composition, Livy, Quintilian, Horace (*Odes*), Latin Composition, Algebra, Euclid, Spherics, History of Rome, Rhetoric.

Sophomore Year.—Electra, The Orations of Demosthenes, Prometheus, Theocritus, Xenophon's *Memorabilia*, Horace (*Satt.* and *Epp.*), Cicero *de Officiis*, Juvenal, Trigonometry, Analytical Geometry, Conic Sections, Elocution, Declamation, Composition, Rhetoric.

Junior Year.—Thucydides, Demosthenes *de Corona*, Tacitus, Mechanics, Disputations, Modern Languages, Logic, Chemistry, Natural Philosophy, the higher branches of Mathematics.

Senior Year.—Metaphysics, Moral Philosophy; higher class of English studies; Guizot's *Civilisation*, Political Economy, Hamilton's *Metaphysics*, Geology, Astronomy, Chemistry, Stewart's *Active and Moral Powers*, Civil Liberty (?), Butler's *Analogy*, Moral Science, Paley's *Natural Theology* and *Evidences*, The Law of Nations.

I cite from an interesting article in the *Fortnightly Review*, October 1867, not having a programme of the college at hand. Probably the college prospectus would explain some things in the above list of subjects which are very puzzling. If the plan is for each student to go through all of these things in four years, the remark in the text (p. 150) is confirmed, as far as Yale University is concerned.

(D, p. 238.)

Since these words were written, I have found the same argument urged with much greater force and precision by Professor Seeley, M.A.—

" The classicists say, and I heartily agree with them, that if you would cultivate the mind, you must imbue it with good literature. If, then, the mind of the classically-educated boy is not imbued with good literature, on their own showing it is not educated. The more you exalt literature, the more you must condemn the classical system. Of what advantage is it, if the boys do not, after all, gain the treasure, to have spent several years in striving after it ? What avail all the merits and beauties of the classics to those who never attain to appreciate them ? If they never arrive, what was the use of their setting out ? That a country is prosperous and pleasant is a reason for going to it, but it is not a reason for going half-way to it. If you cannot get all the way to America, you had better surely go somewhere else. If you are a parent, and think that your son is not fit to go to Cambridge, you send him into the city, or into the army. You do not send him part of the way to Cambridge ; you do not send him to Royston or Bishop-Stortford " (*Macmillan's Magazine*, November 1867).

(E, p. 277.)

The subjects required for the first B.Sc. examination in the University of London are stated annually in the Calendar.

Their enumeration alone occupies five pages. It is the rule of the examination that " Candidates shall not be approved by the examiners unless they show a competent knowledge in the fundamental principles of—1. Mathematics ; 2. Mechanical and Natural Philosophy ; 3. Chemistry ; 4. Biology, including Botany and Vegetable Physiology and Zoology.

" The extent of acquirement expected in Natural Philosophy, Chemistry, and Biology, is such as may fairly be attained by attendance on a course of lectures on each of these subjects, extending through an academical session " (*London University Calendar*, p. 77).

(F, p. 324.)

The fact that it is more than 300 years since the universities ceased to be metropolitan centres of learning and science, seems to throw an unpractical air over the suggestion that they should now become such. What has not been for so long, cannot, it is thought, ever be again. There must be some reason in the nature of things against it. After so long a desuetude, the privilege must have lapsed. To meet this prejudice, it is enough to cite the case of the German universities, which, like ourselves, slept from the Reformation till the latter half of the eighteenth century. We are only now setting about an operation which was gone through, in Germany, a century back. To what causes our delay in the reform of our educational machinery, in all the three grades—elementary, middle, superior—is owing, is sufficiently obvious to all who are acquainted with our internal history during the period. Intelligent statesmen were all along aware of the abuses of the universities. There is *A Memorial relating to the Universities*, printed by Gutch (*Collectanea Curiosa*, ii. 53), as found among the papers of the first Lord Macclesfield. Its authorship is attributed to him ; but " not on sufficient grounds," says Lord Campbell (*Lives of the Chancellors*, vol. iv. p. 563). It is, however, of that date. Lord Macclesfield † 1732.

The memorial proposes as one of its objects—"By what methods learning and industry may be promoted in the universities, setting aside all party considerations."

Setting out the abuses in the elections of Heads of Colleges by the body of fellows, the memorial recommends that they be named for the future by a board, composed of the great officers of State, and such of the archbishops and bishops as shall be thought proper, in conjunction with the visitor.

Commissioners to be appointed to inspect and alter the statutes of the colleges.

All fellowships to be made terminable in twenty years ; except two tutor-fellows in each college, who, after fifteen years of service, might retain their fellowships for life. Every fellow might demand a license of non-residence for six months, and have it renewed ten times, but not oftener ; but no fellow to be dispensed from residence till he has been five years fellow, that he might lay a good foundation in general learning before going out into the world.

The memorial is opposed to doing away the obligation to take orders, though a thing much desired by many. Among other reasons for retaining the obligation, one is, that the "faculty places" are generally filled by younger sons of noble families, or by such as desire to lead a free life. But the memorialist would have, in every college, an equal number of fellows not in orders, to the number of faculty places allowed by the founder ; out of these, when vacancies happened, the faculty places should be supplied.

"Whereas too many fellows live on in the colleges, waiting for their turn of a college living, without endeavouring to improve in learning, as depending upon their being able to pass a legal examination with the bishop ; and whereas most colleges are daily buying in advowsons ; and whereas, by colleges buying in livings of greater value, livings of £120 or £140 per annum, which formerly used to take off fellows, will be despised by them, and come to the share of those of less learning—that the statute forbidding colleges to buy advowsons be made more effectual.

" Whereas, in foreign universities, the study of the law of nature and nations has of late been very much encouraged, and it is of great benefit to mankind, especially to such as design for public employments—that his Majesty would be graciously pleased to found such a professorship in both universities, to have £50 per annum certain salary, and be obliged to read, *v.g.*, twenty public lectures ; and to prevent such professorships from turning into a sinecure, as most of them are, he should have for every such lecture, producing a certificate under the Vice-Chancellor and proctor's hands, of the particular days when he read such lecture, the sum of £5 to be paid for no more than he had read."

Private courses, as in the foreign universities ; " though what answers to these is done by the tutors in respect of classic learning and philosophy ; yet, since no such thing is done in relation to other useful parts of learning, and especially in relation to the great professions ; but the youth are to get through the upper parts of learning as well as they can, without assistance and instruction "—that persons be appointed with pensions of £50 per annum, to give such courses on divinity, civil and canon law, the law of nature and nations ; and at £30 for anatomy, chemistry, mathematics, and natural philosophy.

(G.)

M. Rénan says,—" Une université allemande de dernier ordre avec ses petites habitudes étroites, ses pauvres professeurs à la mine gauche et effarée, ses *privatdocent* [*en*] haves et faméliques fait plus pour l'esprit humain que l'aristocratique université d'Oxford avec ses millions de revenu, ses colléges splendides, ses riches traitemens, ses *fellows* paresseux."— (*Révue des deux Mondes*, Mai 1864.)

A brilliant lecture-list is a paper issue which may, or may

not, be redeemable at par. But it is one constituent of a comparative estimate. I have taken, almost at random, a Leipsic list. Leipsic is a university not by any means " de dernier ordre," yet far from standing in the first rank, and having a *Frequenz* of some 800 to 900.

UNIVERSITY OF LEIPSIC—WINTER SEMESTER OF 1866-7.

1. *Theological Faculty.*

Prof. Ord.	KAHNIS.	History of Dogma.
		History of the Reformation.
		Encyclopædia of Theology.
„	TUCH.	Geography of Palestine.
		Book of Job.
		Hebrew Syntax.
„	BRÜCKNER.	Practical Theology, 2d Part.
		Epistle to the Corinthians.
„	LUTHARDT.	Gospel of St. John.
		Dogmatic.
„	ANGER.	Christian Creeds.
		Epistle to the Ephesians.
„	LECHLER.	History of the Church, 1st Part.
		Epistles of St. Peter.
„	TISCHENDORF.	History of Canon, N. T.
		Greek Palæography.
Prof. Extraord.	HÖLEMANN.	Genesis.
		1 Thessalonians.
„	HOFMANN.	Catechetic.
		Prot. Pädagogik.
„	SCHMIDT.	Harmony of the Gospels.
		Christian Apologetics.
„	FRICKE.	Epistle to the Hebrews.
		Introduction to Dogmatic.

2. *Law Faculty.*

Prof. Ord.	SCHMIDT.	Saxon Municipal Law.
		Use of the Decretals

Prof. Ord.	WÄCHTER.	Pandects.
		Special Principles of the Pandects.
,,	HANEL.	Institutes and Hist. of Rom. Law.
		Pandects, tit. De regulis Juris.
,,	ALBRECHT.	Hist. of German Law.
		Ecclesiastical Law.
		Laws of Marriage.
,,	OSTERLOH.	Saxon Civil Courts.
		Summary Processes.
		Civil Law Process.
,,	MÜLLER.	Principles of Pandects comp. with the Saxon Code.
		Law of Succession.
,,	GERBER.	German State Law.
		Feudal Law.
,,	HEINZE.	Philosophy of Right.
		Penal Law.
,,	SCHLETTER.	Criminal Procedure, General and Saxon.
		International Law ; positive.
Prof. Extraord.	SCHILLING.	Ecclesiastical Law in Germany.
,,	WEISKE.	Mining Law.
,,	HÖCK.	Law of Contracts ; German.
		Punishments.
		Sachsenspiegel.
,,	KUNTZE.	Institutes, and Hist. of Rom. Law.
		Laws of Inheritance ; Pandects.
,,	GÖTZ.	Law of Exchange.
		Commercial Law.
,,	VOIGT.	Institutes, and Hist. of Rom. Law.
		Roman Civil Procedure.
,,	SPRANGER.	German Public Law.
		Do. Penal Law.
		Juristic Encyclopædia.
,,	Dr. LÜDER.	Criminal Procedure.
		International Law.
		Saxon Penal Procedure.

3. *Medical Faculty.*

Prof. Ord.	RUETE.	Ophthalmic.
		Clinic of do.
,,	WEBER.	Intestines.
		Demonstrations in Anatomy.
,,	RADIUS.	Pharmacodynamic.
		Pharmacognosy.
		Hygiene, Public and Private.
,,	GÜNTHER.	Surgical, Clinic.
		Deformed Foot.
,,	WUNDERLICH.	Clinic.
		Constitutional Maladies.
,,	CREDÉ.	Midwifery.
		Do. Operations.
		Do. Demonstrations.
,,	WAGNER.	Pathological Anatomy.
		Policlinic.
,,	LUDWIG.	Experimental Physiology, 2d Part.
Prof. Extraord.	KNESCHKE.	Encyclopædia of Medicine.
		Prescribing.
,,	BOCK.	Pathological Anatomy.
		Do. Diagnostic.
,,	WEBER.	Osteology.
		Myology.
,,	SONNENKALB.	Medical Jurisprudence.
		Insanity in the Law Courts.
,,	STREUBEL.	Surgical, Policlinic.
,,	CARUS.	Reproduction of Species.
		Comparative Anatomy.
		Groups of Mammalia.
,,	WINTER.	Prescribing.
		Introduction to Study of Medicine.
,,	COCCIUS.	Course of Operations on the Pupil.
		Pathology of the Eye.
		Optical Anatomy of the Eye.
,,	GERMANN.	Diseases of Women.
,,	HENNIG.	Diseases of Children.

Prof. Extraord. RECLAM.	Medical Jurisprudence.
	Climate and Mineral Waters.
„ MERKEL.	Diseases of Throat, etc.
	Physiology of Speech.
	Laryngological Policlinic.
	Laryngoscopy.
„ SCHMIDT.	Surgery, 1st Part.
	Surgical Policlinic.
„ BRAUNE.	Principles of Operations.
	Topographical Anatomy.
„ Dr. MEISSNER.	Obstetric Operations—principles.
	Do. Legal Medicine.
„ KÜHN	Syphilis.
„ HAAKE.	Midwifery.
„ HÜPPERT.	Chemical Diagnostic.
	Physiological Chemistry.
	Experimental Physiology—Microscope
„ NAUMANN.	General Pharmaceutics.
„ THOMAS.	Local Diseases.
	Physical Diagnostic.
„ HAGEN.	Diseases of the Ear.
	Anatomy of do.
„ SCHWEIGGER-SEIDEL.	Anatomy of Nervous System.
„ WENDT.	Diseases of Ear.
„ SCHÜPPEL.	Rep. of Pathological Anatomy.

4. *Philosophical Faculty.*

Prof. Ord. WUTTKE.	History of French Revolution and Napoleon I.
„ DROBISCH.	Psychology. Theories of Human Understanding.
„ ERDMANN.	Elements of Organic Chemistry.
„ FECHNER.	Relations of the Material and Spiritual Principle.
„ FLEISCHER.	Translation of Koran. Suras 25-29.
	Modern Arabic.
	Dschami's Beharistan.
	Old Turkish.

Prof. Ord. MÖBIUS.	Higher Arithmetic.	
	Physical Astronomy.	
„ NAUMANN.	Physical Geography.	
	Mineralogy.	
„ WEISSE.	History of Philosophy.	
	Encylopædia of Philosophy.	
„ PÖPPIG.	Zoology, Vertebrata.	
„ ROSCHER.	History of Political Theories.	
	Practical Œconomics.	
	Finance.	
„ BROCKHAUS.	Bopp's Sanskrit Grammar.	
	Lassen. Chrestomathia Sanskrita, 1st Course.	
	Do. 2d Course.	
„ HANKEL.	Physics. Electricity, Magnetism, Heat.	
	Do. Light.	
„ KLOTZ.	History of Latin Literature.	
	Cicero de Natura Deorum.	
	Latin Writing.	
„ ZARNCKE.	The Niebelungen-lied.	
	The Older Edda.	
„ OVERBECK.	Private Antiquities of the Greeks.	
	Theory of Greek Art.	
„ AHRENS.	Logic and Metaphysics.	
	Encyclopædia of Philosophy.	
	Political Philosophy.	
„ CURTIUS.	Greek Grammar.	
	Greek Lyric Fragments.	
„ MASIUS.	History of Pädagogik, 2d Part.	
	Schools in 16th and 17th centuries.	
„ EBERT.	History of Christian Latin Literature to Charlemagne.	
	Introduction to Comparative Theory of the Romance Languages.	
	Provincial Grammar. Bartsch's Reading-book.	

Prof. Ord.	RITSCHL.	Latin Grammar.
„	KOLBE.	Inorganic Chemistry.
„	VOIGT.	History of German Empire from Charlemagne to fall of the Hohenstauffen.
		Alexander the Great and his successors.
Prof. Extraord.	NOBBE.	Sophocles, Œdipus Rex.
		Tacitus, Ann. I.
„	FLATHE.	On the Genius of Shakspeare.
„	MARBACH.	Geometry and Trigonometry.
		Steam Machinery.
„	JACOBI.	Principles of Farming.
		Forest Management.
		Agricultural Profits, Mode of Reckoning.
„	WENCK.	History of Germany, 1648-1790.
		Do. of the West from Fall of the Roman Empire to Charlemagne.
„	SCHEIBNER.	High Equations.
		Determinants.
„	FRITZSCHE.	Greek and Latin Metres.
		Plato. Timæus.
„	BRUHNS.	Stellar Astronomy.
		Trigonometry.
		On Developments in Series.
„	HERMANN.	Introduction to Philosophy.
		Metrical Laws.
		Comparative Examination of Systems of Philosophy.
„	KREHL.	Arabic Grammar, Caspari's.
		Encyclopedia of Semitic Philology.
		Cureton, Spicilegium Syriacum.
„	KNOP.	Agricultural Chemistry.
		Chemical Methods.
„	MINCKWITZ.	History of German Literature since Klopstock.
		Origin of Homeric Poems.
„	ZILLER.	Psychology and Æsthetic.

Prof. Extraord. ECHSTEIN.		History of Superior Education in Germany since the Reformation, with special reference to Saxony.
,,	BRANDES.	Greek Antiquities.
		History of Europe in fifteenth century.
,,	BIEDERMANN.	Constitutional Law.
		Modern History since 1840.
,,	HIRZEL.	Pharmacy.
	Dr. KERNDT.	Agricultural Chemistry.
		Technology.
		Practical Economics.
,,	H. WEISKE.	Experimental Physics.
		Electro-chemistry.
		Meteorology.
,,	SEYDEL.	Ethics.
		History of Mythology.
		Relation between Theology and Philosophy.
,,	PÜCKERT.	History of Saxony.
,,	HANKEL.	Integral Calculus.
		Theories of Analysis with a view to their application in Physics.
,,	SCHÖNE.	Plutarch, Life of Solon.
,,	ZÖLLNER.	Physical Astronomy.
,,	BIRNBAUM.	Principles of Farming.
		Qualities of Land, Land Valuation.

Lecturers—

Prof. FURST.		Isaiah i-xxxix.
		Hebrew Grammar.
		Biblical Literature.
,, LANGER.		Harmonics.
		Theory of musical forms.

This list of lectures is exclusive of the philological seminary; of all the laboratory and dissecting-room work; and of a variety of exercises and practical instruction—*Besprechungen,*

Colloquien, Conversatoria ; and all the modes in which the pro fessor is brought personally into relation with the student.

(H, p. 330.)

As these sheets are passing through press I read that in the discussions, at Cambridge, on the Report of the Syndicate on the Classical Tripos, "Lord Powis defended verse-composition, and objected to the 'alternative' scheme (*i.e.* a proposal to allow candidates a choice between philological questions and a set of verses). He objected to men being pitted against each other on different grounds, which would be the case if one man took the philology paper and another the verse" (*Pall Mall Gazette*, 21st November 1867). This line of argument assumes that students are not examined in that which their teachers think it expedient they should learn, but that they must be taught that in which they can be examined, so as to be pitted against each other. The instruction is to be governed by the examination. Competition, instead of being regarded as a necessary evil, has ousted education from the system, of which it has become the end and purpose.

THE END.

Printed by R. CLARK, *Edinburgh.*

The Academic Profession

An Arno Press Collection

Annan, Noel Gilroy. **Leslie Stephen:** His Thought and Character in Relation to His Time. 1952

Armytage, W. H. G. **Civic Universities:** Aspects of a British Tradition. 1955

Berdahl, Robert O. **British Universities and the State.** 1959

Bleuel, Hans Peter. **Deutschlands Bekenner** (German Men of Knowledge). 1968

Bowman, Claude Charleton. **The College Professor in America.** 1938

Busch, Alexander. **Die Geschichte des Privatdozenten** (History of Privat-Docentens). 1959

Caplow, Theodore and Reece J. McGee. **The Academic Marketplace.** 1958

Carnegie Foundation for the Advancement of Teaching. **The Financial Status of the Professor in America and in Germany.** 1908

Cattell, J. McKeen. **University Control.** 1913

Cheyney, Edward Potts. **History of the University of Pennsylvania:** 1740-1940. 1940

Elliott, Orrin Leslie. **Stanford University:** The First Twenty-Five Years. 1937

Ely, Richard T. **Ground Under Our Feet:** An Autobiography. 1938

Flach, Johannes. **Der Deutsche Professor der Gegenwart** (The German Professor Today). 1886

Hall, G. Stanley. **Life and Confessions of a Psychologist.** 1924

Hardy, G[odfrey] H[arold]. **Bertrand Russell & Trinity:** A College Controversy of the Last War. 1942

Kluge, Alexander. **Die Universitäts-Selbstverwaltung** (University Self-Government). 1958

Kotschnig, Walter M. **Unemployment in the Learned Professions.** 1937

Lazarsfeld, Paul F. and Wagner Thielens, Jr. **The Academic Mind:** Social Scientists in a Time of Crisis. 1958

McLaughlin, Mary Martin. **Intellectual Freedom and Its Limitations in the University of Paris in the Thirteenth and Fourteenth Centuries.** 1977

Metzger, Walter P., editor. **The American Concept of Academic Freedom in Formation:** A Collection of Essays and Reports. 1977

Metzger, Walter P., editor. **The Constitutional Status of Academic Freedom.** 1977

Metzger, Walter P., editor. **The Constitutional Status of Academic Tenure.** 1977

Metzger, Walter P., editor. **Professors on Guard:** The First AAUP Investigations. 1977

Metzger, Walter P., editor. **Reader on the Sociology of the Academic Profession.** 1977

Mims, Edwin. **History of Vanderbilt University.** 1946

Neumann, Franz L., et al. **The Cultural Migration:** The European Scholar in America. 1953

Nitsch, Wolfgang, et al. **Hochschule in der Demokratie** (The University in a Democracy). 1965

Pattison, Mark. **Suggestions on Academical Organization with Especial Reference to Oxford.** 1868

Pollard, Lucille Addison. **Women on College and University Faculties:** A Historical Survey and a Study of Their Present Academic Status. 1977

Proctor, Mortimer R. **The English University Novel.** 1957

Quincy, Josiah. **The History of Harvard University.** Two vols. 1840

Ross, Edward Alsworth. **Seventy Years of It:** An Autobiography. 1936

Rudy, S. Willis. **The College of the City of New York:** A History, 1847-1947. 1949

Slosson, Edwin E. **Great American Universities.** 1910

Smith, Goldwin. **A Plea for the Abolition of Tests in the University of Oxford.** 1864

Willey, Malcolm W. **Depression, Recovery and Higher Education:** A Report by Committee Y of the American Association of University Professors. 1937

Winstanley, D. A. **Early Victorian Cambridge.** 1940

Winstanley, D. A. **Later Victorian Cambridge.** 1947

Winstanley, D. A. **Unreformed Cambridge.** 1935

Yeomans, Henry Aaron. **Abbott Lawrence Lowell: 1856-1943.** 1948